Early Praise for *Small, Sharp Software Tools*

Small, Sharp Software Tools efficiently delivers the practical knowledge you should have if you're a developer who spends any time at all working at the command line. If you've been looking for a text that shows you how to get things done in a Linux or MacOS terminal without slogging through the esoteric things you'll never use, this is the book you should read.

➤ **Trevor Bramble**
Senior Ruby Software Architect

Brian Hogan is gifted at translating high-level command-line concepts into clear and easy to understand terms that anybody can quickly grasp. This book takes the reader on a journey through many of the most powerful command-line tools and utilities in a way that is easy to digest and enjoyable to read. The exercises are practical, useful, empowering, and fun to do. There's something to be learned from this book whether you're brand new to the command line or have been using it for years.

➤ **Greg Myers**
Support Engineer, GitLab

The tricks and tools described in this book will set any developer up to rock the CLI. I challenge anyone to not be more productive after learning these tools!

➤ **Dan Sarauer**
Computer Support Supervisor, City of Eau Claire

Small, Sharp Software Tools

Harness the Combinatoric Power of
Command-Line Tools and Utilities

Brian P. Hogan

The Pragmatic Bookshelf

Raleigh, North Carolina

Our Pragmatic books, screencasts, and audio books can help you and your team create better software and have more fun. Visit us at *https://pragprog.com*.

The team that produced this book includes:

Publisher: Andy Hunt
VP of Operations: Janet Furlow
Managing Editor: Susan Conant
Development Editor: Tammy Coron
Copy Editor: L. Sakhi MacMillan
Indexing: Potomac Indexing, LLC
Layout: Gilson Graphics

For sales, volume licensing, and support, please contact *support@pragprog.com*.

For international rights, please contact *rights@pragprog.com*.

ISBN-13: 978-1-68050-296-1
Book version: P1.0—May 2019

Contents

Acknowledgments

Thank you, Susannah Pfalzer, for working with me on the initial version of this book. We've worked on a lot of things together, and I still hear your editorial voice in my ear every time I write something.

Thank you, Tammy Coron, for editing this book and challenging me to think more deeply about my writing style and my approach. You're great to work with, and I appreciate the effort you put in to keeping me organized and on track!

Thank you, Andy Hunt, for publishing this book. We've talked about something like this for a long time, and I'm glad we're finally getting it done.

Thank you, Janet Furlow, for all you do to make every book we publish amazing. You do so much behind the scenes. I appreciate all you do.

Special thanks to Eric Wackwitz for being a sounding board as I developed and refined the curriculum which led to this book. And thanks to the hundreds of students who explored these exercises in class and in their homework. Your feedback was invaluable.

This book has a lot of content, and explaining it hasn't been easy. Bash is a tricky subject, and various versions of tools make it even more challenging. I'm grateful to Trevor Bramble, Tim Chase, Andrew Herrington, Dan Kacenjar, Will Langford, Andy Lester, Sidharth Masaldaan, Greg Myers, Ryan Palo, Dan Sarauer, and Jessica Stodola for their time and feedback on this book. They caught a lot of mistakes and some poor explanations. I am incredibly grateful for their feedback.

Thank you to my business associates Mitch Bullard, Kevin Gisi, Alex Henry, Jeff Holland, Chris Johnson, Nick LaMuro, Erich Tesky, Myles Steinhauser, Josh Swan, Charley Stran, Mitchell Volk, Chris Warren, Mike Weber, and Andrew Vahey for your continued support.

Thank you, Ana and Lisa, for your love and inspiration.

Finally, thank you, Carissa, for your love and support, and for all you do for our family. I wouldn't be able to write books if it weren't for you.

Preface

The *graphical user interface*, or GUI, is designed for the average user and provides most of the necessary features needed for user interaction. Your smartphone doesn't have a user-accessible command-line interface, or CLI, because it's aimed at the average consumer. You are only able to access basic features. But you're not an average consumer. You're a programmer, a software developer crafting the best code from the finest bits. With command line, you can do everything you can do in the GUI, and more—that is, if you know how.

In this book, you'll learn the basics and use those basic building blocks to tackle more advanced tasks. One of the best features of the CLI is that you can turn those basic commands into scripts that you can execute, meaning you can automate common tasks with ease. That's why popular programming languages and frameworks like Node.js, Ember, React, Elixir, Ruby, Python, and many others rely so heavily on the CLI. With this book, you'll learn how to put this interface to work for you.

A Tale of Many CLIs

When it comes down to it, there are many command-line interfaces. If you've worked on a Linux or Unix server, you've likely had some interaction with its interface. If you're on Windows, chances are you've opened the Command Prompt or PowerShell to run some commands.

Many commands are different. For example, a POSIX system might use the command ls to list the files in a folder, whereas a Windows system uses the dir command instead. The command-line interfaces on macOS and POSIX systems use the rm command to remove files and directories, but the Windows CLI requires different commands for each.

This book covers the Bash command-line interface found on Linux, macOS, and Windows 10 through the Windows Subsystem for Linux.[1] You'll use the

---

1. https://docs.microsoft.com/en-us/windows/wsl/about

Bash shell. While there are other shells popular among developers, like Fish and ZSH, this book focuses on Bash because it's the default on many systems, so setup is minimal. Also, this book uses the GNU version of command-line utilities, instead of the BSD versions found on macOS. However, most of these differences are minor, and I'll point out when things are slightly different and show you how to install the GNU versions of these tools if necessary.

What's In (and not in) This Book

In Chapter 1, Getting Your Feet Wet, on page 1, you'll get a quick tour through some of the most useful parts of the CLI. You'll navigate around the filesystem, run commands as a superuser, learn to install a few programs you'll use in the book using the package managers, create files, learn about streams of text, and learn how to use the help system.

Next, in Chapter 2, Creating an Ubuntu Virtual Machine with VirtualBox, on page 17, you'll create an Ubuntu virtual machine you can use to practice the commands in the rest of this book. While you don't have to follow this chapter, using virtualization is a great way to practice. You'll create the virtual machine, install the Ubuntu operating system, and take a snapshot, so you can restore your environment if something goes wrong.

Chapter 3, Navigating the Filesystem, on page 33, lets you get comfortable moving around the filesystem on the command line. You'll learn where to look for things and how to get around quickly using absolute paths, relative paths, and a few handy shortcuts. You'll also learn where to find things on a Unix-like filesystem, and how to find how much space is available on your filesystem.

Next, in Chapter 4, Working with Files and Directories, on page 55, you'll work with files and directories. You'll expand on what you learned in the first chapter, and do more advanced operations in more detail. You'll concatenate files, read larger files, and manage permissions. You'll move, rename, and copy files and directories, learn about links, and learn about the filesystem itself. You'll learn how to find files quickly, and how to identify file types.

In Chapter 5, Streams of Text, on page 91, you'll dive deeper into redirecting program output and use grep to filter the output. You'll learn how to redirect output to another program, and learn the difference between STDIN, STDOUT, and STDERR. You'll learn about the sed stream editor, xargs, and awk.

In Chapter 6, The Shell and Environment, on page 125, you'll accelerate your workflow by making customizations to your command-line environment. You'll create a custom prompt that tells you information about your session. You'll create aliases for complicated commands so you can type fewer keystrokes.

You'll create configuration files that let you start your session with the customizations you make, and you'll learn how to set environment variables you can refer to later in scripts or applications.

In Chapter 7, Running and Managing Programs, on page 161, you'll explore additional ways to run programs, leverage your command history to reuse commands effectively, and explore subshells. You'll also manage the processes running on your system and run programs in the background.

In Chapter 8, Networking Tools, on page 199, you'll use command-line tools to look up IP addresses and domain names, fetch files and interact with web APIs, transfer files with scp and rsync, inspect open ports, and do low-level network communications with netcat.

In Chapter 9, Automation, on page 231, you'll reduce repetitive tasks and create workflows. You'll use make to build a very basic static site generator that wraps content with headers and footers. Then, you'll use Bash to create an interactive script for creating a web project.

In Chapter 10, Additional Programs, on page 255, you'll explore a handful of tools that can improve how you work. You'll use ranger to navigate and manage files and direnv to set environment variables for specific projects. You'll use some Python CLI tools to keep a journal of your work, run a basic web server, and view source code with syntax highlighting. You'll use jq to process JSON, manipulate documentation with pandoc, run commands when files change with entr, and work with APIs with Siege and HTTPie.

Finally, you'll find two appendices in the book as well. Appendix 1, Command Quick Reference, on page 287, provides a list of the commands used in this book. Appendix 2, Installing GNU Utilities on macOS, on page 291, explains how to install the GNU versions of many of the tools in this book on a Mac.

But you also won't find a few things in this book. First, there are a ton of commands available, and this book won't cover them all. I've selected the tools in this book based on research, interactions with students in classes and workshops, and personal experience. In addition, you'll use only a handful of options for each tool, with the assumption that you'll explore other options on your own. You'll use the Linux versions of these tools, rather than the BSD versions found on OpenBSD or FreeBSD.

I've also left out a few tools that I think are fantastic, but aren't a good fit. This book won't go into using alternative shells, it won't go over Windows or PowerShell command-line tools, and it doesn't spend time using tools like Vim, Emacs, or tmux. You also won't work with Git in this book, except in one case when you'll use it to download and install another tool. When you need to use a command-line based editor, you'll use nano. When talking about running something in a detached terminal, you'll use screen. If you know how to use something different, you should feel comfortable doing so.

You'll work with real-world examples of useful tools that will accelerate your work, and you'll find exercises to practice them. When you're done, you'll know where to go next to learn more about each tool.

How to Use This Book

You can use Windows, Linux, or macOS to follow along with the activities and exercises in this book—as long as you run a Bash shell. Thankfully, that's the default on macOS and most Linux variants, and you can set up Bash on Windows 10. However, you may want to use VirtualBox[2] to install the Ubuntu operating system and use that instead.

Using VirtualBox, you can run the commands in this book without worrying about doing anything to harm your computer, and you can take snapshots of your virtualized environment which you can revert if something goes wrong while you're working on the exercises in this book. You'll also avoid inconsistencies between the various operating systems while you're learning. Chapter 2, Creating an Ubuntu Virtual Machine with VirtualBox, on page 17, explains this in more detail and walks you through setting this up.

Throughout the book, you'll see commands and output. Commands you'll type will look like this:

```
$ echo hello > hello.txt
```

The dollar sign ($) represents the prompt from the Bash shell session. You won't type it when you type the command. It just denotes that this is a command you should type.

Occasionally, you'll see a series of commands. The dollar sign prompts let you see what you should type, and the rest is output from the program:

```
$ ls -l
total 36
drwxr-xr-x 2 brian brian 4096 Mar  2 11:59 Desktop
drwxr-xr-x 2 brian brian 4096 Mar  2 11:59 Documents
drwxr-xr-x 2 brian brian 4096 Mar  2 11:59 Downloads
drwxr-xr-x 2 brian brian 4096 Mar  2 11:59 Music
drwxr-xr-x 2 brian brian 4096 Mar  2 11:59 Pictures
drwxr-xr-x 2 brian brian 4096 Mar  2 11:59 Public
```

2.   https://virtualbox.org

```
drwxr-xr-x 2 brian brian 4096 Mar  2 15:48 sharptools
drwxr-xr-x 2 brian brian 4096 Mar  2 11:59 Templates
drwxr-xr-x 2 brian brian 4096 Mar  2 11:59 Videos
$ mkdir Code
$ cd Code
```

Additionally, sometimes you'll see commands that span multiple lines, like this:

```
$ cat << 'EOF' > hello.txt
> Hello
> World
> EOF
```

The > symbol indicates that the command continues on that line. You'll see the > character in your shell whenever it's waiting for you to continue typing. You won't type that character either.

Finally, each chapter has some exercises for you to try, so you can practice what you learned. In addition, each chapter assumes you have experience with the content in the previous chapter. Feel free to jump around and explore, but don't go so fast that you don't get some practice time in. The commands in this book will help you be more productive, but only once you've practiced them enough so they're second nature.

Online Resources

The book's website[3] has links to download some companion files for this book, including data files you may want for exercises, as well as scripts and configuration files you'll write in this book. You'll download those files from the CLI as you work through the book.

If you're reading the electronic version of this book, you can click the box above the code excerpts to download that source code directly.

In addition, the companion site for the book[4] has supplemental material, including videos and additional tutorials you'll find useful.

With all that out of the way, it's time to dive in. You'll start by doing some very basic command-line stuff on your own machine so you can see how the command-line interface works and what it can do for you.

---

3. https://pragprog.com/titles/bhcldev
4. https://smallsharpsoftwaretools.com

## CHAPTER 1

Getting Your Feet Wet

When you hear about the command-line interface, or CLI, from other developers, you often hear about how much faster it is than a graphical environment. But if you're like most developers, you're probably pretty good with your computer. You know some keyboard shortcuts that help you move even faster. The best way to see the real value of the CLI is to just dive right in to some hands-on activities, while learning a few time-saving techniques along the way. In this chapter, you'll use the command line to do some things you probably know how to do already through the graphical interface. You'll work with files and directories, navigate around a bit, install some software, and get more information about the commands you're typing. We're just going to scratch the surface in this first chapter; we'll go into more detail on many of the topics in the rest of the book, and we'll even review these topics again to help them stick. This chapter is designed to give you a taste of working with the command-line interface.

But first, you have to find the command-line interface.

Accessing the Command-Line Interface

Getting access to the command-line interface, often called the *shell*, varies based on your operating system. Usually, you'll access it through a program called a *terminal*, short for *terminal emulator*.

If you're on a Linux machine with a GUI, you can usually launch its terminal app with `Control`+`Alt`+`t`, or by searching for a Terminal program in your list of programs. When the terminal opens, you'll see something like this:

```
brian@puzzles:~$
```

This is the *prompt*, and it's where you'll enter commands. We'll explore its meaning shortly.

To access the command-line interface on a Mac, hold down the `Command` key on your keyboard and press `Space`. This brings up the Spotlight window. Type `terminal` into the box and press `Enter`. This launches the Terminal program. The prompt you'll see looks like this:

```
puzzles:~ brian$
```

Windows 10 has a few command-line interfaces. The classic Command Prompt and the PowerShell interfaces aren't compatible with the command-line interface on Linux, BSD, or macOS systems. They have their own commands and approaches to solving problems. So you won't be using those interfaces in this book. Instead, you'll use the Bash on Windows feature for Windows 10.

To do this, you'll enable the Windows Subsystem for Linux[1] and then download Ubuntu from the Windows Store. It's a free download that installs a version of Ubuntu on top of your Windows operating system, and it's fully supported by Microsoft. There are other flavors of Linux available, but you'll use Ubuntu in this book.

First, open the Control Panel and select Programs. Then, click Turn Windows Features On Or Off. Locate and enable the option for "Windows Subsystem for Linux." Then reboot your computer.

When the computer reboots, open the Windows Store and search for Ubuntu. Install it and launch it once it installs.

You'll see a console window open and Ubuntu will install some additional components and configure itself:

```
Installing, this may take a few minutes...
Installation successful!
```

Once it finishes extracting, you'll get prompted to create a new user account and password. This new account isn't connected to your Windows account in any way. To keep things easy to remember, use the same username as your Windows user. For the password, choose anything you like. You won't see your password as you type it, as it's hidden for security purposes.

```
Please create a default UNIX user account. The username does not need to match
your Windows username.
For more information visit: https://aka.ms/wslusers
Enter new UNIX username: brian
Enter new UNIX password:
Retype new UNIX password:
passwd: password updated successfully
```

---

1. https://docs.microsoft.com/en-us/windows/wsl/install-win10

```
Default UNIX user set to: brian
To run a command as administrator (user "root"), use "sudo <command>".
See "man sudo_root" for details.
```

You'll then be placed at a Bash prompt. Type exit to close the window.

To open Bash on Windows in the future, open a new Command Prompt or PowerShell window and type bash again. Alternatively, choose Ubuntu from the Start menu.

Now that you have the CLI open, you can start exploring.

Getting Your Bearings

When you first open the CLI, you'll be presented with something that looks like this:

```
brian@puzzles:~$
```

This is the prompt, and it's the CLI's way of telling you it's ready for you to type a command. This prompt is from the Ubuntu operating system. If you're on a Mac, your prompt might look like this:

```
puzzles:~ brian$
```

These prompts may look cryptic at first, but there's valuable information here. The prompts in these examples show the username (brian), the computer's hostname (puzzles), and the *current working directory*, or your current location on the computer's filesystem.

In this case, the current working directory is represented by a tilde (~), which means your *home directory*. Your home directory is where you'll find documents, music, and settings for your programs. You have total control over your home directory. You can create and delete files and directories, move things around, and even install whole programs without administrative privileges. When you launch the CLI, it'll open the session in your home directory.

Why the Tilde Is Used to Represent the Home Directory

 In the 1970s, the Lear-Siegler ADM-3A terminal was in widespread use. On the ADM-3A keyboard, the tilde shared the same key as the Home key.

The computer's disk stores files in a hierarchy of folders, or *directories*, which are called the *filesystem*. You'll explore this in detail in Chapter 3, Navigating the Filesystem, on page 33. When you use the GUI, you click a folder to open it and see its contents, and an indicator at the top of the GUI window tells you where you are on the filesystem.

Your prompt may tell you what directory you're currently viewing. But a clearer way to tell is with the pwd command, which stands for "print working directory."

At the prompt, type:

```
$ pwd
/home/brian
```

The command prints the full *path*, or location on the filesystem, to the current working directory. In this case, the current working directory is your home directory, and the path you see depends on which operating system you're using. For example, on macOS, you'll see /Users instead of /home.

In a GUI, you'd look at the folder name in the top of the file window to see where you are. On the CLI, you use pwd to get that information.

Now that you know where you are, look at the contents of your home directory by using the ls command. This command lists the contents of the directory.

```
$ ls
Desktop Documents Downloads Music Pictures Public Templates Videos
```

You might see different files and directories in your home directory, as each operating system sets things up a little differently.

If your system has a GUI, you'll see a directory named Desktop, and anything you place in that directory will show up on your computer's graphical desktop. After all, any shortcuts, directories, or files on your Desktop have to be stored *somewhere* on your computer, right?

Using the CLI, navigate to your Desktop directory using the cd command. The cd command is short for "change directory." It's somewhat like clicking a folder to open it up in the GUI environment, except it's a little more powerful because you can use it to jump to any directory on your filesystem immediately, without going through any intermediate directory. You'll look at that in Chapter 3, Navigating the Filesystem, on page 33.

Type this command to navigate to the Desktop directory if you're using a Mac or running a Linux distribution with a GUI:

```
$ cd Desktop
```

If you're using Bash on Windows, the Desktop directory isn't located in the same place. The Windows Subsystem for Linux uses its own filesystem that's separate from the one that Windows uses, with its own home directory. However, you can still follow along, as the Windows Subsystem for Linux makes your Windows desktop available. Execute the following command, substituting your_username for your Windows username.

```
$ cd "/mnt/c/Users/your_username/Desktop"
```

You're now in the Desktop directory, which you can verify with the pwd command just to make sure.

Now, let's create a file on your desktop that contains some text.

Creating and Reading Files

The echo command takes text and prints it back to the screen. At the prompt, type the following command:

```
$ echo Hello there
```

You'll see the text you entered printed back to you. You'll use echo in scripts you write to display instructions or output to users. But you can also use it to insert text into files if you combine it with a feature called *redirection*.

Let's create a text file in your Desktop directory that contains the text "Hello". You'll call this file greetings.txt. At the prompt, type:

```
$ echo Hello > greetings.txt
```

When you press the Enter key you won't see any visual feedback because the output of the echo command was redirected to the file you specified. If you look at your computer's graphical desktop, you should see a new icon that wasn't there before for greetings.txt. You just used the command-line interface to create a file that contains some text. Right now it's a cool parlor trick, but the implications are important; this is one way you can programmatically create files on the filesystem.

You can do so much more with redirection, but let's move on and continue your introductory tour. You'll work with echo a lot more soon enough.

But first, make sure that this text file does indeed contain the text you placed inside. You could open this file with a graphical text editor, but you can display the contents of any file from the command line quickly with the cat command:

```
$ cat greetings.txt
```

This command reads the contents of a given file and displays them on the screen.

Since the file was small, it all fit on one screen. But try reading the contents of a much larger file and see what happens. On macOS and Ubuntu, there's a dictionary of words located at /usr/share/dict/words. Use the cat command to display its contents:

```
$ cat /usr/share/dict/words
```

If you're using Ubuntu on Windows 10, you might not have this file, but you can try using a different file for this exercise instead.

You'll see the contents of the file scroll by until it reaches the end. You'll encounter this a lot when working on the command line. You might have the source code to a program you're working on, a document you're editing, or a log file you're using to diagnose an issue.

You can use the more and less commands to read longer files one page at a time. Use the less command to read the contents of that huge dictionary file:

```
$ less /usr/share/dict/words
```

You'll see the first page of the file on the screen. Use the Enter key to display the next line, the Spacebar to jump to the next page, and the q key to exit and return to your prompt.

Since you're using less, you can use the arrow keys to move forward and backward through the file. On most systems, the less and more commands run the same program. The more command is a legacy program with limited features, but it's still quite popular in documentation and on some minimalist operating systems due to its smaller size.

Now, let's look at redirecting program output to files and other programs, something you'll find yourself doing quite often.

Redirecting Streams of Text

When you used the echo command to create a file, you took the output of one command and directed it somewhere else. Let's look at this in more detail.

Execute this command to view all of the running processes on your computer:

```
$ ps -ef
```

The ps command shows you the processes running on your computer, and the -ef options show you the processes for every user in all sessions. Once again, the output of the command streams by.

This problem can be solved in a couple of ways. The first approach would be to capture the output to a file by using the > operator, just like you did to create a text file with echo:

```
$ ps -ef > processes.txt
```

You could then open that file in your favorite text editor and read its contents, or you could use less to view it one page at a time.

But a better way involves less steps. You can redirect the output of the ps command to the less command by using the pipe (|) character. Give it a try:

```
$ ps -ef | less
```

Now you can read the output more easily.

Clearing and Resetting Your Terminal

After typing several commands, your terminal might become a little harder to read. Type the clear command to clear the contents of the screen. Everything in the terminal will be wiped away and your prompt will start at the top of the screen just as if you'd opened a new terminal.

In some cases, you may need to do more than just clear your screen. Your terminal might begin behaving strangely after you've run some programs—for example, if you accidentally used the cat command to read an executable file. Instead of closing the terminal and starting a new one, try the reset command, which resets your terminal session and usually fixes the problem. The reset command works in conjunction with your Terminal program, so its actual behavior depends on how your Terminal program is configured.

As you work on the command line, you'll find yourself taking the output of one program and sending it off to another program, which will then output something new. Sometimes you might use three or four programs together to achieve a result. Imagine the data that flows as a stream of text that can be processed by programs. Each program that processes the text does one thing. You'll learn more detail about this concept later in the book. For now, turn your attention back to files and directories.

Creating Directories

Directories help you organize your files and projects. The mkdir command lets you create a directory. Let's use it to create a directory called website on the Desktop. At the prompt, assuming you're still in your Desktop directory, type:

```
$ mkdir website
```

If your computer's graphical desktop is visible, you'll see the directory appear. Otherwise, use the ls command to view it:

```
$ ls
```

Once you've created the directory, you can use the cd command to navigate into that directory:

```
$ cd website
```

You can then create new directories inside of this directory for images, style sheets, and scripts. You'll explore more efficient ways to create complex directory structures for projects later. For now, take a look at how you can get back to your home directory.

Going Home

No matter where you are, you can execute a single command that will take you back to your home directory. As you recall, the tilde (~) always refers to *your* home directory.

So if you type

```
$ cd ~
```

you'll return to your home directory regardless of where you are on the filesystem.

You can save a couple of keystrokes, because entering cd followed by Enter will do the same thing. Try it out:

```
$ cd
```

Either of these methods will always take you back to your home directory, no matter where you are on the filesystem.

Using Autocompletion

If you need to reference a filename or directory in a command, you can type part of the name, followed by the Tab key, and the CLI will attempt to auto-complete the word for you. Try this out. Switch to the Documents directory in your home directory like this:

```
$ cd ~/Doc<Tab>
```

As soon as you press Tab, the word Documents will expand. This technique serves two purposes. First, it saves you from typing the whole name, which means you'll make less typos. But second, the CLI only completes filenames and directory names it can find. If it can't complete it, there's a good chance it doesn't have enough information, or the file doesn't actually exist. Try this out. Navigate to your home directory:

```
$ cd
```

Then type:

```
$ cd D<Tab>
```

You won't see anything. This is because Bash doesn't have enough information to do the completion, because you probably have a Documents directory as well as a Downloads directory.

But if you press Tab again, you'll see a list of possible options:

```
Desktop/    Documents/ Downloads/
```

Type a few more characters and press Tab to let it autocomplete the rest of the directory name.

Now, try autocompleting var from your Home directory:

```
$ cd va<Tab>
```

This time, pressing Tab doesn't do anything. And pressing it a second time doesn't either, since there's no var directory within the current directory. You can use this as a good test while you're learning how to navigate around; if you can't autocomplete the filename or directory, you might not be looking in the right spot.

Some tasks, like creating files outside of your home directory, or installing programs system-wide, require that you run commands with additional privileges.

Elevating Privileges

You have complete and total control over all of the files in your home directory. But you don't have free reign over directories and files across the whole disk. You can only do certain things with superuser privileges. On Linux, Unix, BSD, and macOS systems, this is called the *root* user. To keep things more secure and to prevent accidents, regular user accounts are restricted from modifying things outside of their home directories.

Try to create a new directory called /var/website:

```
$ mkdir /var/website
```

This command will fail with the following error:

```
mkdir: /var/website: Permission denied
```

You're not allowed to create files in the /var directory; only certain users can do that. But thanks to the sudo command, you can execute a single command as the root user, without logging in as that user. To use it, prefix the previous command with sudo, like this:

```
$ sudo mkdir /var/website
```

Think of this sudo command as "superuser do mkdir /var/website." The command will complete successfully, and you can verify that it exists by using the ls command to view the contents of the /var directory:

```
$ ls /var/
backups  cache  crash  lib  local  lock  log  mail  metrics  opt  run  snap
spool  tmp  website
```

The website directory is now listed in the output.

The sudo command is powerful but dangerous. You're running the command as a privileged user, so if the command does something sinister, you could be in a lot of trouble. It also bypasses any file permission restrictions, meaning you could accidentally alter or delete files owned by anyone if you accidentally ran the wrong command. Use this with care!

One place you're likely to use sudo is when modifying system-wide configuration files, or, as you'll try next, installing additional programs or tools on your operating system.

Installing Additional Programs with a Package Manager

Your operating system has a bunch of programs already installed, but you'll want to install more. You might be used to going to an "app store" or downloading some files from a website and installing them, but POSIX systems traditionally offer *package managers* to make downloading and installing software easy. Each operating system has its own package manager. Debian and Ubuntu use the apt package manager, while Fedora and CentOS use yum.

If you're using Bash on Windows, you'll use apt, as the Bash environment is based on Ubuntu.

If you're on macOS, you don't have a package manager installed. You should install Homebrew[2] by following the directions on its official homepage.

You'll install a few programs throughout this book using package managers, so let's make sure everything works.

Whenever you use the package manager to install a program, make sure you have the latest list of packages. The package manager will have a command that fetches that list for you. If you're using apt, you'll use this command:

```
$ sudo apt update
```

---

2. https://brew.sh

If you're using yum, the command is similar:

```
$ sudo yum update
```

And for macOS with Homebrew, you'll use this command:

```
$ brew update
```

However, Homebrew updates its packages automatically before installing a package. Also, notice that you don't need the sudo command with Homebrew. Homebrew installs programs into a directory within the /usr/local directory, and during the Homebrew installation process, it modifies the permissions on that directory so your user has access to modify its contents.

Let's install the tree package, which lets you visualize a directory structure. You'll use it in the next chapter. For systems using apt, install it with the following command:

```
$ sudo apt install tree
```

If you're using yum, install tree with this command:

```
$ sudo yum install tree
```

And for macOS with Homebrew, use this command:

```
$ brew install tree
```

The package manager will install the program. It may ask you to confirm the installation, which you should accept. Once the package is installed, you'll be able to use the tree command. Try it out.

```
$ tree --version
tree v1.8.0 (c) 1996 - 2018 by Steve Baker, Thomas Moore, Francesc Rocher,
Florian Sesser, Kyosuke Tokoro
```

You'll use the tree command throughout this book to visualize directory structures.

Now let's look at how to download files from the CLI.

Downloading Files

This book has some code examples and data files you can use as you work through the book. Instead of using a browser to download these files, you can download them right from the command line.

The curl command, which you'll learn about in detail in Making Web Requests with cURL, on page 208, lets you download documents from web servers to your machine, just like a browser would. And the unzip command will let you unzip archives you downloaded.

First, check to see if curl is installed. You can use the which command to do that. You'll learn more about this command later in Locating Executables with PATH, on page 129.

```
$ which curl
```

If the result is blank, install curl using your package manager just like you did with tree.

Then, check to see if you have the unzip command on your machine:

```
$ which unzip
```

If you don't see any results, install unzip with your package manager.

Now let's download those example files. First, ensure that you are in your home directory. Then, make a new directory to hold the files and switch to this new directory:

```
$ cd
$ mkdir sharptools
$ cd sharptools
```

You'll find the URL for the book's companion files by visiting the book's web page.[3] Find the download for the ZIP version and look at its URL. It should be https://media.pragprog.com/titles/bhcldev/code/bhcldev-code.zip. Use that URL with the curl command to download the file:

```
$ curl -O https://media.pragprog.com/titles/bhcldev/code/bhcldev-code.zip
```

This downloads the file from the specified URL and saves it to your current working directory. The -O option (uppercase letter, not zero) tells curl to use the original filename as the filename.

The examples are compressed in an archive. The unzip command extracts them.

```
$ unzip bhcldev-code.zip
```

This creates a code directory in your current directory. Explore its contents using the tree command. You'll use a few of the files in this directory throughout the book.

As you'll see later, you can use curl to do a lot more than just download files.

---

3.   https://pragprog.com/titles/bhcldev

You've already worked with quite a few commands so far, but you only saw their basic usage. You can learn more about those commands using the built-in documentation system.

Read the Friendly Manual

Provided your operating system hasn't been set up by a sinister monster of a system administrator, the documentation for the commands you're learning is available to you thanks to the man command, which is shorthand for "manual." For example, you've played around with the echo command a little, so type the following command to learn more about echo:

```
$ man echo
```

You'll see what the program does, along with its options. In some cases, you might even see some example usage.

Press q to return to your prompt.

Some commands you use, like cd, don't have their own man page, as they are "built-in" commands. You can see those with man builtins.

You're just about done with your introductory tour, but before we wrap up, there are a few shortcuts you should know about that will come in handy as you play around.

Useful Shortcuts

You've already learned that typing cd returns you to your home directory. This is just one of the many shortcuts available on the command line.

First, if you press the Up arrow key on your keyboard, the previous command you issued will appear on the command line. Press Enter to execute it again. Or press Up again to see the command you typed before that. Keep pressing Up to move through the history of commands you've typed. Pressing Down will move forward through your command history.

Second, you can see all the commands you've typed with the history command. Each one will be listed with a number:

```
$ history
  1  tree --version
  2  man echo
  3  history
```

You can execute any of these commands again by typing !, followed by the number associated with the command:

```
$ !1
tree --version
tree v1.8.0 (c) 1996 - 2018 by Steve Baker, Thomas Moore, Francesc Rocher,
Florian Sesser, Kyosuke Tokoro
```

You can always rerun the most recent command with !!:

```
$ !!
tree --version
tree v1.8.0 (c) 1996 - 2018 by Steve Baker, Thomas Moore, Francesc Rocher,
Florian Sesser, Kyosuke Tokoro
```

This comes in handy if you execute a command that should have been run with sudo:

```
$ mkdir /var/website
mkdir: /var/website: Permission denied
$ sudo !!
```

This way you don't have to type the whole command over again.

Finally, there are a handful of keyboard shortcuts you'll find useful:

- Ctrl+a jumps to the first character of the line.

- Ctrl+e jumps to the end of the line.

- Ctrl+l clears the screen's contents, similar to typing the clear command. This works even if you're in the middle of typing a new command.

- Ctrl+r lets you search through your command history and execute a command.

- Ctrl+u removes a command you're typing. It's great if you decide you don't want to complete the current command and want to start over.

Practice with these shortcuts; they'll make it much easier as you work through this book, as well as your own projects.

Your Turn

1. Review the following commands and write down what each does:

   a. pwd
   b. cd Desktop
   c. cd ~
   d. cd
   e. echo
   f. echo Hi there > greetings.txt
   g. cat greetings.txt
   h. mkdir /var/website
   i. !!

2. Explain the difference between cat, more, and less. Use the man command to explore the more and less commands. When would you use one command over another?

3. The history command will show you the recent commands you typed. Create a log for your notes of the commands by saving the result of the history command to a text file called history.txt.

4. The cal and ncal commands give you a small calendar right in your terminal. Explore both of these commands and then use each to display a calendar for two years in the future.

What You Learned

In this chapter, you learned the basics of working with the CLI. You created a file by redirecting output, you created a directory, and you installed a program with the package manager. You learned a few shortcuts, and you should now feel a little more comfortable with the CLI. But you're just getting started. You'll revisit many of these topics in more detail throughout the rest of the book.

Next, you'll set up a test environment so you can explore the CLI without worrying about accidentally deleting files or messing up your computer.

## CHAPTER 2

Creating an Ubuntu Virtual Machine with VirtualBox

If you're worried about messing up your computer while you're trying to learn to use the command-line interface, you can install software that lets you create virtual machines. This software borrows your computer's CPU, memory, and other resources and allocates it to an emulated computer. Virtual machines are great for development and testing; you can install a separate operating system on a virtual machine, and you can then do all of your work in this virtual environment without affecting the host operating system.

In this chapter, you'll create a test environment that you'll use for the rest of this book. You'll install VirtualBox—a free, open-source application that creates virtual machines—and create a virtual machine running the Ubuntu operating system, a popular and user-friendly Linux-based OS. You'll use Ubuntu 18.04 LTS for this chapter, as well as the rest of the book. You'll then create snapshots, which let you save the state of the machine so you can return to it later if you run into problems. Finally, you'll configure some networking options for the machine so you can connect to it remotely.

If you are already comfortable with setting up virtual machines, or you're feeling adventurous and want to try out the exercises in the rest of this book on your actual computer instead of a virtual one, you can skip this chapter. However, I'll assume you're using this machine in the rest of the book, especially in Chapter 8, Networking Tools, on page 199. By using the virtual machine running Ubuntu, you'll be able to replicate what you see in this book, practice without accidentally damaging your real OS, and gain confidence with the CLI.

Creating a New Virtual Machine

To create Ubuntu virtual machines, you'll need two pieces of software. First, you'll need the Ubuntu operating system itself. Visit Ubuntu's downloads page[1] and select the Desktop version of Ubuntu 18.04 LTS. The file is quite large and may take a while to download. Save this file to your Downloads folder.

Next, you'll need VirtualBox, the software you'll use to create and manage our virtual machine. Visit VirtualBox's download page[2] and download the version for your operating system. Once the software downloads, run the installer and accept all of the default options. The installer may ask for permission to install additional drivers or components, which you should allow.

Once the installation completes, run VirtualBox. You'll see a menu across the top of the screen that looks like this:

Select the New button to create your machine. VirtualBox displays a wizard that walks you through creating your machine.

The first screen asks for a name for your machine and the operating system you plan to install.

---

1. https://www.ubuntu.com/download/desktop
2. https://virtualbox.org

Enter the following into the form:

- For the Name, enter "Ubuntu1804" or something more descriptive.
- For Type, choose Linux.
- For Version, choose Ubuntu (64-bit).

When you're ready, click Continue.

The next screen asks you to choose the amount of memory you want to allocate to the virtual machine. For a smooth experience, choose at least 1024 MB of RAM. If you have 8 GB of RAM on your machine, consider choosing 2048 MB of RAM instead. Once you've set the RAM, click Continue.

Next, you'll create a hard disk for your virtual machine. This hard disk is nothing more than a big data file on your computer's hard drive, but the operating system you install in VirtualBox will think it's a real physical hard drive. It'll see this hard drive instead of the real one on your computer. Select the default setting of "Create a virtual hard disk now" and click Create.

The wizard then asks you for the hard disk file type. Choose the default of VDI (VirtualBox Disk Image), and press Continue.

The next screen asks you how VirtualBox should create the disk. VirtualBox can create a "fixed" disk, which allocates all of the space right away, or it can dynamically allocate space as needed. A fixed disk results in slightly better performance when your machine is running because it doesn't have to do any calculations to expand the size of the disk. A dynamic disk saves disk space. Performance isn't a concern here, so you can save disk space and let VirtualBox dynamically allocate space as needed. Select the option and click Continue.

Next, VirtualBox asks you for the filename and location of the disk and how big you want the disk to be, as shown in the first figure on page 20.

VirtualBox automatically uses the name of your virtual machine as the name of the disk, and it places the disk's file in the default folder that VirtualBox uses for virtual machines. While you can change this, it's best to leave it alone.

Set the size of the disk to 32 GB or more. The default 8 GB of space isn't enough since you'll install some additional programs. Then, click Create.

VirtualBox creates the new machine, which appears in the list of machines in VirtualBox's interface. When you select the machine, you'll see a summary of the machine's attributes as shown in the second figure on page 20.

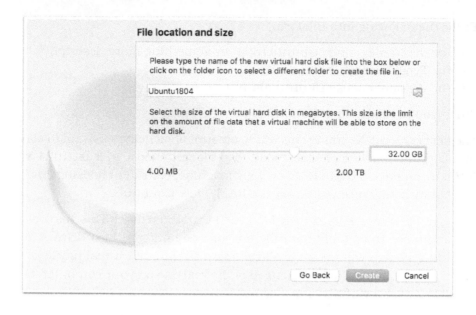

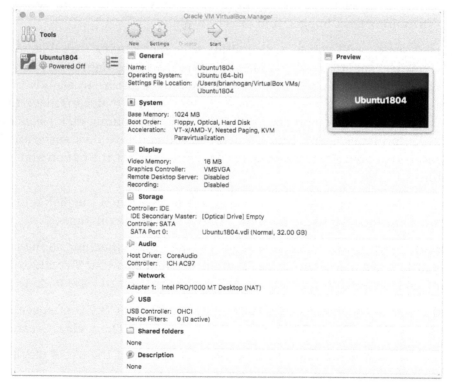

Let's set up the network interfaces next.

Configuring a Network

In Chapter 8, Networking Tools, on page 199, you will learn how to use some tools to communicate with other computers. You will install the OpenSSH server so you can transfer files, and install a small server so you can test the web server connections. To access those services in your virtual machine from your host OS, you have to let VirtualBox know how to route the traffic.

VirtualBox has a few different networking modes. The default mode, NAT, short for *Network Address Translation*, works like the router you might have in your home. The operating system in the virtual machine can access the outside network by forwarding the requests to the host operating system, just like how your home router lets you use a single Internet connection across all of your devices. The downside with this approach is that you can't access any services running inside of the virtual machine from the host OS unless you configure port forwarding. This is doable, but you can make things easier on yourself by using VirtualBox's "Host-only" networking option to create a private network between the host machine running VirtualBox and the guest machine running inside of VirtualBox.

First, go to the File menu and select the Host Network Manager tab. Double-click the network listed and set the IPv4 address to 192.168.99.1. If you have a different value in this box, change it to this new value so you can follow along with the rest of the book. And if there's no network defined, press the Create button to add one as shown in the first figure on page 22.

The 192.168. address range is reserved for small private networks, which is exactly what we're creating here. You'll learn more about this in Chapter 8, Networking Tools, on page 199.

Next, select the DHCP tab. The DHCP tab configures how VirtualBox assigns IP addresses to guests on this private network. Ensure the DHCP server is enabled and set the DHCP Server address to 192.168.99.1. Ensure the Subnet Mask is 255.255.255.0. Then set the Lower Address Bound to 192.168.99.100 and the Upper Address Bound to 192.168.99.254. As shown in the second figure on page 22.

Press Apply to save the changes. Then press Close to close the window.

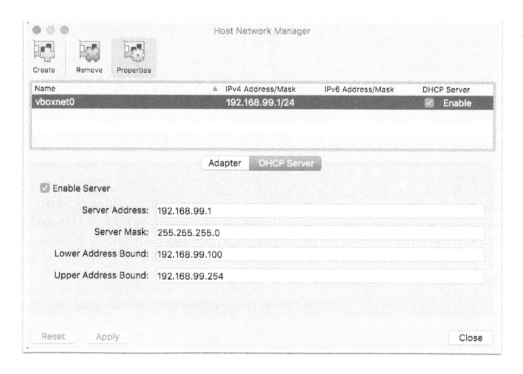

Now you can configure your virtual machine to use this new network. Select your Ubuntu virtual machine in the main VirtualBox window, click the Settings icon, and select the Network tab. You'll see that Adapter 1 is enabled and configured to use NAT for its network type. Leave this setting alone, as this is what allows your guest machine to access the Internet.

Instead, select the Adapter 2 tab and check the box to enable the adapter. Then choose Host-only Adapter for the type. Your configuration should look like this:

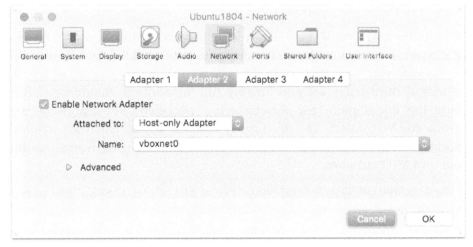

Press OK to configure the machine.

These settings ensure that you'll be able to access your guest operating system from your host operating system, and vice-versa.

You now have a virtual computer configured, but it won't do much until you install your operating system. Let's do that now.

Installing the Guest Operating System

VirtualBox creates "guest" machines that run on top of a "host" machine. The host machine is the machine running VirtualBox. It "hosts" various virtual machines running as "guests" inside of VirtualBox. Once you define a virtual machine, you install an operating system, much like you would if you were installing a real operating system on your computer. Let's install Ubuntu on this machine using the disk image you downloaded.

When you first start your virtual machine, VirtualBox detects that there's no operating system and prompts you to install one. To start the machine, select your Ubuntu virtual machine from the list of machines and press the green Start button at the top of the VirtualBox interface.

VirtualBox prompts you for a virtual disk or optical disk that holds the installation media. Select the folder icon at the bottom right to open a file dialog. Navigate to your Downloads folder and select the Ubuntu ISO file you downloaded. Once you've selected the installation media, press the Start button.

The machine boots, and the Ubuntu installation program starts, displaying a welcome screen. Choose the Install Ubuntu option on the Welcome screen.

You'll be prompted to select your keyboard layout from the list. Click Continue once you've made your selection.

The installer asks you if you'd like to do a normal installation or a minimal installation. Do a minimal installation, as you can install other things later if you decide you want them. It'll also ask if you'd like to download updates and install third-party software during the installation. Installing updates during the installation can prevent some incompatibility issues between Ubuntu and VirtualBox. The third-party software option tells the installer to include packages that have additional restrictive licensing terms, such as Flash and MP3 support.

On the Installation Type screen, you will see this screen, asking you to erase your disk.

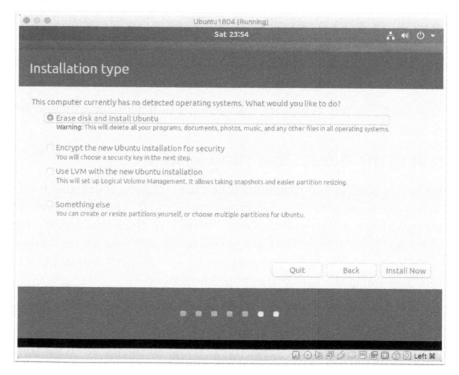

Don't worry, you won't be erasing your actual computer's hard disk. You're just erasing the already blank virtual disk you created for your Ubuntu virtual machine. The virtual disk you created doesn't have a filesystem on it, and Ubuntu needs to format the disk so it can add one.

Select the Erase disk option and click the Install Now button to continue.

You'll see a confirmation box telling you that the installer will create two partitions on the disk. The first partition is the main storage partition which will hold your operating system files and data. The second partition is the swap partition, a special partition Linux systems use as temporary memory in case you run out of RAM.

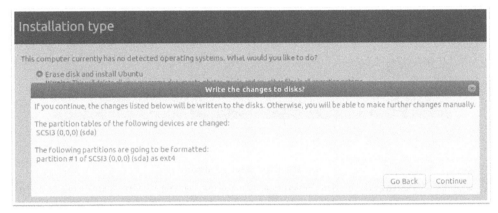

Click Continue to start the installation process. While the files copy, you'll see a few additional prompts.

The first asks for your time zone. Select your time zone on the map and press Continue.

Next, the installation prompts you to create a user and name the computer as shown in the figure on page 26. This creates the user account you'll use to log in to Ubuntu.

Choose a password that you'll remember, and choose whether you want to require the password to log in to the machine, then press Continue. The installer copies the rest of the operating system files. Once it's done, click the Restart Now button to restart the virtual machine.

The screen will display a message asking you to remove the installation disk. If you don't, the installation will start over when you reboot. In many cases, VirtualBox will do this for you, but double-check this by clicking the Devices menu in VirtualBox, selecting Optical Drives, and then clicking Remove Disk from Virtual Drive. Press Enter to continue, and the virtual machine will reboot.

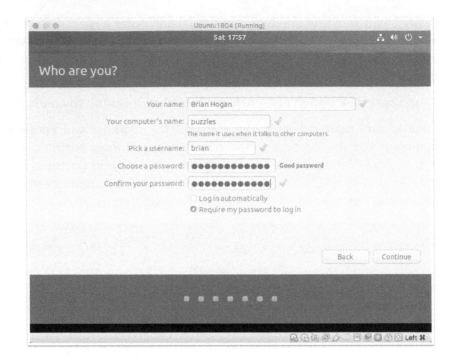

Locating the Devices Menu

On macOS, VirtualBox uses a unified menu at the top of the screen like other macOS applications. You'll find the Devices menu and other options in that menu when your virtual machine has focus. On Windows, you'll find the Devices menu entry at the top of the virtual machine window itself, instead of on the VirtualBox window where you create and manage machines.

Once the machine restarts, Ubuntu loads, and you're presented with a login screen. But before you log in, let's create a snapshot so you can reset your machine if something goes wrong.

Working with Snapshots

Setting up a new virtual machine and running the installation process for an operating system takes time. You can save the state of a machine by taking a snapshot, and then you can revert the machine to that snapshot later. You can think of these like save points in a video game. This comes in handy if you goof up the machine's configuration, install some software that messes things up, or if you just want to start over without going through the entire installation process again. Snapshots are great for testing software in pristine environments, too.

To create your first snapshot, navigate to the Machine menu in VirtualBox and select Take Snapshot. In the dialog that appears, enter a name and a description for the snapshot so you can identify it later.

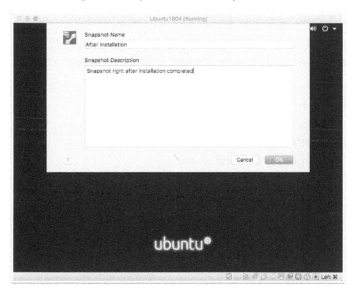

Then, press OK to create the snapshot. This process takes only a few seconds.

Now that you have a new snapshot, let's make some modifications to the virtual machine, and then restore the machine back to its original state.

Log in to Ubuntu using the username and password you created during the installation. You'll be presented with the Ubuntu Desktop.

If you're presented with a dialog to install software updates, skip this for now.

Once logged in, make a mess of your Desktop. Right-click on the desktop and choose New Folder. Give the new folder a name like "Junk folder." Repeat this a few times to place several more folders on the desktop.

Let's also mess up the default menu items in the sidebar. Right-click any of the icons on the sidebar and choose Remove from Favorites to make it disappear.

Now, undo everything you just did by restoring the snapshot you took earlier. You can take a snapshot while the machine is running, but you have to shut the virtual machine down to restore one. From VirtualBox's Machine menu, choose ACPI Shutdown. This sends the shutdown signal to the machine and Ubuntu will prompt you to shut down.

Select your Ubuntu virtual machine in VirtualBox and then select the Snapshots tab in the upper right corner. You will see something similar to the following figure:

Select the snapshot you created and then press the Restore button.

You'll be asked to confirm that you want to restore this snapshot, and you'll also have a chance to save the current state as a new snapshot in case you want to keep that mess you made as its own save point. Uncheck that option and press Restore.

Once the restore completes, you can restart the machine. Log in again, and the icons you removed will be restored, and the folders you created will be gone.

You now have a snapshot you can use to reset the machine to the point right after you completed the installation. You can move forward with confidence knowing that if anything goes wrong, you can put everything back the way it was in just a couple of clicks. You should make periodic snapshots as you work. It'll save tons of time and give you the freedom to explore knowing that you can go back in time and reset things.

Let's do a few more things to this new virtual machine to get it ready for the rest of the book.

Installing Software with the Package Manager

In Installing Additional Programs with a Package Manager, on page 10, you learned how to use the apt package manager that's built into Ubuntu to install the tree command. You'll want this program installed on your virtual machine so you can use it in the next chapter to visualize directory structures. You'll also want the unzip command so you can uncompress archives. Going through this process again will give you more practice installing additional software through package managers.

Log in to your Ubuntu machine and open a new terminal. Press Ctrl+Alt+t to bring up the terminal, or click the Ubuntu logo on the sidebar and type "Terminal" into the text box that appears, followed by the Enter key. You'll see a new Terminal window like the following:

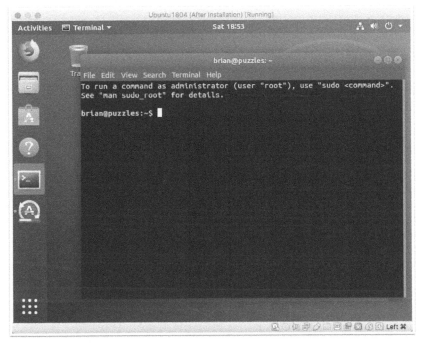

First, make sure you have the most recent list of packages available. Packages can only be managed and installed by the root account on Ubuntu, but it's a bad security practice to do anything with the root user. That's why you used the sudo command in Elevating Privileges, on page 9, to run commands with root privileges.

Ubuntu configured the user you set up during installation so it can use the sudo command to execute commands as the superuser.

Ubuntu's package manager uses a list of available packages to know what's available. Execute the following command to tell the package manager to download the latest list of available packages. Without this, you might not get the latest version of the software. Or worse, you might not be able to find the software you want to install.

```
$ sudo apt update
```

You'll be prompted for your password. Enter it, and the package manager will update the list of available software packages. Once the list of packages downloads, install the tree command. using sudo again:

```
$ sudo apt install tree
```

This time you won't be asked for your password; Ubuntu's default configuration only makes you reenter your password every fifteen minutes.

Once the installation finishes, run the tree command to view the contents of your home folder.

```
$ tree
```

You'll see the following output, displaying the directories and files in your home directory:

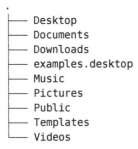

```
.
├── Desktop
├── Documents
├── Downloads
├── examples.desktop
├── Music
├── Pictures
├── Public
├── Templates
└── Videos
```

You will install additional applications and commands with this package manager throughout this book. But now let's install another component for VirtualBox that makes things run a little more smoothly.

Improving Performance by Installing Guest Additions

To get better performance out of your machine, install the VirtualBox Guest Additions, a collection of drivers and programs provided by VirtualBox. With the Guest Additions installed, you'll get better video performance, and you'll also be able to share files with the host operating system, or copy and paste text between your host and guest operating systems.

To install these additions, first open a terminal and install the make and gcc packages. These packages will let VirtualBox modify the Ubuntu kernel when you install the Guest Additions:

```
$ sudo apt install make gcc perl dkms
```

Once those packages install, select the Devices menu in VirtualBox and choose Insert Guest Addition CD Image from the menu. Ubuntu will then display a message asking you if you want to run the software. Choose Run to start the installation process.

You'll be prompted for your password. The installation process will begin once you enter it.

Once the installation completes, restart Ubuntu by typing the following in the Ubuntu terminal:

```
$ sudo reboot
```

You can set your shared folders and clipboard settings under the Devices menu. Review the VirtualBox documentation for more on how those options work.

You now have an environment you can use to practice working on the command line. But before you move on, do the exercises that follow. These exercises will let you practice working with your machine so you're comfortable with how VirtualBox and Ubuntu work, as you'll use this environment for the rest of the book.

Your Turn

Exercise 1: Snapshots

Get comfortable working with snapshots in VirtualBox.

1. Take a new snapshot of the machine, called "Ready for Practice". This way you won't have to reinstall the tree command and the Guest Additions.

2. Power down the machine, and restore your original "After Installation" snapshot. Don't create a new snapshot of the current state.

3. Boot the machine and execute the tree command. It should tell you it's not found.

4. Power down the machine, and restore the "Ready for Practice" snapshot once again.

5. Boot the machine and execute the tree command from the terminal. The command now works.

Exercise 2: Review

Review the following concepts from the previous chapter and work with them on your Ubuntu virtual machine for practice:

1. List the contents of your home directory.

2. Create a file called greetings.txt in the ~/Desktop folder containing any text you want.

3. List the running processes using ps -ef.

4. Use the sudo command to create a directory called /var/website.

5. Install the unzip and curl programs with the apt tool.

6. Download the supporting files and resources for this book using curl like you did in Downloading Files, on page 11. You'll want these available on your virtual machine as you work through the rest of the book.

What You Learned

In this chapter, you set up a virtual machine using VirtualBox. You'll use this machine as your playground in the rest of the book, but you can use VirtualBox to install other operating systems so you can test applications or websites on multiple platforms, experiment with new features, and work without fear of wrecking your actual work machine.

In the next chapter, you'll navigate around your filesystem on the command line instead of a graphical file manager.

## CHAPTER 3

Navigating the Filesystem

When you're looking for a specific file or directory, you probably pop open a graphical tool and click on icons, drilling down to where you need to go. But you can do this much more quickly using the command-line interface once you know how. In this chapter, you'll explore how to work with files and directories, and you'll get comfortable navigating around your computer's filesystem using the CLI.

Let's start by looking at one of the most basic commands for working with files and directories on the CLI.

Listing Files and Directories

The ls command shows you the contents of a directory. By default, it only shows you part of the story. You can get a more descriptive listing by passing some additional arguments to the command. In your home directory, execute the command ls -l. (That's a lowercase L.)

```
$ ls -l
total 36
drwxr-xr-x 2 brian brian 4096 Mar  2 11:59 Desktop
drwxr-xr x 2 brian brian 4096 Mar  2 11:59 Documents
drwxr-xr-x 2 brian brian 4096 Mar  2 11:59 Downloads
drwxr-xr-x 2 brian brian 4096 Mar  2 11:59 Music
drwxr-xr-x 2 brian brian 4096 Mar  2 11:59 Pictures
drwxr-xr-x 2 brian brian 4096 Mar  2 11:59 Public
drwxr-xr-x 2 brian brian 4096 Mar  2 15:48 sharptools
drwxr-xr-x 2 brian brian 4096 Mar  2 11:59 Templates
drwxr-xr-x 2 brian brian 4096 Mar  2 11:59 Videos
```

This gives you a "long listing" of the current directory's contents. The filenames are all the way on the right side, preceded by some additional information. How it breaks down is shown in the figure on page 34.

Type	Permissions	Links	User Owner	Group	Size	Modified Date	Filename
d	rwxr-xr-x	2	brian	brian	4096	Mar 2 11:59	Desktop

The first character tells you the type of the entry. A d indicates it's a directory, a dash (-) lets you know it's a file, and l tells you that the entry is a link, which is a special type of entry that points to another file elsewhere.

The next set of characters is the file permissions. In this example, you see rwxr-xr-x, which specify the read (r), write (w), and execute (x) permissions for the user that owns the file, the group, and other users on the system, in that order. Here's how they break down:

User	Group	Others
rwx	r-x	r-x

In this case, the user that owns the file has full access to the file. The members of the group associated with the file can read and execute the file, and everyone else can read and execute the file.

The r, w, and x on a directory mean slightly different things. r means the user can list the contents of the directory, w means they can add, modify, or delete things in the directory, and x means they can navigate to that directory. The permissions on the Desktop directory are rwxr-xr-x, which tells you that your user has full access, and everyone else can list the contents and navigate there, but they can't change the contents of the directory. You'll get into changing owners, groups, and permissions in the next chapter.

After the permissions, there's a number indicating the number of *links*, or places in the filesystem that point to the the file or directory. Directories will have a minimum of two links: one for the directory itself and another for the parent directory. If the directory contains other subdirectories, the number will increase by one for each immediate subdirectory.

After the links, you'll see the user that owns the file, followed by the group that can access the file. Then you'll see the size of the file, the last modified date, and the filename itself.

Improving the Listing's Readability

The output for the file size is shown in bytes, which isn't too helpful given how large modern files can get. But if you use the -h flag in conjunction with the -l flag, you can get a more "human-readable" output:

```
$ ls -l -h
total 36K
drwxr-xr-x 2 brian brian 4.0K Mar  2 11:59 Desktop
drwxr-xr-x 2 brian brian 4.0K Mar  2 11:59 Documents
drwxr-xr-x 2 brian brian 4.0K Mar  2 11:59 Downloads
drwxr-xr-x 2 brian brian 4.0K Mar  2 11:59 Music
drwxr-xr-x 2 brian brian 4.0K Mar  2 11:59 Pictures
drwxr-xr-x 2 brian brian 4.0K Mar  2 11:59 Public
drwxr-xr-x 2 brian brian 4.0K Mar  2 15:48 sharptools
drwxr-xr-x 2 brian brian 4.0K Mar  2 11:59 Templates
drwxr-xr-x 2 brian brian 4.0K Mar  2 11:59 Videos
```

To save a few keystrokes, you can combine single-letter arguments, like this:

```
$ ls -lh
```

You'll use this convention throughout the rest of the book.

Showing Hidden Files

Any filename or directory name that begins with a dot will be hidden from directory listings. They're also often hidden in the GUI unless you change how you've set things up. Configuration files for your shell or programs often use this naming convention, commonly referred to as *dotfiles*. Your system has a few of these hidden files in your home directory. To view them, add the a flag to your ls command:

```
$ ls -alh
total 96K
drwxr-xr-x 15 brian brian 4.0K Mar  2 16:05 .
drwxr-xr-x  3 root  root  4.0K Mar  2 17:59 ..
-rw-------  1 brian brian  103 Mar  2 22:28 .bash_history
-rw-r--r--  1 brian brian  220 Mar  2 11:38 .bash_logout
-rw-r--r--  1 brian brian 3.7K Mar  2 11:38 .bashrc
...
```

This time, your directory listing returns many more files.

Listing Specific Files and Directories

The ls command isn't limited to showing you the contents of the current directory; you can also use it to get information about a specific file.

On Ubuntu, your home folder has a file named .bashrc which contains commands that run when you start a shell session. You'll work with this file in detail in Customizing Your Shell Session, on page 138, later in this book. To get information about this file, execute this command:

```
$ ls -alh .bashrc
-rw-r--r-- 1 brian brian 3.7K Mar  2 11:38 .bashrc
```

If the file doesn't exist, ls will let you know.

You can also use ls to get a listing of any other directory on your system by specifying the name of the directory. View the contents of the Documents folder:

```
$ ls -lh Documents
total 0
```

In this case, the Documents folder doesn't have any files in it.

When you pass ls a filename, it shows you the details about a file. When you pass a directory, ls displays the directory's contents. If you wanted the ls command to show you the information about the directory rather than its contents, add the -d argument, like this:

```
$ ls -lhd Documents
drwxr-xr-x 2 brian brian 4.0K Mar  2 11:59 Documents/
```

The * character is a wildcard character, which means it can stand in for one or more characters. You can use it with the ls command to view only certain types of files. Want to list all files with the .txt extension in the current folder? Use this command:

```
$ ls *.txt
```

Wildcards even work with directories. Try this command to list all directories starting with D:

```
$ ls -lh D*
Desktop:
total 4.0K
-rw-r--r-- 1 brian brian 12 Mar  2 12:05 greetings.txt

Documents:
total 0

Downloads:
total 0
```

This time, the ls command showed the contents of three directories at once.

Recursive File Listings

You can use the -R flag to make the ls command list the contents of the current folder, as well as the contents of each folder within the current folder.

```
$ ls -lhR
.:
total 36K
drwxr-xr-x 2 brian brian 4.0K Mar  2 12:25 Desktop
drwxr-xr-x 2 brian brian 4.0K Mar  2 11:59 Documents

...

./Templates:
total 0
./Videos:
total 0
```

If you have a lot of files, you won't be able to read all of the contents easily unless you redirect the output to a file, or pipe the output to the more command, like you learned about in Redirecting Streams of Text, on page 6. You can also press Ctrl+c to abort the listing.

The output of the command isn't the easiest to read, so if you do need to get a recursive listing of a directory structure, use the tree command you installed in Installing Additional Programs with a Package Manager, on page 10:

```
$ tree
.
├── Desktop
│   ├── greetings.txt
│   └── website
├── Documents
├── Downloads
├── Music
├── Pictures
├── Public
├── sharptools
│   └── bhcldev-code.zip
├── Templates
└── Videos

10 directories, 2 files
```

This shows you a nice clean listing of the directories and files contained within your current directory. You can use tree -a to see the hidden files and directories, and tree -h to see the size of each entry next to its name.

You know how to list files and you've poked around in your home folder a bit, but there are files and folders all over your computer. Let's get comfortable moving around the filesystem.

Navigating Files and Folders

The cd command lets you change directories. It's the tool for changing our current working directory, or the "location" on the filesystem. As you've already seen, using cd by itself takes you straight to your home directory. Execute this command in your shell right now:

```
$ cd
```

Then, execute the pwd command to check your location. You will then see a file path displayed:

```
$ pwd
/home/brian
```

Each slash in the path represents a part of the hierarchy. So, /home/brian is just another way to represent this:

```
/
└── home/
      └── brian
```

If you've built a website and referenced images or CSS files, or written code to work with files, you're already familiar with the concept of specifying paths to files.

Your home directory is just one part of the *filesystem*. The filesystem is a hierarchy of files and directories, all starting at the *root directory*, which you represent with the forward slash character (/).

Other disks and filesystems are mounted as child directories on this filesystem. If you're familiar with Windows operating systems, you may be used to having a C: drive or a D: drive, each with its own collection of files and directories. But on a Unix-like system, disks are *mounted*, or attached, to a single tree of directories and files. This includes optical media like DVDs and external disks. To access them, you will navigate to the directory that points to the device.

The *root filesystem* is the name given to the filesystem on a Unix-like system that contains the *root* directory (/) and where all other disks and filesystems are mounted.

The following figure illustrates this hierarchy:

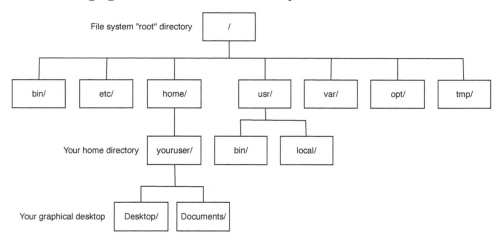

This figure shows the most common directories on a Unix-like filesystem. Here's what each folder is for:

- The *filesystem root* is represented by /, a single forward slash.

- The /bin folder traditionally contains base commands and programs necessary to operate the operating system.

- The /etc folder contains configuration files for system-wide applications, such as web servers or database servers.

- The /home folder contains the home folders for users on the system. On macOS, this folder is called Users instead.

- The /usr/bin folder contains additional commands and programs that build on top of those in the bin folder.

- The /usr/local folder is where you can install your own system-wide commands and utilities.

- The /opt folder is often where you'll find, or install, software installed from source. This is a good place to put alternative versions of software so they won't conflict with existing versions.

- The /var folder is where programs typically put their data. For example, on many Linux systems, log files for various programs are stored in the /var/log directory. On a web server, you'll often find web pages in /var/www.

- The /tmp folder is a system-wide place for temporary files. It's readable and writable by everyone on the system.

Using the cd command, you can navigate to any place on the filesystem using a single command. To jump to the root of the filesystem, execute this command:

```
$ cd /
```

Use the pwd command and you'll see that the current working directory is /. Use the ls command to get a list of the directories and you'll see something like the following:

```
$ ls
bin     dev    initrd.img      lib64       mnt    root  snap      sys  var
boot    etc    initrd.img.old  lost+found  opt    run   srv       tmp  vmlinuz
cdrom   home   lib             media       proc   sbin  swapfile  usr
```

You'll see the bin folder, the var folder, and the usr folder you saw in the preceding figure.

Use the cd command to navigate into the /var folder:

```
$ cd var
```

The prompt changes, and you can also use pwd to verify that you're now in the /var directory.

```
$ pwd
/var
```

Now, use the ls command again to see the contents of the var folder:

```
$ ls
backups   crash   local   log    metrics   run    spool   website
cache     lib     lock    mail   opt       snap   tmp
```

Use the cd command to navigate into the log directory within this directory:

```
$ cd log
$ pwd
/var/log
```

Notice that you moved to the var folder first, and then went into the log folder. You can shorten that a bit by telling cd to change to the child folder directly by specifying the path var/log. Return to the filesystem root and try it out:

```
$ cd /
$ cd var/log
$ pwd
/var/log
```

From here you can use cd / to jump back to the root of the filesystem, or use cd to get to your home directory. But what if you wanted to get back to the var directory?

Relative and Absolute Paths

So far, you've been navigating using "relative paths." That means you've been specifying the destination relative to your current working directory, or your current location on the filesystem. When you're at the root of the filesystem, and you type cd var, the var directory is something you can see with the ls command. You and the var directory are in the same location on the filesystem, and the command you specified said "Switch to the var directory that's in the same folder that I'm currently working in."

You can navigate the filesystem much more quickly by using the entire path to a directory from the root of the filesystem. Let's navigate to the /usr/bin directory. In a GUI, you'd have to go to the /usr folder first, and then open the bin directory. But the cd command can take entire file paths, so you can jump to the /usr/bin directory in a single command.

```
$ cd /usr/bin
```

This command says:

1. Go to the root of the filesystem.
2. Then go into the usr folder.
3. Finally, go into the bin folder.

Try moving around to a few locations this way. Navigate to the /usr/lib directory, and then back to the /var directory:

```
$ cd /usr/lib
$ pwd
/usr/lib
$ cd /var
$ pwd
/var
```

In this example, you didn't have to navigate back up to the parent directory, or jump back to the filesystem's root. You included the root of the filesystem in the path to the file by specifying the leading forward slash.

So instead of specifying a directory relative to your current working directory, you specify the absolute location of the directory.

Dots and Double Dots

Two shortcuts help us work with files and directory paths when working on the command line; the dot (.) and the double dot (..).

Switch to the /var directory and use the ls -alh command to get a list of the files in the current directory, including the hidden ones:

```
$ cd /var
$ ls -alh
```

Take a look at the top two entries in the listing:

```
total 56K
drwxr-xr-x 14 root root    4.0K Mar  2 18:20 .
drwxr-xr-x 24 root root    4.0K Mar  2 11:39 ..
...
```

The first entry is a dot (.). It represents the *current directory*. The second entry, the double dot (..), represents the directory that contains the current directory. This is referred to as the *parent* directory.

To quickly change to the parent directory, /, execute the command cd ..:

```
$ cd ..
$ pwd
/
```

The command cd .. changes your working directory to the parent directory, regardless of where you're currently located on the filesystem. But if you need to quickly visit the directory above the parent, you can execute this command:

```
$ cd ../..
```

Each .. entry in this command means "up one folder."

Try it out. Return to your home folder, then navigate to the /home directory's parent folder (which should be the filesystem root) using the double dot shortcut:

```
$ cd
$ pwd
/home/brian
$ cd ../..
$ pwd
/
```

Using that command, you've jumped to the root directory of the filesystem.

You can take this a step further if you like. Change the current working directory to the /usr/bin folder, and then navigate to the /var folder using the shortcuts in a single command:

```
$ cd /usr/bin
$ cd ../../var
$ pwd
/var
```

Use Pen and Paper

It can be a little difficult to visualize how the .. notation works. One trick that helps even experienced command-line users is to sketch out a directory structure on paper or a whiteboard and use it as a reference. Place your pen on the starting point, and trace up the hierarchy one level for each double dot. Do this a few times and you'll probably be able to visualize this structure in your head.

In this example, you're telling the cd command to go up two folders and then go into the var folder. But that's a lot of typing. This kind of relative path navigation works well in applications and websites where you might move the files around and you want things to be relative to where you've stored them. But when navigating around on a filesystem on the terminal, it's sometimes quicker to just use the cd command with an absolute path like cd /var—much less typing.

Try this little exercise to make sure you're comfortable navigating around using the double-dot syntax:

1. Use cd to go to your home folder.
2. Use cd ../../var to go to the /var folder.
3. Use cd ../usr to get to the /usr folder.
4. Use cd local to get to the /usr/local folder.
5. Use cd ../bin to get to the /usr/bin folder.
6. Return to your home folder with cd.

Using the .. notation can sometimes help you move around a little more quickly than typing the entire path each time. Other times it might be quicker to use the absolute path instead. Knowing both ways will help you move as quickly as possible no matter what situation you find yourself in.

Using the cd command, you can get from one part of the filesystem to another in a single command. But sometimes you'll find yourself switching back and forth between just a few locations. Let's look at some more efficient ways to do that.

Switching Between Directories

In the last few examples, you moved between the /var and /usr/bin directories by specifying either relative or absolute paths. Switching back and forth between two directories is something you'll do more often than you'd think. This has a nice shortcut command. Whenever you change to a new working directory, your shell stores the previous directory.

To switch back to the previous directory, use cd -. This command retrieves the value of the previous directory and uses it to change the directory.

Try this exercise out. First, go to your home directory. Then, navigate to the /var directory. Use cd - to switch back and forth between the two:

```
$ cd
$ cd /var
$ cd -
/home/brian
$ cd -
/var
```

When you use the cd - command, it automatically prints the new current working directory, so you don't have to use the pwd command manually.

Now you can switch between two working directories with ease. But you may find yourself moving between a few locations. You can change your working directory in another way.

Using pushd and popd to Manage a Stack of Directories

The pushd command, short for "push directory," changes your current working directory and adds it to a directory stack, or a list of directories. You can then view this stack or easily jump to an entry in the stack. Try it out. First, navigate to your home directory.

```
$ cd
```

Now use pushd to switch to the /var folder:

```
$ pushd /var
/var ~
```

The pushd command switches your working directory, but it also displays the contents of the directory stack. The current directory is listed first, followed by the previous directory. Use pushd to navigate to the /tmp directory:

```
$ pushd /tmp
/tmp /var ~
```

Your location changes, and the directory stack has a new entry at the front. Now switch to the /usr folder with pushd:

```
$ pushd /usr
/usr /tmp /var ~
```

The popd command removes the first entry from the stack, and then changes your location to the new first entry:

```
$ popd
/tmp /var ~
```

This places you in the /tmp directory now, and the stack reflects this. You can keep using popd to traverse backward through your previous locations.

Use pushd to navigate to the /usr/bin directory:

```
$ pushd /usr/bin
/usr/bin /tmp /var ~
```

You can view the directory stack with the dirs command, and if you use the -v switch, you'll see the index associated with each entry in the stack:

```
$ dirs -v
0   /usr/bin
1   /tmp
2   /var
3   ~
```

You can use these indexes to jump from one folder to another. Jump to the /var folder with:

```
$ pushd +2
/var ~ /usr/bin /tmp
$ pwd
/var
```

This moves the /var folder to the top of the stack. If you wanted to switch to the /tmp folder with pushd, what index would you use?

You'd use 3:

```
$ pushd +3
/tmp /var ~ /usr/bin
$ pwd
/tmp
```

Using pushd and an index doesn't add or remove entries from the stack, but it does change the order of the entries. In fact, it rotates them.

You can also use the cd command to switch to an entry in the stack, but this does modify the stack. The command cd ~3 will take you to the /usr/bin directory:

```
$ cd ~3
$ pwd
/usr/bin
```

But look at the directory stack now:

```
$ dirs -v
  0   /usr/bin
  1   /var
  2   ~
  3   /usr/bin
```

The entry for /tmp, which was the first entry in the stack, has been replaced with the new current directory.

Now, use the popd command to get back to your home directory. The first time you use it, you'll navigate to /var. Use it again, and you're back home:

```
$ popd
/var ~ /usr/bin
$ popd
~ /usr/bin
$ pwd
/home/brian
```

You're probably wondering why there are so many different ways to do things, and the easiest answer is that this allows for more flexibility. In some situations using cd to change directories is faster, and in other cases, like when creating complex scripts to automate tasks, pushd and popd make more sense. Knowing how to use both methods, and understanding how they work, will let you choose what works best in a given situation.

Navigating around the filesystem is one thing, but knowing where files are is another. Let's look at how to search for files and do something with the results.

Finding Files

Sometimes you just don't know where to look for a file. Maybe you've misplaced it, or maybe you're like me and you save everything you've ever done and have lost track of the file several months ago. GUI interfaces usually have some tool that can search through your disk and find files. A tool on the CLI does that too, and it's the appropriately named find command.

With find, you can locate files by name, last modified date, or even by the content they contain.

In Creating and Reading Files, on page 5, you created a file named greetings.txt in the ~/Desktop directory. Let's use the find command to look for that file in the Desktop folder:

```
$ find ~/Desktop -name "greetings.txt"
/home/brian/Desktop/greetings.txt
```

The find command displays the full path to the file. The -name argument lets you specify the filename you're looking for.

If you don't know the entire name of the file, you can use the wildcard character (*) in the filename, like this:

```
$ find ~/Desktop -name "gr*.txt"
/home/brian/Desktop/greetings.txt
```

This searches the Desktop folder for any files that start with gr and end with .txt.

The find command searches a directory and its subdirectories by default. Use find to display all the files with the .log extension in the /var/log folder:

```
$ find /var/log -name "*.log"
```

This displays a longer list of results.

Filenames can contain both uppercase and lowercase letters, but the -name argument is case-sensitive. You can use -iname instead if you to find anything that matches, regardless of case. Search for files in the Desktop folder that start with GR using the -name flag. It'll return no results:

```
$ find ~/Desktop -name "GR*.txt"
$
```

But if you use the -iname flag, the greetings.txt file will show up:

```
$ find ~/Desktop -iname "GR*.txt"
/home/brian/Desktop/greetings.txt
```

The find command searches directories recursively, so it can take a considerable amount of time if you start your search on a directory structure with lots of subdirectories, like your home directory or the filesystem root. You can tell find to only search a certain depth with the -maxdepth argument:

```
$ find ~ -maxdepth 2 -iname "GR*.txt"
/home/brian/Desktop/greetings.txt
```

The -maxdepth option has to come before you test for matching filenames.

You can also use find to look for files that recently changed. Let's look for files in the /var/log folder that changed in the last 30 minutes. This could be a nice way to figure out what logs on your operating system were recently active.

```
$ find /var/log -mmin -30
```

The mmin argument looks for things that were modified a specified number of minutes ago. Using a minus sign in front of the number makes the search look for files from the current time backward to the specified number of minutes. If you leave the minus sign off, you'd be looking for files that changed *exactly* that many minutes ago. If you used a plus sign, you'd be looking for things that changed more than 30 minutes ago.

When you look for files, you might want to see their attributes like you would when you run the ls command. The find command provides the ls argument to do just that. Try it out by finding anything in the /var/log directory that changed within the last 30 minutes:

```
$ find /var/log -mmin -30 -ls
```

You'll get a long listing of the files similar to what you'd get if you ran the ls -l command. If you're picky and want to see the file sizes in sizes other than bytes, you'll have to use find's exec argument, which can execute a command based on the results of the search. Try this command out, which performs the same search but gives you a slightly different directory listing:

```
$ find /var/log -mmin -30 -exec ls -ldh {} \;
```

A lot's going on with this command. ls -ldh is the command you execute for each file. The -d switch tells ls to treat a directory as a file rather than listing its contents. Since find may also return directories, you don't want ls to list the contents of directories it finds; you just want to see the names of those directories. The {} is a placeholder for the file that gets passed to the program. The \; at the end tells find to run the command on each file it finds. You have to use the backslash to escape the semicolon.

Run that command, and you'll see something like this:

```
drwxrwxr-x 11 root syslog 4.0K Mar  2 12:10 /var/log
-rw-r--r-- 1 root root 1.3M Mar  2 12:08 /var/log/dpkg.log
-rw-r----- 1 syslog adm 7.2K Mar  2 12:17 /var/log/auth.log
-rw-rw-r-- 1 root utmp 286K Mar  2 12:11 /var/log/lastlog
```

If you change the \; to a +, the find command will attempt to group the arguments into a single call. This can be more efficient:

```
$ find /var/log -mmin -30 -exec ls -ldh {} +
drwxrwxr-x 11 root    syslog   4.0K Mar  2 12:10 /var/log
-rw-r--r-- 1 root    root      30K Mar  2 12:08 /var/log/alternatives.log
-rw-r--r-- 1 root    root     113K Mar  2 12:08 /var/log/apt/history.log
-rw-r----- 1 root    adm       52K Mar  2 12:08 /var/log/apt/term.log
-rw-r----- 1 syslog adm      7.2K Mar  2 12:17 /var/log/auth.log
-rw-r----- 1 root    adm      984 Mar  2 12:12 /var/log/cups/access_log
```

In this example, the ls command runs only once, instead of once for each file in the list. Since all the files and directories are passed to the ls command, the output looks prettier; the columns are lined up because only a single command ran.

Finding Files Faster with the locate Command

The locate command, available on macOS and some Linux operating systems, creates an index of the files on your filesystem so you can search for them more quickly. Unfortunately, because locate isn't available on every platform, and because it doesn't work the same way on various operating systems, we're not going dig into all of its uses. But you can research it on your own by using man locate to view the documentation and see how to get it working for you.

Once you have locate set up and an initial index built, you look for files by filename or with wildcards. For example, to find all of your MP3 files, use locate '*.mp3'. To find the greetings.txt file, just use locate greetings.txt.

On many systems, a background task will periodically scan your disk for files and update the index. But to do this manually, you'd typically execute the command updatedb.

The locate utility is incredibly powerful, and it's worth learning how to use it on your own systems.

You can use find to find files for specific users, groups, and more. You can even use it to delete files it finds. But before you see how to modify files on the filesystem, let's look at how to find information about disks and free space.

Identifying Available Disk Space

Every file you save takes up additional disk space, and while using the ls -lh command will tell you how much space the files in a directory consume, it doesn't give you a holistic view of the filesystem. The df and du commands will give you more insight into where your space is going. These commands represent disk space and usage in slightly different ways.

The df command will show you the filesystems, size, used space, available space, and where it's mounted on the filesystem. By default, it shows everything in bytes. If you use the -h flag, you'll see all of the sizes represented clearly, similarly to how the -h flag worked for the ls command. Execute the df -h command to see the results on your system:

```
$ df -h
Filesystem      Size  Used Avail Use% Mounted on
udev            967M     0  967M   0% /dev
tmpfs           200M  1.5M  198M   1% /run
/dev/sda1        32G  6.8G   24G  23% /
tmpfs           997M     0  997M   0% /dev/shm
tmpfs           5.0M  4.0K  5.0M   1% /run/lock
tmpfs           997M     0  997M   0% /sys/fs/cgroup
tmpfs           200M   28K  200M   1% /run/user/121
tmpfs           200M   20K  200M   1% /run/user/1000
```

The system in this example has several devices and disks that store files. Remember that each disk or storage device on the system is mounted somewhere on the main filesystem. The output of this command shows each device or filesystem, its total available space, the amount used, and where it's mounted on the main filesystem.

The tempfs entries represent virtual-memory filesystems, or RAM disks.

If you had a DVD inserted, or a portable USB drive, you'd see it in this list as well. And to access it, you'd use the path listed in the *Mounted on* column.

But the only entry in this list you're really interested in is the device that's mounted to the root of the filesystem. In this case, it's the one called /dev/sda1.

The dev directory, short for *devices*, contains a node for each physical device connected to your computer. On Linux-based systems, disks typically start with sd for SATA hard drives and hd for IDE hard drives. The rest of the name tells you more information about the disk and partition. a is the first disk in the system, b is the second. 1 is the first partition on the disk, 2 is the second, and so on.

For example, dev/sda1 refers to the first partition of the first SATA drive of our computer. dev/sdb2 refers to the second partition of the second SATA drive.

BSD and macOS-based systems use different naming conventions for their disks and partitions, but you'll still find their device files in the /dev directory.

Look at the entry for /dev/sda1 in the output of df -h again:

```
Filesystem      Size  Used Avail Use% Mounted on
...
/dev/sda1        32G  6.8G   24G  23% /
...
```

The output shows the disk is 32 GB in size, and it's 23% full. What's taking up the space though?

The du command lets you look at disk usage, the df command looks at the filesystem metadata. Using du, you can find out where your space is going.

Use du -h on your home directory to show how much disk space each directory in your home directory is taking up. Be warned though, if you have a lot of files, this will take quite a while to scan them all:

```
$ du -h
76K     ./.local/share/gvfs-metadata
296K    ./.local/share/gnome-software
...
4.0K    ./Videos
4.0K    ./Pictures
4.0K    ./sharptools
4.0K    ./Desktop/website
12K       ./Desktop
...
4.0K    ./Music
4.0K    ./Downloads
4.0K    ./Documents
4.0K    ./Public
4.4M    .
```

You'll get quite the list, but next to each entry, you'll see how much space each entry uses.

This output only shows directories that take up space. If you wanted to see the files as well, add the -a switch to see all files.

The very last item in the list is a total of the space used for that directory and its children. If you just want to see this summary, without all of the files, use du -sh:

```
$ du -sh
4.4M    .
```

A lot of times, what you're really looking for is a breakdown of the directories and their sizes at a high level. You can control the depth with the -d switch. Execute this command to show the space used by each directory:

```
$ du -h -d 1
1.8M    ./.local
4.0K    ./Videos
4.0K    ./Pictures
4.0K    ./sharptools
12K     ./Desktop
2.4M    ./.cache
16K     ./.gnupg
4.0K    ./Templates
168K    ./.config
```

```
4.0K    ./.ssh
4.0K    ./Music
4.0K    ./Downloads
4.0K    ./Documents
4.0K    ./Public
4.4M    .
```

You still get the summary at the bottom, but it doesn't drill down and show you the contents of each child directory.

The du command accepts multiple directories, which is great for getting a single list of directory sizes for your most common places. Use this to see the size of your Music, Pictures, and Videos directories:

```
$ du -h -d 1 Music Pictures Videos
4.0K    Music
4.0K    Pictures
4.0K    Videos
```

And if you add the -c switch, du will give you a grand total of the space used:

```
$ du -c -h -d 1 Music Pictures Videos
4.0K    Music
4.0K    Pictures
4.0K    Videos
12K     total
```

Out of Space with Free Space Left

I was managing an application server that hosted several Ruby on Rails web applications. The developers deployed the apps with a tool called Capistrano that copied a new version of the code to the server each time they deployed. After a few deployments, our team got notifications from the monitoring software that the disk was full. Overnight, the logs rotated on the server, but the server couldn't create the log file for the new day.

When I looked at the output of df -h, it reported that there was plenty of free space. Unfortunately, we were out of *inodes*. An inode holds the metadata for a file or directory. It stores the attributes and location of the data on the disk. Directories are just a list of names that point to inodes, and a directory uses an inode for itself, its parent, and all its children.

Every time we deployed the application to the server, we created a whole bunch of new files and new directories, which used up our available inodes.

The df -i command displays the available and free inodes on the system. Using that command, I found out we were completely out. We purged the old versions of the app and modified our deployment script to only keep a couple of previous versions.

You can also exclude certain types of files using --exclude. For example, you could filter out HTML files so you can see how much space the other files take up with du -h --exclude="*.html".

The du and df commands produce different output. Remember that df is looking at free space as reported by the metadata for the filesystem itself, while du is looking at the directories and files on the disk and counting up the bytes used. If you delete a file that's in use by a running program and it hasn't completely been removed yet, df might still report that the space hasn't been freed up yet, but du doesn't see the file, so it reports that the file isn't there anymore. In most cases, you won't notice these differences, but now you know why results may differ if you run into this later.

Your Turn

Before you move on to creating and managing your own files and directories, make sure you're comfortable navigating around the filesystem. Once you are, you'll be able to use absolute and relative paths with many other commands without having to stop and think. Do the following exercises to practice moving around your filesystem:

1. Navigate to your home directory.

2. Use the ls command to list the contents of the /var/log directory.

3. In a single command, switch to the /usr/local/bin folder.

4. Switch to the /var/log folder in a single command using double-dot syntax.

5. Switch to the home directory in a single command by using double-dot syntax.

6. Use the pushd command to navigate to /opt. Use pushd again to navigate to /var/log. Then use popd to return to your home directory.

7. Using man find, figure out how to find all the files your user has changed in the last 24 hours. Try to do this without looking on the Internet or other resources. Learning to read the built-in documentation is helpful when exploring more advanced features.

See if you can answer these questions before moving on:

1. What's the difference between the /usr/bin and /usr/local/bin directories?

2. What kind of data is usually stored in the /var directory?

3. Explain the difference between the following commands:

    - cd
    - cd ..
    - cd .
    - cd /

4. Explain the difference between pushd +2 and cd ~2.

5. Explain the difference between the df and du commands.

What You Learned

You should be much more comfortable navigating around your filesystem on the command line. After working through this chapter, you know how to change directories, and you now know several shortcuts to move around more quickly. You can also find files and directories by name. Keep practicing these commands and they'll become second nature to you. You'll be able to zip around your entire filesystem much faster than you ever could with your graphical file manager.

In the next chapter, you'll create your own files and directory structures, and you'll perform more advanced operations to manipulate your filesystem.

## CHAPTER 4

Working with Files and Directories

You probably spend a lot of your time working with files and directories. You write programs, change configuration files, copy and move files around your projects, rename files, and maybe even back things up.

In the last chapter, you learned how to use the CLI to move around the filesystem. In this chapter, you'll manipulate that filesystem. You'll concatenate files, read larger files, and manage permissions. You'll move, rename, and copy files and directories, all without ever using a graphical tool.

Creating Files

In Creating and Reading Files, on page 5, you learned how to use the echo command and redirection to create files. This is one of many ways to create files on the command line. Let's look at a few alternatives.

If you only need to create an empty file, you can use the touch command. This command is designed to update the timestamp of a file. It's common for programs to watch a file for changes and then react to those changes by executing a process. For example, you might have a process that runs tests whenever a file changes, but you don't actually want to open the file and make a change. You can use touch to modify the file without actually changing the contents. This would then trigger the program or process monitoring the file.

However, if the specified file doesn't exist, the touch command creates the file. This makes touch a very popular tool for creating files quickly.

Test it out. Navigate to your home directory:

```
$ cd
```

Now, use touch to create a new file named file.txt:

```
$ touch file.txt
```

Verify that it exists by using the ls -lh command:

```
$ ls -lh file.txt
-rw-r--r-- 1 brian brian 0 Mar  2 12:50 file.txt
```

The file doesn't have any contents, but it was created successfully. This is a handy way to create a blank file that you can then modify elsewhere.

Remember that touch updates a file's timestamp whenever you run it. Wait a minute and run the touch command on this file again. Then get a new listing:

```
$ touch file.txt
$ ls -alh file.txt
-rw-r--r-- 1 brian brian 0 Mar  2 12:51 file.txt
```

You'll notice that the timestamp has changed.

You can use touch to operate on more than one file at once. All you have to do is provide it with a list of filenames, separated with spaces. Give it a try:

```
$ touch index.html about.html style.css
```

This creates the three files, index.html, about.html, and style.css in the current directory. Verify this with the ls command:

```
$ ls file.txt index.html about.html style.css
about.html  file.txt  index.html  style.css
```

You're not limited in where you create the files. You can create a file in the current directory and in the Documents directory as well, all with a single command:

```
$ touch this_goes_in_home.txt Documents/this_goes_in_Documents.txt
```

By specifying a relative path or a full path to a directory, you can create files anywhere on your filesystem.

Creating Files with Content

The touch command creates blank text files, and as you already know, you can capture the output of programs to a text file by redirecting the program's output to a file. Let's review this by creating a new text file in the current directory that contains the text "Hello, World". Use the echo command to print out the text and then redirect it to a file:

```
$ echo 'Hello, World' > hello.txt
```

If the file hello.txt doesn't exist, it gets created. If it does exist, *it gets overwritten.* So you have to be incredibly careful with this command. You could accidentally erase a file's contents this way.

To append text to the file instead of overwriting its contents, use >> instead of >. So, to append another line to the file hello.txt, you can do this:

```
$ echo 'How are you today' >> hello.txt
```

You can use the > and >> symbols to redirect any program's output messages to a file. For example, if you wanted to save the list of files in the current directory to a file, it's as easy as:

```
$ ls -alh > files.txt
```

You can then append the output of another command to the same file using >>:

```
$ ls -alh ~/Documents >> files.txt
```

The files.txt file will contain the output of both commands. You'll dive into how this works in greater detail in Chapter 5, Streams of Text, on page 91.

Writing Multiple Lines to a File

You can create files from program output, and you can create a new file with a line of text, but you can also create a new file with multiple lines of text right from the command line, without opening a text editor.

In Creating and Reading Files, on page 5, you used the cat command to view the contents of files. The cat command reads the contents of files and displays them to the screen. However, you can use cat to create new files. Let's create a simple text file with several lines. Execute this command:

```
$ cat > names.txt
```

After pressing Enter, you'll see a different prompt and a flashing cursor:

```
>
```

The cat command is waiting for input. Type the following lines, pressing Enter after each one:

```
> Homer
> Marge
> Bart
> Lisa
> Maggie
```

After the last line of the file, press Enter one more time, then press Ctrl+d. This saves the contents to the file.

Use cat again to view the file to ensure the contents were saved:

```
$ cat names.txt
Homer
Marge
Bart
Lisa
Maggie
```

Here's how that worked. You told cat to start accepting text from the keyboard. Every time you pressed the Enter key, cat saved the line to the file. Pressing Enter after the last line (Maggie) saved *that* line to the file as well. The sequence Ctrl+d exits the process. If you forget to press Enter after the last line, you won't save the last line to the file.

To avoid that issue entirely, tell cat to terminate when it sees a specific string on its own line. Try this command:

```
$ cat << 'EOF' > names.txt
> Homer
> Marge
> Bart
> Lisa
> Maggie
> EOF
```

Instead of a blank line at the end, you use the text EOF. Then, when you invoke cat, you tell it to take in keyboard input until it sees the line EOF. The text EOF is short for "end of file," and it's mostly a convention; you can use any combination of characters you want, like DONE or END.

This is a great way to create files without switching to your GUI and breaking your flow. You'll use this throughout the book and explore how it works in Chapter 5, Streams of Text, on page 91.

Combining Files

The cat command is the go-to tool for looking at the contents of small files. If you send multiple files to the cat command, it will read them all in the order you specified. Try it. Create two files in your current directory:

```
$ echo "Hello" > hello.txt
$ echo "Goodbye" > goodbye.txt
```

Now, use the cat command to read both files:

```
$ cat hello.txt goodbye.txt
Hello
Goodbye
```

As you can see, the output shows the content of both files. The cat command is actually designed to concatenate files. And as you've seen already, you can redirect standard output to a file using the > symbol.

Let's see this in action. Websites often have a common header and footer, and instead of repeating that content in every file, you can store the common contents in templates, and then place the page-specific bits in their own files. Try it out.

First, use cat to create a new file named header.html with the following content:

```
files/header.html
<!DOCTYPE html>
<html lang="en-US">
  <head>
    <meta charset="utf-8">
    <title>My Site</title>
  </head>
  <body>
    <div class="content">
      <header>
        <h1>AwesomeCo</h1>
      </header>
```

Create it with the following command:

```
$ cat << 'EOF' > header.html
> <!DOCTYPE html>
> <html lang="en-US">
>   <head>
>     <meta charset="utf-8">
>     <title>My Site</title>
>   </head>
>   <body>
>     <div class="content">
>       <header>
>         <h1>AwesomeCo</h1>
>       </header>
> EOF
```

Next, create a file named footer.html with the following content:

```
files/footer.html
      <footer>
        <small>Copyright &copy; 2019 AwesomeCo</small>
      </footer>
    </div>
  </body>
</html>
```

Use the same method to create this file too:

```
$ cat << 'EOF' > footer.html
>       <footer>
>         <small>Copyright &copy; 2019 AwesomeCo</small>
>       </footer>
>     </div>
>   </body>
> </html>
> EOF
```

Finally, create a file named main.html that contains this:

```
files/main.html
<main>
  <h2>Welcome!</h2>
  <p>This is the main page!</p>
</main>
```

Here's the command:

```
$ cat << 'EOF' > main.html
> <main>
>   <h2>Welcome!</h2>
>   <p>This is the main page!</p>
> </main>
> EOF
```

Now, join the three files to create a new file named index.html using cat:

```
$ cat header.html main.html footer.html > index.html
```

Print out the contents of the new file to verify that it contains the output you expected:

```
$ cat index.html
<!DOCTYPE html>
<html lang="en-US">
  <head>
    <meta charset="utf-8">
    <title>My Site</title>
  </head>
  <body>
    <div class="content">
      <header>
        <h1>AwesomeCo</h1>
      </header>
<main>
  <h2>Welcome!</h2>
  <p>This is the main page!</p>
</main>
```

```
    <footer>
      <small>Copyright &copy; 2019 AwesomeCo</small>
    </footer>
  </div>
 </body>
</html>
```

The lines in all three files were combined into a single file. The indentation looks off since we didn't indent the contents of the main.html in this example.

Reading small files is easy. Let's explore looking at larger ones.

Reading Larger Files

The cat command reads small files nicely. But as you learned in Redirecting Streams of Text, on page 6, some files are too large to read with cat because they scroll off the screen, so you can use the more command to display a file one page at a time. Let's review that command to explore the contents of the system log, the log that holds messages from various applications and operating system processes.

On Ubuntu, you'll find this in /var/log/syslog:

```
$ more /var/log/syslog
```

On macOS, the system log is located at /var/log/system.log instead:

```
$ more /var/log/system.log
```

The first page of the file will display on the screen. Press the Enter key to see the next line of the file, and the Spacebar key to jump to the next page. Press q to quit, or page to the end of the file to return to your prompt.

The more command is a legacy program designed to read a file forward only, with no way to go backward. That's why you have the newer less command.

Less Is More

The less program was introduced to overcome some of the limitations more comes with. With less, you can navigate through the file using arrow keys and even perform some searches. For example, pressing / and typing in a search term followed by the Enter key jumps to the first occurrence of the search term and highlights the other entries.

On many systems, the more command is simply an alias of the less command, which causes some confusion. If you don't see any difference between these programs on your system, then that's probably what's going on.

less has many more features, and as a result it's also a lot bigger. Some smaller Linux distributions don't include it at all, so it's good to know the differences between these commands. But for daily use, your OS includes the less command, so you should be comfortable using that.

Both less and more are handy ways to read through a large amount of text, but sometimes you don't need to see the whole file. Sometimes you only want to look at the beginning or the end.

Reading the Beginning and End of a File

Sometimes the most interesting information in a file is in the first few lines or in the last few lines. That's where the head and tail commands come in handy.

The head command reads the first ten lines from a file and displays them to the screen:

```
$ head /var/log/syslog
```

If you want a different number of lines from the file, use the -n argument to specify the number of lines you want to see. To grab the first line in the /var/log/syslog file, use this command:

```
$ head -n 1 /var/log/syslog
```

The tail command displays the *last* ten lines from a file by default.

```
$ tail /var/log/syslog
```

Like head, tail also supports specifying the number of lines you want to view by using the -n switch. However, with tail, the count starts from the end of the file. Try it out with the names.txt file you created in Writing Multiple Lines to a File, on page 57. Use the -n switch to show only the last two names in the file:

```
$ tail -n 2 names.txt
Lisa
Maggie
```

If you specify the number with a plus sign, tail will start counting from that line and display everything until the end of the file. Give it a try. Read the names.txt file but don't display the first two lines. Instead, tell tail to start with the third line:

```
$ tail -n +3 names.txt
Bart
Lisa
Maggie
```

Reading Larger Files • 63

The first two lines are skipped. This is also a handy way of removing lines from a file or splitting a file. Use the > symbol to send the result to a new file instead of to the screen:

```
$ tail -n +3 names.txt > children.txt
$ cat children.txt
Bart
Lisa
Maggie
```

tail has another powerful feature that comes in handy when you're debugging things. You can use tail to "follow" a file and see its changes on the screen. Give it a try:

```
$ tail -f /var/log/syslog
```

You'll see the last few lines of the file displayed on your screen, but you won't be returned to your prompt. As changes happen in the file, your screen will update, displaying the new lines. This is incredibly helpful when viewing the logs for an application or other process in real time.

Press Ctrl+c to stop watching the file and return to your prompt.

You'll work with less, head, and tail again in Creating Pipelines of Data, on page 94. But let's shift focus and look at creating files outside of the home directory.

Creating Files on the Rest of the Filesystem

So far, you've worked in your home directory, where you have permission to write files. But sometimes you'll need to create files in other directories, like /etc or /var.

Try to create a file named mylog.txt in the /var directory:

```
$ touch /var/mylog.txt
touch: cannot touch '/var/mylog.txt': Permission denied
```

Since you don't have write permissions to the /var directory, the command fails. You'll have to run the command as an administrative user.

In Elevating Privileges, on page 9, you used the sudo prefix, which lets you execute commands with elevated privileges. Rerun the command with sudo:

```
$ sudo touch /var/mylog.txt
[sudo] password for brian:
```

You're prompted to enter the password for your user account. This is your password, not the administrator's password. This is a security precaution; it prevents someone else from doing bad things to your computer if you've left it on. Once you enter the password, the file gets created. But if you look at the permissions for the file, you'll see that it's owned by the root user:

```
$ ls -l /var/mylog.txt
-rw-r--r-- 1 root root 0 Mar  2 13:03 /var/mylog.txt
```

To modify the file in the future, you'll have to either modify the file's permissions or ownership, which you'll learn how to do in Managing File and Directory Permissions, on page 73, or continue to use sudo.

Setting Up sudo

Your user account must be granted access to use the sudo command. On Bash for Windows and macOS, your user will most likely have access. On Ubuntu, the user you create during installation has access. But if you run a command with sudo and see a message like this—

```
brian is not in the sudoers file.  This incident will be reported.
```

—then you are not allowed to use sudo. You will need to set up access for this user from a privileged account. On macOS, this means you need to set the user up as an administrator. On Ubuntu systems, you will execute the command sudo usermod -aG sudo your_username from a privileged account. On other systems, you will need to consult the documentation.

There's one other catch. You can use touch to create a blank file, but if you wanted to create a file with contents by using the redirection method or cat, it's not as simple. Try to append some text to the /var/mylog.txt file:

```
$ sudo echo "Line one" >> /var/mylog.txt
bash: /var/mylog.txt: Permission denied
```

Permission denied? But you used sudo! Why doesn't it work? Well, you used sudo for the echo command. But the redirection happened as your regular user—it wasn't part of the sudo process.

One way to get around this is with the tee command. The tee command takes a program's output and redirects it to the screen and a file. You'll learn how to do that in Splitting Streams with tee, on page 96. It's a bit of a hack, so we'll move on for now.

You've spent a lot of time looking at the various ways to work with files. Let's look at how to work with directories so you can manage those files.

Creating Directories

While you can create files several ways, you will use a single command to create directories: mkdir. You learned how to use this command in Creating Directories, on page 7, but let's dig in a little deeper by performing a common task: setting up a hierarchy of directories to store documents.

Navigate to your home directory, and then create a directory named files:

```
$ cd
$ mkdir files
```

Then, use the ls command to verify the new directory exists:

```
$ ls -l
total 72
-rw-r--r-- 1 brian brian     0 Mar  2 12:51 about.html
-rw-r--r-- 1 brian brian    17 Mar  2 12:54 children.txt
drwxr-xr-x 2 brian brian  4096 Mar  2 12:25 Desktop
drwxr-xr-x 2 brian brian  4096 Mar  2 12:52 Documents
drwxr-xr-x 2 brian brian  4096 Mar  2 11:59 Downloads
drwxr-xr-x 2 brian brian  4096 Mar  2 13:04 files
...
```

Now, create a directory inside of the files directory called photos. Based on what you've learned so far, your first instinct might be to do this by changing the working directory to the files directory and then issuing another mkdir command, but that's not efficient. Instead, specify the full relative path to the new directory:

```
$ mkdir files/photos
```

Like the ls, cat, and cd commands, the mkdir command accepts both relative and absolute paths, and it supports the double-dot syntax for parent directories. You don't have to change your working directory when you want to manipulate files or directories in other locations.

Let's create two more directories underneath files: one for movies and one for music files. You can pass multiple paths to the mkdir command, so you can create both directories like this:

```
$ mkdir files/movies files/music
```

You have to specify the path to each new directory, though. If you'd executed the command mkdir files/movies music, then the movies directory would be placed under files, but the music directory would end up in your current working directory.

Let's create a structure to hold documents like Markdown files and diagrams. Specifically, let's make the structure look like this:

```
files
├── docs
│   ├── diagrams
│   └── markdown
├── movies
├── music
└── photos
```

You might be thinking you can do this:

```
$ mkdir files/docs/diagrams files/docs/markdown
```

Unfortunately, you'll see this error message:

```
mkdir: cannot create directory 'files/docs/diagrams': No such file or directory
mkdir: cannot create directory 'files/docs/markdown': No such file or directory
```

To create a directory with the mkdir command, the parent directory must exist first. The files directory exists, but the docs directory doesn't. So you could create the docs directory and then issue these two commands again, but you don't have to.

The -p switch tells mkdir to create the entire path, including any directories that don't yet exist. Try it out:

```
$ mkdir -p files/docs/diagrams files/docs/markdown
```

That's pretty handy. The -p switch also suppresses errors if you attempt to create a directory that already exists. For example, if you tried to execute this command again:

```
$ mkdir files
```

You'll get an error:

```
mkdir: cannot create directory 'files': File exists
```

But if you use the -p switch, you'll get no errors. This comes in handy when you automate things with scripts, which you'll do in Chapter 9, Automation, on page 231.

Let's add one more structure—a place for the source code. You'll make a dev directory, and beneath it, you'll create the directories elm, go, and js. And instead of specifying each path, you'll use a handy shortcut named *brace expansion*. You can place the four directories you want to create inside of curly braces, separated by commas, like this:

```
$ mkdir -p files/code/{elm,go,js}
```

This command creates all three directories under the files/code directory by taking the prefix files/code and appending it to each entry in the list between the braces. It's a powerful shortcut, and you can use it in many places.

Use tree to ensure that your completed directory structure now looks like this:

```
$ tree files
files
├── code
│   ├── elm
│   ├── go
│   └── js
├── docs
│   ├── diagrams
│   └── markdown
├── movies
├── music
└── photos
```

If you're really trying to save time, you could create this entire structure in a single command since you can nest braces inside of braces:

```
$ mkdir -p files/{movies,music,photos,docs/{diagrams,markdown},code/{go,js,elm}}
```

But that's just showing off.

You built this entire tree with a series of commands without ever leaving your current working directory. This ends up being a huge time-saver if you find yourself creating structures like this for projects. You can use the mkdir command to create directory structures anywhere on the filesystem as long as you have access to the parent directory. And you can prefix the mkdir command with sudo if you need to create the directory elsewhere.

Now that you have a directory structure to play with, it's time to look at how you can manipulate files and directories.

Copying, Moving, and Deleting Files and Directories

Creating files and directories is only part of the story. In the GUI, you'll drag files and directories to move them to new locations, and you'll use the mouse to copy files from one place to another. And sometimes you'll want to get rid of a file or an entire directory's worth of files. You can do all of these from the CLI more quickly than you can with the GUI.

In the previous section, you created a directory structure that looks like this:

```
files
├── code
│   ├── elm
│   ├── go
│   └── js
├── docs
│   ├── diagrams
│   └── markdown
├── movies
├── music
└── photos
```

Let's create a few files in there. First, create some empty files in each subdirectory of the code directory. Use brace expansion to create these files quickly:

```
$ touch files/code/{elm/main.elm,go/main.go,js/app.js}
```

Create the files chapter1.md, chapter2.md, and chapter3.md in the files/docs/markdown directory. You can use brace expansion here too:

```
$ touch files/docs/markdown/chapter{1,2,3}.md
```

In fact, since the numbers for the chapters are sequential, you can use this command instead:

```
$ touch files/docs/markdown/chapter{1..3}.md
```

That's pretty handy if you need to create a bunch of numbered files; Bash will expand the range automatically.

Before moving on, verify that your structure looks like this:

```
$ tree files
files
├── code
│   ├── elm
│   │   └── main.elm
│   ├── go
│   │   └── main.go
│   └── js
│       └── app.js
├── docs
│   ├── diagrams
│   └── markdown
│       ├── chapter1.md
│       ├── chapter2.md
│       └── chapter3.md
├── movies
├── music
└── photos
```

Now that the structure is in place, let's copy some files around.

Copying Files

To copy a file, use the cp command, and specify the source and destination paths.

Try this out by creating a README.md file in the files/code/elm directory. You'll then copy that file to the other code directories:

```
$ echo "# Project README" > files/code/elm/README.md
```

To copy this file to the files/code/go directory, use the cp command and specify the source path, files/code/elm/README.md, and then the destination path, files/code/go/README.md:

```
$ cp files/code/elm/README.md files/code/go/README.md
```

The file is copied to the new location.

You don't actually need to specify the destination filename. Copy the same README.md file to the files/code/js directory, but this time, don't specify the destination filename:

```
$ cp files/code/elm/README.md files/code/js/
```

When you don't specify a filename, the cp command uses the source filename.

However, specifying the destination name lets you copy the file and rename the new version at the same time. In the files/documents directory, you have three Markdown files. Create a fourth one by copying chapter1.md to chapter4.md:

```
$ cp files/docs/markdown/chapter1.md files/docs/markdown/chapter4.md
```

The cp command always replaces the destination file if it exists. Run the command again:

```
$ cp files/docs/markdown/chapter1.md files/docs/markdown/chapter4.md
```

You get absolutely no warning. Be careful when copying files around; it's very easy to specify the wrong destination and lose data. If you don't like the default behavior, you can alter it with the -i switch, which will ask you to confirm your actions:

```
$ cp -i files/docs/markdown/chapter1.md files/docs/markdown/chapter4.md
cp: overwrite 'files/docs/markdown/chapter4.md'? y
```

The cp command also accepts wildcard characters. That means you can copy all of the Markdown documents to a new directory with a single command. Let's do that.

First, create a new directory called backups under the files directory:

```
$ mkdir files/backups
```

Then use the cp command to copy all of the Markdown files from the files/documents/markdown directory to the files/backups directory:

```
$ cp files/docs/markdown/*.md files/backups
```

Verify the files are in the files/backups directory using either the ls command or the tree command.

Copying Directories

When you copy a directory, you're making a duplicate of the directory and its contents, including all files and subdirectories. Let's demonstrate by making a backup of the code directory in our structure. Try copying files/code to files/backups/code:

```
$ cp files/code files/backups/code
cp: -r not specified; omitting directory 'files/code'
```

It doesn't work as expected because the cp command only copies files by default.

Try again, but this time, use the -r switch, which tells cp to recursively copy a directory and its contents:

```
$ cp -r files/code files/backups/code
```

This results in the following structure, which you can verify with the tree command:

```
$ tree files
files
├── backups
│   ├── chapter1.md
│   ├── chapter2.md
│   ├── chapter3.md
│   ├── chapter4.md
│   └── code
│       ├── elm
│       │   ├── main.elm
│       │   └── README.md
│       ├── go
│       │   ├── main.go
│       │   └── README.md
│       └── js
│           ├── app.js
│           └── README.md
...
```

Notice that you specified the destination directory. If the destination directory doesn't exist, the cp command creates it. However, run the same command again:

```
$ cp -r files/code files/backups/code
```

Now, check out the results. It's probably not what you'd expect:

```
$ tree files/backups
files/backups
...
└── code
    ├── code
    │   ├── elm
    │   │   ├── main.elm
    │   │   └── README.md
    │   ├── go
    │   │   ├── main.go
    │   │   └── README.md
    │   └── js
    │       ├── app.js
    │       └── README.md
    ...
```

Rather than overwrite the files you just copied, the command placed a new copy of the code directory *inside* of the existing one.

If you *don't* specify the destination directory, the cp command still creates the destination directory:

```
$ cp -r files/code/ files/backups
```

Running this command again will produce the same results.

Of course, you can specify a new destination name entirely. Just keep in mind that if the destination directory you specify already exists, you'll get a nested file structure.

Moving and Renaming Files and Directories

Filenames need to change, and things need occasional reorganization. You use the mv file to perform both of these operations. It works almost exactly like the cp command, except that the syntax is identical for moving files and directories. To move a file, you specify the source path and the destination path. Try it out.

First, rename the files/documents/markdown directory. Name it employee_handbook instead:

```
$ mv files/docs/markdown files/docs/employee_handbook
```

Next, create a manuals directory under files/docs and move the employee_handbook underneath it:

```
$ mkdir files/docs/manuals
$ mv files/docs/employee_handbook files/docs/manuals
```

That's all there is to moving an entire directory structure. Moving individual files works the same way, and like the cp command, you can use wildcards to move multiple files.

Deleting Files and Directories

In the GUI, you delete files by dragging them to the Trash, the Recycle Bin, or some other metaphor for reclaiming disk space. On the command line, you typically skip that intermediate step and directly remove the files or directory.

To delete a file, you use the rm command. Let's delete the chapter1.md file in the files/backups/ directory:

```
$ rm files/backups/chapter1.md
```

Like the other commands, you can use wildcards to delete multiple files. Delete the rest of the Markdown files in the files/backups directory:

```
$ rm files/backups/chapter*.md
```

To delete directories, you'll have to use the -r switch to tell the rm command to delete recursively, even if there's nothing in the directory. Let's explore this by cleaning up the files/backups directory.

First, delete the files/backups/code directory and all of its contents:

```
$ rm -r files/backups/code
```

On Ubuntu and macOS, this deletes the entire directory and its files. On other operating systems, you may be prompted to confirm you want to delete each file and directory. If that's the case, you can add the -f flag to the command:

```
$ rm -rf files/backups/code
```

Be Careful with rm

The rm command is dangerous; there's no easy way to undo it. You'll have to resort to a backup. And rm -rf will forcibly delete files that are write-protected too. You'll find lots of examples online that use rm -rf, but unless your OS prompts you to delete files you own, it's safer to skip the -f flag. You can also use the -i flag and rm will ask you to confirm each deletion.

If you need to delete a bunch of files or directories in different locations, you can pass the paths to the rm command, and you can use brace expansion or wildcards as well. Let's clean up some of the files we made. Run this command to delete the HTML and text files you made in your home directory, along with the style.css file and the text file you created in the Documents folder:

```
$ rm *.html style.css *.txt Documents/this_goes_in_Documents.txt
```

You can create, move, rename, and remove files and directories on any path on your system. Of course, unless you own the parent directory, you have to use sudo to perform those operations. But you can fix that if you change the permissions.

Managing File and Directory Permissions

If you're the administrator of the system, or if you can run the sudo command, you can change the permissions on files and directories anywhere on your system.

The files structure you made in your home directory is something other users on the machine could use, so let's copy the structure into the /var directory so others can access it. Use the sudo command since you don't have write access to the var directory:

```
$ sudo cp -r ~/files /var/files
```

Next, get a long listing of the /var/files directory, showing all hidden files. This lets you view the permissions of the /var/files directory itself:

```
$ ls -alh /var/files
total 32K
drwxr-xr-x  8 root root 4.0K Mar  2 13:25 .
drwxr-xr-x 16 root root 4.0K Mar  2 13:25 ..
drwxr-xr-x  2 root root 4.0K Mar  2 13:25 backups
drwxr-xr-x  5 root root 4.0K Mar  2 13:25 code
drwxr-xr-x  4 root root 4.0K Mar  2 13:25 docs
drwxr-xr-x  2 root root 4.0K Mar  2 13:25 movies
drwxr-xr-x  2 root root 4.0K Mar  2 13:25 music
drwxr-xr-x  2 root root 4.0K Mar  2 13:25 photos
```

As you recall from Listing Files and Directories, on page 33, the first entry in the list, (.), represents the directory itself, in this case, /var/files:

```
drwxr-xr-x  8 root root 4.0K Mar  2 13:25 .
```

If you recall, the permissions break down like this:

User	Group	Others
rwx	r-x	r-x

In this case, the root user can read, write, and execute files in this directory. Other users on the system can read from this directory structure and execute any files there, but they won't be able to create new files or even make changes to the contents of the files. Execute permissions on directories also allow users to list their contents.

There are two methods you can use to alter access to this structure. You can change the permissions, or you can change the owner.

Let's change the owner first so your user can manipulate this structure.

Changing Ownership

Changing ownership is the easier method, and it's often the only method you need. In most cases, the permissions are set correctly, but they're applied to the wrong user and group. That's the case here, as well.

The chown command lets you change the owner and group of a directory.

```
$ sudo chown brian:brian /var/files
```

Get a new directory listing to check the ownership:

```
$ ls -alh /var/files/
total 36K
drwxr-xr-x  8 brian brian 4.0K Mar  2 13:25 .
drwxr-xr-x 16 root  root  4.0K Mar  2 13:25 ..
drwxr-xr-x  2 root  root  4.0K Mar  2 13:25 backups
drwxr-xr-x  5 root  root  4.0K Mar  2 13:25 code
drwxr-xr-x  4 root  root  4.0K Mar  2 13:25 docs
drwxr-xr-x  2 root  root  4.0K Mar  2 13:25 movies
drwxr-xr-x  2 root  root  4.0K Mar  2 13:25 music
drwxr-xr-x  2 root  root  4.0K Mar  2 13:25 photos
```

The chown command changed the ownership on the /var/files directory. Unfortunately, it didn't do anything to the directory's contents. To do that, add the -R switch:

```
$ sudo chown -R brian:brian /var/files
```

Then get a new directory listing:

```
$ ls -alh /var/files/
total 32K
drwxr-xr-x  8 brian brian 4.0K Mar  2 13:25 .
drwxr-xr-x 16 root  root  4.0K Mar  2 13:25 ..
drwxr-xr-x  2 brian brian 4.0K Mar  2 13:25 backups
drwxr-xr-x  5 brian brian 4.0K Mar  2 13:25 code
drwxr-xr-x  4 brian brian 4.0K Mar  2 13:25 docs
drwxr-xr-x  2 brian brian 4.0K Mar  2 13:25 movies
drwxr-xr-x  2 brian brian 4.0K Mar  2 13:25 music
drwxr-xr-x  2 brian brian 4.0K Mar  2 13:25 photos
```

You can now make modifications to the directory without using sudo. Try it out: add a new directory named dropbox, which you'll use to let every user on the system write files. Create this directory *without* using the sudo command:

```
$ mkdir /var/files/dropbox
```

The command completes without any error messages. Use ls -alh to look at the permissions for the new directory as well as its parent:

```
$ ls -alh /var/files/dropbox
total 8.0K
drwxr-xr-x 2 brian brian 4.0K Mar  2 13:28 .
drwxr-xr-x 9 brian brian 4.0K Mar  2 13:28 ..
```

The new directory inherits the permissions from the parent directory. Your user has full access to the directory, while your group and all other users can only list the contents and navigate there. Let's change who can modify files in this directory.

Changing Permissions

To change file or directory permissions, use the chmod command. You can set permissions a couple of ways. Let's look at *symbolic mode* first. In symbolic mode, you will use combinations of letters and symbols to add or remove permissions.

Time to experiment. Create a file in the /var/files/dropbox directory named permissions.txt:

```
$ touch /var/files/dropbox/permissions.txt
```

Then look at its permissions:

```
$ ls -lh /var/files/dropbox/permissions.txt
-rw-r--r-- 1 brian brian 0 Mar  2 13:29 /var/files/dropbox/permissions.txt
```

The permissions for this file give read and write permissions to your user and allow everyone else access to read the file.

To remove the ability to write to this file for your user, use the chmod -w command:

```
$ chmod -w /var/files/dropbox/permissions.txt
$ ls -lh /var/files/dropbox/permissions.txt
-r--r--r-- 1 brian brian 0 Mar  2 13:29 /var/files/dropbox/permissions.txt
```

To add write permission back for your user, use chmod +w:

```
$ chmod +w /var/files/dropbox/permissions.txt
$ ls -alh /var/files/dropbox/permissions.txt
-rw-r--r-- 1 brian brian 0 Mar  2 13:29 /var/files/dropbox/permissions.txt
```

Notice that this only changed the permissions for your user. To allow other members of the associated group to write to the file, prefix the permission with the letter g:

```
$ chmod g+w /var/files/dropbox/permissions.txt
$ ls -lh /var/files/dropbox/permissions.txt
-rw-rw-r-- 1 brian brian 0 Mar  2 13:29 /var/files/dropbox/permissions.txt
```

To add the ability for others to write to this file, prefix the permission with the letter o, for "others":

```
$ chmod o+w /var/files/dropbox/permissions.txt
$ ls -lh /var/files/dropbox/permissions.txt
-rw-rw-rw- 1 brian brian 0 Mar  2 13:29 /var/files/dropbox/permissions.txt
```

Now everyone has access to write to the file.

You can remove write access for yourself, your group, and everyone, all at once. Use the u prefix to reference your user, and the g and o prefixes for your group and everyone else:

```
$ chmod ugo-w /var/files/dropbox/permissions.txt
$ ls -lh /var/files/dropbox/permissions.txt
-r--r--r-- 1 brian brian 0 Mar  2 13:37 /var/files/dropbox/permissions.txt
```

Now add that write permission back with +w:

```
$ chmod ugo+w /var/files/dropbox/permissions.txt
$ ls -lh /var/files/dropbox/permissions.txt
-rw-rw-rw- 1 brian brian 0 Mar  2 13:37 /var/files/dropbox/permissions.txt
```

You've controlled access to a file, but what about the directory itself? Use ls -lhd to view the current permissions for the /var/files/dropbox directory:

```
$ ls -lhd /var/files/dropbox/
drwxr-xr-x 2 brian brian 4.0K Mar  2 13:37 /var/files/dropbox/
```

Right now, your user has full access, but nobody else does. Use chmod on the directory to grant write permissions for everyone so they can add or remove files:

```
$ chmod go+w /var/files/dropbox/
```

Then use ls -lhd to view the directory to review its permissions:

```
$ ls -lhd /var/files/dropbox
drwxrwxrwx 2 brian brian 4.0K Mar  2 13:37 /var/files/dropbox/
```

Now everyone has access to modify files here.

The chmod command can also act recursively if you use the -R switch, so to remove write permissions from the /var/files/dropbox directory and all of its contents for other users, execute this command:

```
$ chmod -R o-w /var/files/dropbox/
$ ls -alh /var/files/dropbox/
total 8.0K
drwxrwxr-x 2 brian brian 4.0K Mar  2 13:37 .
drwxr-xr-x 9 brian brian 4.0K Mar  2 13:28 ..
-rw-rw-r-- 1 brian brian    0 Mar  2 13:37 permissions.txt
```

Notice that the permissions.txt also lost write permissions. The permissions set at the directory were applied recursively to the files in the directory. You'll want to be very mindful about this when you set permissions recursively, especially since file permissions and directory permissions work differently.

Things get a little tricker when you want to assign completely different permissions for yourself and everyone else. The easiest way to do that is by changing the permission bits.

Changing Permission Bits

One of the most common ways to change permissions is to use *absolute mode*, where you specify numbers to set the permissions. This can be more effective if you need to make more granular changes.

When you're looking at the permissions for a file, you know you can break them down like this:

User	Group	Others
rwx	r-x	r-x

The first three letters are the permissions for the user that owns the file, the next three are for the group, and the last three are for all the other users. In this case, the user has full access (rwx), while the group and other users have read and execute access (r-x).

If you think of each one of these as a switch, where 1 is "on" and 0 is "off," you can represent the permissions as a bunch of bits, like so:

User			Group			Others		
r	w	x	r	-	x	r	-	x
1	1	1	1	0	1	1	0	1

If you convert each group of three to decimal numbers, it'll look like this:

User	Group	Others
rwx	r-x	r-x
111	101	101
7	5	5

Converting binary to decimal is beyond the scope of this book. If you're not comfortable converting binary numbers to decimal numbers, you can use this table for now, and then brush up on that later:

Binary	000	001	010	011	100	101	110	111
Decimal	0	1	2	3	4	5	6	7

To apply these permissions to a file, you pass all three numbers to the chmod command. Let's apply these permissions to the permissions.txt file:

```
$ chmod 755 /var/files/dropbox/permissions.txt
$ ls -lh /var/files/dropbox/permissions.txt
-rwxr-xr-x 1 brian brian 0 Mar  2 13:37 /var/files/dropbox/permissions.txt
```

Using this approach, you can quickly assign different sets of permissions to a file or group of files.

If you wanted to give yourself read and write access but only allow others to read the file, you'd figure this out the same way:

User	Group	Others
rw-	r--	r--
110	100	100
6	4	4

The permissions end up being 644. Apply the new permissions to the file:

```
$ chmod 644 /var/files/dropbox/permissions.txt
$ ls -lh /var/files/dropbox/permissions.txt
-rw-r--r-- 1 brian brian 0 Mar  2 13:37 /var/files/dropbox/permissions.txt
```

Finally, since the chmod command lets you set permissions recursively, you can set permissions for the entire contents of a directory. Let's make sure nobody else can read the source code we put in the /var/files/code directory. Retain full control for your user, but revoke access from others:

```
$ chmod -R 700 /var/files/code
```

Now check the permissions on the /var/files/code directory:

```
$ ls -alh /var/files/code
total 20K
drwx------ 5 brian brian 4.0K Mar  2 13:25 .
drwxr-xr-x 9 brian brian 4.0K Mar  2 13:28 ..
drwx------ 2 brian brian 4.0K Mar  2 13:25 elm
drwx------ 2 brian brian 4.0K Mar  2 13:25 go
drwx------ 2 brian brian 4.0K Mar  2 13:25 js
```

Your user is now the only user who can access these files.

Before wrapping up, make sure that everyone can read and write files in the /var/files/dropbox directory. And since it's a directory, you'll want to make it executable so people can switch to it:

```
$ chmod -R 777 /var/files/dropbox
```

Now, check the permissions:

```
$ ls -alh /var/files/dropbox
total 8.0K
drwxrwxrwx 2 brian brian 4.0K Mar  2 15:36 .
drwxr-xr-x 9 brian brian 4.0K Mar  2 15:26 ..
-rwxrwxrwx 1 brian brian    0 Mar  2 15:36 permissions.txt
```

Look at the permissions for the permissions.txt file. The permissions.txt file is readable, writable, and executable by everyone, since that's what you told the chmod command to do; it recursively set all permissions on all of the files and directories.

Be Careful with chmod

Opening up permissions on a file or directory can have devastating results. It gives everyone access to read and execute files, and if those files are accessible through a web server or a shared disk, you could be in some serious trouble. Before you reach for the chmod command, see if you can find another solution.

If you ever see anyone suggest running chmod -R 777 anywhere, you can probably ignore that advice, since it opens things up to everyone. A better solution than that is almost always available.

Generally, you don't want files to be executable, and we probably don't need everyone else reading this file's contents, so change the permissions on that file back to being readable and writable by you, but only readable by everyone else:

```
$ chmod 644 /var/files/dropbox/permissions.txt
```

Verify the permissions one last time to make sure they're what you want:

```
$ ls -alh /var/files/dropbox
drwxrwxrwx 2 brian brian 4.0K Mar  2 15:36 .
drwxr-xr-x 9 brian brian 4.0K Mar  2 15:26 ..
-rw-r--r-- 1 brian brian    0 Mar  2 15:36 permissions.txt
```

To avoid situations like this in the future, where you accidentally set the wrong permissions recursively, you could set the permissions on the directory without using the -R option so it won't apply recursively, or use letters instead of permission bits. For example, the command chmod -R go+rwX /var/files/dropbox would apply read and write permissions on all files and directories, but the capital X would only apply execute permissions to directories.

Permissions on a Unix-based system is a very complex topic. You have used both symbolic mode and absolute mode to set file permissions, and you will find yourself using both methods depending on the situation you are in. View the documentation for the chmod and chown commands by using man chmod and man chown respectively, and practice changing permissions on files until it becomes second nature.

Next, let's explore links, which let you create a filesystem object that points to another object.

Working with Links

Sometimes it's helpful to create a shortcut to a file. For example, you may want to keep a configuration file in an easy-to-access location, but a piece of software expects to find that file in a specific location. You can use links to create shortcuts to files.

In Out of Space with Free Space Left, on page 52, you learned about inodes, which are data structures that hold information about filesystem objects such as files and directories. Each inode stores the location of the object's data on the disk, as well as information like the last modification date and file permissions.

When you create a file, you're creating a link to an inode. Create a new file named greetings.txt that contains some text:

```
$ echo "Hi there!" > greetings.txt
```

Now, use the ls -i command to look at the inode associated with the file:

```
$ ls -i greetings.txt
534335 greetings.txt
```

You can create two types of shortcuts, or links, to files. *Hard links*, which are pointers to the actual inode, and *symbolic links*, or *symlinks*, which are links to another file. Hard links only work for files, whereas symbolic links work for files and directories.

You'll look at hard links first. Using the ln command, create a hard link called salutations that points to greetings.txt:

```
$ ln greetings.txt salutations
```

The order of the arguments is important. The ln command works just like the cp command. The source comes first, followed by the name of the link you want to create.

Now, execute the ls -i command again to view the inodes for greetings.txt and salutations. You'll see that both entries have the same inode number:

```
$ ls -i greetings.txt salutations
534335 greetings.txt  534335 salutations
```

Both of these links point to the same inode. They're two names for the same reference on disk.

If you delete greetings.txt, the salutations file still exists. Try it out:

```
$ rm greetings.txt
$ cat salutations
Hi there!
```

Since both greetings.txt and salutations pointed to the same inode, which points to the same location on disk, deleting one doesn't affect the other.

Now let's look at symbolic links, or symlinks, which work a little differently. A symlink doesn't point directly to an inode. It points to an existing file or directory instead. Create a symlink from salutations to greetings.txt:

```
$ ln -s salutations greetings.txt
```

Now, look at the inodes of both files. They each point to a different inode:

```
$ ls -i salutations greetings.txt
538374 greetings.txt   534335 salutations
```

The symlink is an independent filesystem object with its own inode.

Use ls -l to view a long listing for greetings.txt:

```
$ ls -l greetings.txt
lrwxrwxrwx 1 brian brian 11 Mar  2 16:09 greetings.txt -> salutations
```

The output shows that greetings.txt points to salutations. Also note that the first character on the line is an l, indicating it's a link.

A symlink is quite similar to a traditional desktop shortcut in a GUI. If you remove the underlying file, it no longer works. Delete the salutations file and then try to view greetings.txt with cat:

```
$ rm salutations
$ cat greetings.txt
cat: greetings.txt: No such file or directory
```

The output informs you that there's no such file, but if you use ls -l, you'll see that the symlink still exists:

```
$ ls -l greetings.txt
lrwxrwxrwx 1 brian brian 11 Mar  2 16:09 greetings.txt -> salutations
```

You can restore the functionality of the symlink by re-creating the file to which it points. You can also delete it with rm. Go ahead and delete greetings.txt before moving on.

```
$ rm greetings.txt
```

Unlike hard links, you can use symlinks with directories. One of the most useful uses for this is to give you quick access to deeply nested directory structures.

Create the following directory structure:

```
app
├── v1
├── v2
└── v3
```

You can do that quickly with a little brace expansion:

```
$ mkdir -p app/v{1,2,3}
```

Use a symlink to create a current directory under app/ that points to the v3 directory:

```
$ ln -s app/v3 app/current
```

Now, use the tree command to view the app directory structure and you'll see your symlink, along with its destination:

```
$ tree app
app
├── current -> app/v3
├── v1
├── v2
└── v3

3 directories, 1 file
```

You can use the ln -s command to point the symlink to the v1 or v2 directories, or even to a new v4 directory you create later. This way, you only have to think about the app/current directory. This is the process a lot of deployment tools use when you set things up on servers. The web server points to a current directory, and the deployment software places the new version of the application into a new directory and updates the symlink. If anything goes wrong, rolling back means changing the symlink back to the previous directory. In addition, you can use symlinks for logs and configuration files. You can create an app/logs directory that holds the production logs for your application. When you deploy a new version, you can create a symlink in app/current/logs which points to your central app/logs directory. Then when you deploy new versions, re-create the symlink again. Deployment solutions often take care of this piece for you as well, but now you have a deeper understanding of how it works.

You can also use symlinks to manage your shell configuration files, which is something you will look at in Chapter 6, The Shell and Environment, on page 125.

One last thing we should look at before we move on is how to see more detailed info about files and directories, including how to identify what type of file you're dealing with.

Getting More Information About Filesystem Objects

You might be used to being able to tell what type of file you're working with by looking at its filename. Typically, a three or four-letter extension gives it away. For example, foo.pdf is a PDF file, logo.png is a graphics file, and foo.txt is a plain-text file. But sometimes there's no extension, and sometimes the files are named incorrectly.

The file command can help you figure out what type of file you're working with. Try it out by pointing it at the greetings.txt file you created in the Desktop directory within your home directory:

```
$ file ~/Desktop/greetings.txt
/home/brian/Desktop/greetings.txt: ASCII text
```

The output tells you what's in the file by looking at its content. Create a file called test.html in your home directory with touch and try to identify it:

```
$ touch ~/test.html
$ file ~/test.html
/home/brian/test.html: empty
```

This time file tells you it's an empty file, despite having the .html extension. Now throw some HTML into the file:

```
$ echo '<h1>this is a test</h1>' > test.html
$ file test.html
/home/brian/test.html: ASCII text
```

Now it says it's an ASCII text file. You might have expected it to report something like "HTML file", but that's not quite how it works. Sure, there's HTML in it, but find looks at the first few bytes of the file to try to determine what it is, and it isn't quite sure.

Put an HTML5 doctype at the beginning of the file:

```
$ echo '<!DOCTYPE html><h1>this is a test</h1>' > test.html
```

This time, file tells you it's an HTML document:

```
$ file test.html
/home/brian/test.html: HTML document, ASCII text
```

Since file is looking at the contents of the file instead of the filename, it's great for figuring out files that have been mislabeled, like graphics files with a png extension that are actually jpeg files. You can use file to identify the correct type and rename the file appropriately.

The file command is great for determining the type of file, but you might want more information about the file itself, such as when it was last accessed. The ls command is fine for collecting basic information about a file, directory, or other filesystem object, but the stat command will tell you much more.

Use the stat command to view details about the test.html file you just worked with:

```
$ stat test.html
  File: test.html
  Size: 39          Blocks: 8        IO Block: 4096    regular file
Device: 801h/2049d    Inode: 538539      Links: 1
Access: (0644/-rw-r--r--)  Uid: ( 1000/   brian)   Gid: ( 1000/    brian)
Access: 2019-03-02 16:15:26.506004475 -0600
Modify: 2019-03-02 16:15:25.150004475 -0600
Change: 2019-03-02 16:15:25.150004475 -0600
 Birth: -
```

---

macOS Has Different Output and Options

The stat command on macOS doesn't produce the same output as the one on Ubuntu by default. Use stat -x instead, or install the GNU version on your Mac by following Installing coreutils, on page 291.

This gives you a nice detailed view of the file, its size on disk, what type of file it is (a regular file in this case), the inode, permissions, ownership, user and group IDs, and timestamps for when the file was last accessed, modified, or changed.

The Access timestamp is the last time something read the file. The Modify timestamp shows the last time the file's contents changed. The Change timestamp reflects when the file's inode changes, such as when permissions or other metadata about the file is updated. This can also include the file's content.

Time to experiment. Add a line of text to the file:

```
$ echo '<p>How are you today?</p>' >> test.html
```

Now, run the stat command again. Since you changed the file, both the Modify and Change fields updated, but the Access timestamp did not:

```
$ stat test.html
  File: test.html
  Size: 65            Blocks: 8          IO Block: 4096    regular file
Device: 801h/2049d    Inode: 538539      Links: 1
Access: (0644/-rw-r--r--)  Uid: ( 1000/   brian)  Gid: ( 1000/   brian)
Access: 2019-03-02 16:15:26.506004475 -0600
Modify: 2019-03-02 16:18:38.674004475 -0600
Change: 2019-03-02 16:18:38.674004475 -0600
 Birth: -
```

Display the file with cat and run stat again. The Access timestamp has changed.

```
$ cat test.html
$ stat test.html
  File: test.html
  Size: 65            Blocks: 8          IO Block: 4096    regular file
Device: 801h/2049d    Inode: 538539      Links: 1
Access: (0644/-rw-r--r--)  Uid: ( 1000/   brian)  Gid: ( 1000/   brian)
Access: 2019-03-02 16:19:48.258004475 -0600
Modify: 2019-03-02 16:18:38.674004475 -0600
Change: 2019-03-02 16:18:38.674004475 -0600
 Birth: -
```

This makes sense, since you didn't change anything. Still, you're probably wondering why both the Modify and Change timestamps updated when you added content, even though you only changed the file's contents. Remember that the Change time reflects a change to the underlying inode, so a change to the content affects both the Modify time and the Change time. But if you change the permissions on the file, you'll see that reflected only in the Change time. Give it a try. Change permissions on the file so that your user is the only person with access:

```
$ chmod 700 test.html
```

Now run stat again:

```
$ stat test.html
  File: test.html
  Size: 65            Blocks: 8          IO Block: 4096    regular file
Device: 801h/2049d    Inode: 538539      Links: 1
Access: (0700/-rwx------)  Uid: ( 1000/   brian)  Gid: ( 1000/   brian)
Access: 2019-03-02 16:19:48.258004475 -0600
Modify: 2019-03-02 16:18:38.674004475 -0600
Change: 2019-03-02 16:21:02.950004475 -0600
 Birth: -
```

This time, the Change entry is the only timestamp that's updated. Note that the output also shows the updated permissions.

The stat command works on directories as well. Run the stat command against the app directory you created in Working with Links, on page 81:

```
$ stat app
  File: app
➤ Size: 4096          Blocks: 8          IO Block: 4096    directory
Device: 801h/2049d    Inode: 534335      Links: 5
...
```

This time, the output reports that you're looking at a directory. Now run stat on the app/current directory, which is a symlink:

```
$ stat app/current
  File: app/current -> app/v3
➤ Size: 6             Blocks: 0          IO Block: 4096    symbolic link
Device: 801h/2049d    Inode: 538538      Links: 1
...
```

The output shows you're looking at a symlink.

You can also use stat to get information about the underlying filesystem by using the -f flag:

```
$ stat -f test.html
  File: "test.html"
    ID: 7e65dd4d07bdafb7 Namelen: 255      Type: ext2/ext3
Block size: 4096       Fundamental block size: 4096
Blocks: Total: 2563397    Free: 1471084    Available: 1335942
Inodes: Total: 655360     Free: 521858
```

Finally, you can control the output you want to see. On Linux versions of stat, you do this using the --printf option. For example, use this command to print out the access time:

```
$ stat --printf '%x\n' test.html
2018-11-14 22:28:57.257636803 +0530
```

The %x value shows the human-readable access time, and \n adds a line break. You can add other text, as well, to create a label:

```
$ stat --printf 'Access: %x\n' test.html
Access: 2019-03-02 16:19:48.258004475 -0600
```

If you use %y and %z, you can display the modified and changed times, respectively:

```
$ stat --printf 'Access: %x\nModify: %y\nChange: %z\n' test.html
Access: 2019-03-02 16:19:48.258004475 -0600
```

```
Modify: 2019-03-02 16:18:38.674004475 -0600
Change: 2019-03-02 16:21:02.950004475 -0600
```

On macOS or BSD versions of stat, you'll use different formatting options. Use the man stat command to see the values you can display for your version of stat.

The stat command can give you insight into when a file was updated or accessed, and tell you more about the underlying filesystem, which can be very helpful when debugging a file access issue.

Your Turn

You worked with a lot of new concepts in this chapter. See if you can answer these questions:

1. Review each of the commands below and write down what it does:

   - cp
   - cp -r
   - mv
   - head
   - tail
   - ln

2. What's the difference between using touch and echo > to create a new text document?

3. What's the difference between the chmod and chown commands?

Now for some additional practice, try these exercises.

Exercise 1: Navigating Directories

Perform the following list of actions exactly as you see here. Don't change your working directory unless you see a step informing you to do so.

1. Navigate to the /var/log directory.

2. Use the echo command and redirection to create a file in your home directory with the text "Created from var/log".

3. Navigate to the /usr/local directory.

4. Use the cat command to view the contents of the file created in step 2.

5. Use the touch command to create two files in your home directory named one.txt and two.txt. Create both files with a single command. Be careful here. You need to specify the full path to each file you want to create.

6. Navigate to your home directory.

7. Use the sudo command to create the directory /opt/test/.

8. Use touch to create three files in the /opt/test directory.

9. Rename the /opt/test directory to /opt/testing.

10. Use a single command to remove all of the files you created in this exercise, but be sure to leave the /opt directory in place.

Exercise 2: Identifying Files

In the files directory of the companion files for this book, you'll find three files: mystery1, mystery2, and mystery3. Use the file command to determine the file type.

Exercise 3: Creating a Website

Using only command-line tools, and without changing your working directory, create a simple website by following these steps:

1. Create this file and directory structure in your home directory using as few commands as possible:

```
website/
├── about/
├── images/
├── products/
└── stylesheets/
    └── style.css
```

2. Copy this directory structure to /opt/website.

3. Change the permissions on /opt/website and all of its files so that your user has full permissions.

4. Create a new file in the /opt/website directory named index.html file that contains the following contents:

```
<!DOCTYPE html>
<html lang="en-US">
  <head>
    <title>My web page</title>
  </head>
  <body>
    <h1>My web page</h1>
  </body>
</html>
```

5. Copy the new index.html page to the about and products directories.

6. Rename the products directory to products_and_services.

7. Remove the website directory from your home directory and replace it with a symlink called website that points to /opt/website.

What You Learned

You can now create, move, copy, rename, and delete files and directories, and you can manage permissions to control access. You'll use the techniques shown here in the rest of this book as well as daily in your work. In the next chapter, you'll use some powerful utilities to manipulate text, whether it's in files or the output from a program.

CHAPTER 5

Streams of Text

Long ago, if you wanted output from a program, you had to write specific instructions into your code. If you wanted the program to take input from a keyboard, you had to write that code as well. This tightly coupled the program to the hardware on which it ran, making things pretty specialized and not easily portable. Unix introduced the concept of standard streams of data at the OS level, which meant that programs could write to these standard streams, and the OS would take care of the rest, either handling the input or displaying the output appropriately.

There are three standard streams you'll encounter when working on the CLI on a Unix-based system:

- *Standard Output (stdout)*: Output from a program.
- *Standard Input (stdin)*: Input to a program.
- *Standard Error (stderr)*: Errors from a program.

When you start a program in the CLI, the standard input is connected to your terminal's input (your keyboard), while the standard output and standard error streams are connected to your terminal's output (the screen). However, you can change how these connections work. You can send the output to a log, discard the output entirely, or even send the output of one program to another program as its input stream. You can create basic or complex workflows using a handful of basic tools.

You've already seen a few of the concepts used in this chapter elsewhere in the book, but you'll now dive a little deeper. You'll start by reviewing how to redirect these streams, and then you'll learn about programs specifically designed to process text on the command line.

Redirecting Input and Output with File Descriptors

When you execute the history command, the program's output is displayed on the screen. The history command writes its output to standard output, and standard output is mapped to your terminal screen by default.

You've already used the > and >> symbols to redirect a program's output to a file. For example, you can save the contents of your shell history to a file:

```
$ history > commands.txt
```

You also know that the >> symbol appends text to an existing file. For example, you can append today's date to the file you just created:

```
$ date >> commands.txt
```

Here's how this concept works. The > and >> symbols redirect content to *file descriptors*, an abstract way for the OS to talk to the kernel and manage files. On Unix systems, each file opened by any process returns a file descriptor to the process as an integer. The kernel keeps track of all these file descriptors in a table. However, there are three file descriptors reserved. 0 is mapped to standard input, 1 is mapped to standard output, and 2 is mapped to standard error.

When sending a program's output to a file using standard output, you can omit the integer, and most people do. That's why you'll see history > commands.txt instead of history 1> commands.txt.

Sometimes you don't even care about the output of a program. You know it'll work and you don't need to see the response. Unix-based operating systems have a special device designed specifically for this purpose: /dev/null. Instead of redirecting the output to a file, redirect it to /dev/null:

```
$ ls > /dev/null
```

You don't see any output on the screen because you redirected it, but it also doesn't end up in a file. It's completely discarded.

This isn't very practical by itself, but the concept will make more sense when you work with errors shortly. Right now, let's look at how to process input from files.

Unix-based programs accept input from a few places; one of those places is the standard input stream.

When you use the cat command to display a file, you specify the file to read as an argument to the program:

```
$ cat commands.txt
```

However, cat also accepts data from standard input. That means you can use a file descriptor instead of specifying a file. The file descriptor for standard input is 0<, but you can use < instead, which is what you'll typically see.

```
$ cat < commands.txt
```

You'll see the output displayed on the screen, just as if you'd passed it in as an argument. This particular example isn't entirely practical, since cat lets you specify the filename directly with one less character. But when you use <, the file is opened and its content is sent to cat; and if the file doesn't exist, cat doesn't execute. Try this out:

```
$ cat windows.txt
cat: windows.txt: No such file or directory
$ cat < windows.txt
-bash: windows.txt: No such file or directory
```

In the first attempt, cat opens the file. In the second attempt, the shell tries to open the file before passing it to the cat command.

It's common for many command-line utilities to receive data from files via standard input. For example, the command-line tool for the MySQL database lets you run a series of SQL commands using standard input. If you're setting up a new database for an app, you'll often see instructions like this:

```
$ mysql -u root -p < tables.sql
```

The tables.sql file contains a bunch of SQL statements to create tables. The program reads them in and executes them. If you've ever encountered that kind of command, you now know how it works.

You can send input to programs in a few other ways. Throughout the book, you've used cat as a quick method to build files:

```
$ cat << 'EOF' > names.txt
> Homer
> Marge
> Bart
> Lisa
> Maggie
> EOF
```

The << symbol defines a "here-document" or *heredoc*, a block of text that programs treat as if it were a separate file. The EOF characters in this example specify the end of the heredoc. EOF is a convention, short for "end of file." You can use any sequence you want.

The data gets passed to the cat program as if it were an input file. The > symbol then redirects the output to standard output, saving it in the specified file.

Using cat with a heredoc is a useful hack for creating a file, and now you have a deeper understanding of how it works.

A "herestring," which lets you create a premade string as input to a program, is another option. Let's use the bc program as an example.

bc is a command-line calculator. When launched, you can do interactive math:

```
$ bc
bc
bc 1.07.1
Copyright 1991-1994, 1997, 1998, 2000, 2004, 2006, 2008,
2012-2017 Free Software Foundation, Inc.
This is free software with ABSOLUTELY NO WARRANTY.
For details type `warranty'.
2 + 2
4
quit
```

If you wanted to use bc in a noninteractive way, you can use a herestring, which you specify with <<<:

```
$ bc <<< "2 + 2"
4
```

Herestrings and heredocs can save you a few steps when you're feeding input into programs.

Now let's look at another way to get input into programs. In addition to sending a program to a file, you can send it to another program as its input.

Creating Pipelines of Data

One of the main foundations of a Unix-based system is that programs work together like a pipeline; the output of one program can be the input of another. In other words, you send the standard output of one program to the standard input of another.

The less command makes it easy to navigate through a large file by reading it one page at a time, but less also accepts input from standard input. If you have a very long directory listing, you can send the output from the ls -alh command to the less command to paginate the results. Give this a try:

```
$ ls -alh /usr/bin | less
```

So how does this work? The | symbol, or the *pipe*, connects the programs. The results of the ls command, which get sent to standard output, are "piped" to the less command which sees the stream as standard input.

Remember the head and tail commands you used in Reading the Beginning and End of a File, on page 62? You can pipe output to these as well.

To see only the first three entries in a long directory listing, try this:

```
$ ls -alh /usr/bin | head -n 3
total 241M
drwxr-xr-x  2 root root    44K Mar  8 11:56 .
drwxr-xr-x 10 root root   4.0K Feb  9 18:12 ..
```

The output of the ls command gets sent to the head command, which displays only the first three of lines of output, as specified by the -n argument.

Using this concept, you can use head and tail together to view a single line from output if you know where it's located. Display only the third entry from the directory listing by using the tail command to start at the third line of the file, and then pipe the results to the head command to read only the first line:

```
$ ls -alh /usr/bin/ | tail -n +3 | head -n 1
drwxr-xr-x 10 root root   4.0K Feb  9 18:12 ..
```

You can keep piping output from one program to the next, creating long pipelines of text that you process. You'll see a few examples of this throughout the rest of the book, but here's one example you can try now, which prints the most-used commands on your system by looking at your history, grouping identical commands, and sorting them:

```
$ history | awk '{c[$2]++}END{for(i in c){print c[i] " " i}}' | sort -rn | head
```

This command sends the output of history to the awk command, which parses out the commands and counts up how many times each one is used, producing an output of each command and its frequency, like this:

```
37 ls
12 chmod
11 cat
9 stat
9 mkdir
9 echo
8 cd
7 touch
7 rm
7 cp
```

You'll learn about awk at the end of the chapter.

It then sends the output to the sort command which sorts the output in reverse order. The output then gets sent to the head command which displays the first ten results.

This demonstrates a key philosophy of Unix-based systems: use small, focused tools that do a single thing well, and chain them together. Let the data flow through a pipeline of tools.

If you write code, you probably apply this same approach to the functions or objects in your system. You know that when you make a function do too many things, it becomes more difficult to maintain; and when you have systems that are too tightly coupled, they tend to resist change. That's the idea behind how these tools interact.

Let's look at another practical use for piping data to another program.

Splitting Streams with tee

When you redirect the output to a file, it no longer displays on the screen. To see the output on the screen and send it to a file, you could use the cat or less commands to view the file, but you can also use the tee command. The tee command gets its name from plumbing—a T-shaped pipe fitting that splits the water off in two directions. The tee command takes input and splits the stream to the screen and to a file.

Execute the history command and pipe its data to the tee command:

```
$ history | tee commands.txt
```

Instead of redirecting the output to a file, you're piping it to tee, which receives the data as standard input. This time, you see the results on the screen. The commands.txt file will also have the latest version of your history inside.

The tee command overwrites the target file each time. But if you use the -a flag, you can append to the file instead:

```
$ date | tee -a commands.txt
```

The date displays on the screen and is appended to the end of the file:

```
$ tail -n 2 commands.txt
  191  history | tee commands.txt
Sat Mar  2 03:53:24 UTC 2019
```

The tee command has another benefit—you can use it to write to places where normal redirection won't let you. Remember in Creating Files on the Rest of the Filesystem, on page 63, you tried to create a file with content in the /var folder but it didn't work? Time to review that.

Try to save the history to a file in the /var directory. The command fails because your user doesn't have access to write a file there:

```
$ history > /var/commands.txt
-bash: /var/commands.txt: Permission denied
```

You might think that you can use sudo to get this to work, but sudo runs the history command as a privileged user rather than your user, and the redirection isn't part of the sudo process:

```
$ sudo history > /var/commands.txt
-bash: /var/commands.txt: Permission denied
```

But you can get around this using sudo tee:

```
$ history | sudo tee /var/commands.txt
```

This time, the file gets created. This works with echo as well:

```
$ sudo echo "Line one" >> /var/mylog.txt
bash: /var/mylog.txt: Permission denied
$ echo "Line one" | sudo tee -a /var/mylog.txt
Line one
```

One drawback to this approach is that you still see the output on the screen. But you can suppress the output by sending it to /dev/null instead of a file:

```
$ echo "Line two" | sudo tee -a /var/mylog.txt > /dev/null
```

You can use tee to create multiline files with sudo, similar to how you did it with cat:

```
$ sudo tee -a /var/mylog.txt << EOF > /dev/null
```

You'll be presented with a blank cursor, as tee is waiting for data from standard input. Type the following lines, pressing Enter after each line:

```
Line three
Line four
EOF
```

The two new lines get written to the file.

If all of this seems too much like a hack, it's because it is. It's often just easier to create files in your home directory and use sudo to move them where you want them:

```
$ echo "some text" > ~/myfile.txt
$ sudo mv ~/myfile.txt /var/myfile
```

You've worked with two of the three standard streams in detail. You know how to redirect streams to files or other programs, so let's look at how to handle error messages.

Working with GUI Clipboards

You can send text from the command-line interface to your system's clipboard so you can work with it in other graphical programs.

On macOS, the pbcopy command takes input and places it on the macOS clipboard. For example, pipe the output of a command to pbcopy:

```
$ ls -alh | pbcopy
```

The pbpaste command sends the clipboard output as standard output. That means you can save the contents of the clipboard to a file:

```
$ pbpaste > file.txt
```

On Linux systems, install the xclip command with your package manager. To save things to the clipboard, use this command:

```
$ ls -alh | xclip -selection c
```

And use xclip -o to display the contents of the clipboard:

```
$ xclip -o > file.txt
```

You can use xclip or pbpaste with command substitution too. If your clipboard contained the text ls -alh, you could execute it with $(xclip) on Linux or $(pbpaste) on macOS.

Clipboard integration makes it incredibly easy to pipe the output of programs to your system clipboard so you can share output logs or other data with others over Slack, email, or forums.

Handling Standard Error Streams

When errors occur in commands, you'll see both the standard output and standard error streams displayed on your screen. This makes it easier for you to see when something went wrong, but it makes it more difficult for you to send the output to a file or another program. To get around this, well-behaved programs separate diagnostics messages and other error messages to the standard error stream and leave it up to you to split them out. Like output, you'll use a file descriptor to either send the errors to a file or suppress the messages.

Let's look at an example of this in action. Use the find command to look at the contents of the /root folder, which you don't have access to view:

```
$ find /root/
/root/
find: `/root/': Permission denied
```

The output shows the root directory, and then tells you that you're not allowed to see the contents. You're seeing both standard output and standard error here. Let's separate the errors from the regular messages.

You already know that the > symbol represents the standard output stream. To use the error stream, use 2> instead. Unlike standard input and standard output, you have to specify the integer for the file descriptor so the shell knows you're talking about the error stream rather than the standard output stream. Run this command to put the error messages into a text file named errors.txt:

```
$ find /root/ 2> errors.txt
/root
```

You still see the output, but the error messages are now in the errors.txt file.

If you wanted the standard output to go to a file instead of the screen, just use the > file descriptor:

```
$ find /root/ > output.txt
find: `/root/': Permission denied
```

When you do that, the error stream shows up on the screen. So, how can you get errors in one file and the regular output to another? Take a moment to think about what you've learned so far about how data flows through programs and you might already see the solution. When you sent the output to a file, the errors still appeared on your screen. When you sent the errors to a file, the standard output still appeared on the screen. So, what if you did two redirections?

```
$ find /root/ > output.txt 2> errors.txt
$ cat output.txt
/root/
$ cat errors.txt
find: `/root/': Permission denied
```

Sometimes you want all of the program output you see on the screen to be logged to the same file. One common way you'll see is to redirect the standard error stream to the standard output stream, and then log the standard output stream to a file, like this:

```
$ find /root/ > log.txt 2>&1
$ cat log.txt
/root/
find: `/root/': Permission denied
```

The characters 2>&1 tell the shell to take file descriptor 2, the error stream, and send it to file descriptor 1, the standard output stream. The &1 piece is how you reference the target. The actual redirection happens with > log.txt, which you specify *before* you tell the shell how to combine the streams. If you specify the output file after you specify how to join the streams, it won't work. This is a common mistake.

Note that this overwrites log.txt. Use find /root/ >> log.txt 2>&1 to append to the file.

On more recent version of Bash, you can redirect both the error and output streams in a much more concise way:

```
$ find /root/ &> log.txt
$ cat log.txt
/root/
find: `/root/': Permission denied
```

This version overwrites log.txt. To append to it, you'd use &>> log.txt, although this only works on Bash 4. Check the value of BASH_VERSION to see which version you have. If you have a previous version, you'll have to use the longer form.

Sometimes you don't care at all about the errors from a program, and it's not worth logging them to a file just to separate them. Instead of sending the error stream to a file, send it to /dev/null:

```
$ find /root/ 2> /dev/null
/root/
```

You can also pipe this combined output to another program using a similar technique. To send the results of this command to the less program, execute this command:

```
$ find /var/log -mmin -30 | less 2>&1
```

This opens less and displays the combined streams.

You've explored how to process the output from a program to a file, or to another program as input. Let's take things a step further and explore additional programs that can transform, filter, and otherwise manipulate the output you see. Next, you'll look at a few of the most common programs.

Filtering with grep

When you're dealing with program output, you'll often want to filter the results. The grep command lets you search text for characters or phrases. You can use grep to search through program output or a file. Let's explore grep by working with some files.

Create a file named words.txt that contains several words, each on its own line:

```
$ cat << 'EOF' > words.txt
> blue
> apple
> candy
> hand
> fork
> EOF
```

Now use grep to search the file for the word and:

```
$ grep 'and' words.txt
candy
hand
```

This displays the two lines of the file that show the string you specified. You get both results because they contain the string and somewhere on the line. This is the most simple form of searching. Surrounding the search term in quotes isn't always necessary, but it's a good habit to get into because you can run into some strange edge cases with special characters if you don't.

You can also tell grep to remove lines containing that text. The -v option instructs grep to only show lines that *don't* contain the search pattern you specified.

```
$ grep 'and' -v words.txt
blue
apple
fork
```

grep reads the file in and processes its contents, but you're not limited to using grep on just files. You can use it to process output from other programs, which means you can use it to filter the streams of text other programs display.

Try it out by using grep to show you all the ls commands in your history:

```
$ history | grep 'ls'
...
  471  ls
  479  ls
  484  ls
  500  history | grep 'ls'
```

When you ran the command on your machine, you probably saw a lot of results, and the last result was the history | grep command. You can filter that last command out by piping the output to grep again:

```
$ history | grep 'ls' | grep -v 'grep'
...
  471  ls
  479  ls
  484  ls
```

If there are too many commands for you to see, you can always pipe the output to less:

```
$ history | grep 'ls' | grep -v 'grep' | less
```

grep supports searching multiple files as well. Create another file with some more words:

```
$ cat << 'EOF' > words2.txt
> blue car
> apple pie
> candy bar
> hand in hand
> fork in the road
> EOF
```

Then, use grep to search both files for the word blue:

```
$ grep 'blue' words.txt words2.txt
words.txt:blue
words2.txt:blue car
```

This time, grep shows the word, along with the name of the file that contains the word.

The grep command only shows the exact line containing the match, but you can tell it to give you a little more context. Using the -A and -B switches, you can specify the number of lines above and below the match:

```
$ grep 'candy' -A 2 -B 2 words*
words2.txt-blue car
words2.txt-apple pie
words2.txt:candy bar
words2.txt-hand in hand
words2.txt-fork in the road
--
words.txt-blue
words.txt-apple
words.txt:candy
words.txt-hand
words.txt-fork
```

The output separates the matches clearly.

In this example, you selected the same amount of lines before and after the matched line. In cases like this, you can shorten the command by using the -C switch instead of specifying both -A and -B:

```
$ grep 'candy' -C 2 words*
```

The resulting output is the same as before. The -C switch shows the "context" around the results.

Adding the -n flag will show you the line number where the match was found:

```
$ grep 'candy' -C 2 -n words*
words2.txt-1-blue car
words2.txt-2-apple pie
words2.txt:3:candy bar
words2.txt-4-hand in hand
words2.txt-5-fork in the road
--
words.txt-1-blue
words.txt-2-apple
words.txt:3:candy
words.txt-4-hand
words.txt-5-fork
```

This is helpful when working with source code. You can use grep to look at your entire codebase and find phrases or keywords quickly, as grep can read directories recursively.

To demonstrate this, use grep to scan the contents of the /var/log folder for instances of your username:

```
$ sudo grep 'brian' -r /var/log
...
/var/log/auth.log:Mar  3 15:40:29 puzzles sudo:    brian : TTY=pts/8 ;
PWD=/home/brian ; USER=root ; COMMAND=/bin/grep brian -r /var/log/
/var/log/auth.log:Mar  3 15:40:29 puzzles sudo: pam_unix(sudo:session):
session opened for user root by brian(uid=0)
Binary file /var/log/btmp matches
Binary file /var/log/wtmp matches
Binary file /var/log/auth.log.1 matches
```

You'll see a stream of data returned, displaying events from your system logs.

All of the searches you performed so far are simple text searches, but you can use *regular expressions*, or *regexes* as well. A regex is a sequence of characters that defines a pattern for finding text.

This book doesn't go into a ton of detail on regular expressions. However, you'll use regular expressions a few more times throughout this book, so I'll explain what's going on with each one.

If you'd like more information on regular expressions, lots of online resources will help get you started, including Regex101,[1] an interactive online tool for building and debugging regular expressions.

For now, let's try out regular expression with grep. If you search both files for the letter b, you get all of the lines containing that word:

```
$ grep 'b' words*
words.txt:blue
words2.txt:blue car
words2.txt:candy bar
```

But if you use the regular expression ^b, which means "look for the lower-case letter b at the beginning of the line," you only see two results: blue and blue car:

```
$ grep '^b' words*
words.txt:blue
words2.txt:blue car
```

Similarly, if you use the expression e$, which means "look for any line ending with the letter e," you see these three results:

```
$ grep 'e$' words*
words.txt:blue
words.txt:apple
words2.txt:apple pie
```

Likewise, use the regular expression blue|apple to search for lines that contain "blue" or "apple". To use this regular expression with grep, use the -E switch:

```
$ grep -E 'blue|apple' words*
words.txt:blue
words.txt:apple
words2.txt:blue car
words2.txt:apple pie
```

The -E switch lets you use extended regular expressions, which means that the characters |, ?, +, {, (, and) are supported in the expression. These characters let you create more advanced search patterns. For example, the expression a(n|r) will look for any lines containing either "an" or "ar":

```
$ grep -E 'a(n|r)' words*
words2.txt:blue car
words2.txt:candy bar
words2.txt:hand in hand
words.txt:candy
words.txt:hand
```

---

1. https://regex101.com

grep is a general purpose text search tool, and while there are some other options out there like ack[2] or ripgrep,[3] which have additional features aimed at working with source code, you should be comfortable using grep since it's universally available.

Next, you'll look at how to remove characters from output.

Removing Characters from Output with cut

The cut command lets you remove text from the output stream or from a file.

Give it a try:

```
$ echo 'hello world' | cut -c 2-4
ell
```

Here's how it works. The -c flag tells cut to cut at characters, rather than bytes. The value is 2-4, which tells cut to cut out everything other than characters 2 through 4.

You can also specify that you want everything from the beginning of the string until the specified position. For example, to grab just the first five characters, use -c -5:

```
$ echo 'hello world' | cut -c -5
hello
```

Using -c 7-, you can grab everything from the seventh character until the end of the line:

```
$ echo 'hello world' | cut -c 7-
world
```

Let's try something more practical by using cut to manipulate the output of the history command. As you recall, when you execute history, you'll see two columns of output—the history number and the command:

```
$ history
    5  ls
    6  cd Documents/
    7  cd
    8  history
    ...
```

---

2.   https://beyondgrep.com/
3.   https://github.com/BurntSushi/ripgrep

You can use the cut command to remove the numerical column:

```
$ history | cut -c 8-
ls
cd Documents/
cd
history
...
```

Notice that cut operates on each line of the output. Combine this with redirection to save this to a text file:

```
$ history | cut -c 8- > commands.txt
```

The cut command can also operate on fields. It uses tabs by default. Try it out. Use the echo command with the -e switch to print out a string with some tabs, using \t for the tab character. Then, use cut to pull out the individual fields:

```
$ echo -e "hello\tworld" | cut -f 1
hello
$ echo -e "hello\tworld" | cut -f 2
world
```

You can specify a different delimiter, like a comma, using the -d switch. Create a quick CSV file:

```
$ cat << 'EOF' > contacts.txt
> Homer,Simpson,939-555-4795,742 Evergreen Terrace
> EOF
```

Then, use cut to pull out the third field in the file:

```
$ cut -d ',' -f 3 contacts.txt
939-555-4795
```

The cut command is a good fit for simple use cases where you're working with uniform content, but it's not always the best tool for the job. For example, it's not the best tool for extracting fields from the ls -l command, as that output is separated by spaces. Tools like awk are a better fit for that, and you'll get to that later in this chapter.

But first, let's look at how to sort results.

Sorting Output

The sort command can sort output alphabetically or numerically. Not every program sorts its output, but you can pipe the output to sort when needed.

Remember the words.txt file you created earlier?

```
$ cat words.txt
blue
apple
candy
hand
fork
```

Use sort to sort the lines of the file alphabetically:

```
$ sort words.txt
apple
blue
candy
fork
hand
```

Using the -r switch, you can sort the file in reverse:

```
$ sort -r words.txt
hand
fork
candy
blue
apple
```

Using the -R flag will sort the lines randomly.

sort on macOS

The -R option is only available on the GNU version of sort. If you're on a Mac, you won't have this option, as it comes with the BSD version. You can use Homebrew to install the GNU version of sort and other tools by using brew install coreutils. See Installing coreutils, on page 291, for how to do that.

```
$ sort -R words.txt
apple
blue
candy
fork
hand
```

Like other programs, you can use sort in a pipeline, which means you can use it to sort output of another command.

Next, let's look at sed, a tool that lets you edit streams of text on the fly.

Editing Streams with sed

If you need to modify text in a pipeline or in a file, sed is your best friend. Its name is short for "stream editor" and it's very handy. While you can do many things with sed, the most common use is to replace some text with other text, similar to how you'd use the find and replace feature in your text editor.

Like other tools, sed can read its input from a file or from standard input. Try it out. Print out "Hello World" and use sed to replace "Hello" with "Goodbye":

```
$ echo "Hello World" | sed -e 's/Hello/Goodbye/'
Goodbye World
```

In this example, you're sending "Hello World" via a pipe and then using the -e flag to specify an expression. The expression s/Hello/Goodbye/ is a basic substitution. The / characters are the delimiter. "Hello" is the regular expression, and "Goodbye" is the string you'll insert as the replacement.

This basic substitution only works on the first occurrence on each line. Let's take a closer look at this. Create a Markdown file called document.md that contains this text:

streams_of_text/document.md
```
This is *very* important text with *very* important words.

* These words are not important.
* Neither are these.

You can *always* tell very important text because it's in italics
```

Use cat to create the file:

```
$ cat << 'EOF' > document.md
> This is *very* important text with *very* important words.
>
> * These words are not important.
> * Neither are these.
>
> You can *always* tell very important text because it's in italics.
> EOF
```

Use sed to replace occurrences of the word "very" with "really". (In reality, you should remove the superfluous adverb entirely, but humor me for a moment.)

```
$ sed -e 's/very/really/' document.md
This is *really* important text with *very* important words.

* These words are not important.
* Neither are these.

You can *always* tell really important text because it's in italics.
```

Notice that one of the instances of "very" didn't get replaced. On closer inspection, the first instance on the first line was replaced, but the second one was not. Add the g operator to the end of the substitution expression to replace both:

```
$ sed -e 's/very/really/g' document.md
```
➤ This is *really* important text with *really* important words.

```
* These words are not important.
* Neither are these.
```

➤ You can *always* tell really important text because it's in italics.

sed doesn't modify the original file. Let's look at how to save changes.

Saving Changes

To keep the changes you've made with sed, you have two options. Your first option is to redirect the output to a new file using redirection.

Execute this command to transform all instances of "very" to "really" and save the results to the file new_document.md:

```
$ sed -e 's/very/really/g' document.md > new_document.md
```

The new_document.md file contains the transformed file. Don't try to redirect the output to the original filename though. You'll end up with a blank file.

The other option for saving changes is to modify the document in place by using the -i switch.

sed on macOS

On macOS, the version of sed you get is the BSD version. It has slightly different options, which can be confusing if you're trying to follow along with examples you see online or even in this book. You can use Homebrew to install the GNU version of sed. See Installing GNU Versions of awk, sed, and grep, on page 292, for how to do that.

Execute this command to replace all instances of "really" with "very" in the file new_document.md:

```
$ sed -i -e 's/really/very/g' new_document.md
```

In practice, modifying the file in place is more dangerous, so you should run the command without the -i switch first and verify you're getting what you want. Then, run the command again with the -i switch.

Ready to look at manipulating specific lines of a file?

Editing Specific Lines

In Markdown documents, you can italicize words or phrases by surrounding them with asterisks or underscores, depending on the Markdown processor you're using. In your document, you're using asterisks to bold words:

streams_of_text/document.md
```
This is *very* important text with *very* important words.

* These words are not important.
* Neither are these.

You can *always* tell very important text because it's in italics
```

Try using a basic substitution to replace them:

```
$ sed -e 's/*/_/g' document.md
This is _very_ important text with _very_ important words.

_ These words are not important.
_ Neither are these.

You can _always_ tell very important text because it's in italics.
```

Whoops. That's not quite right. Markdown uses asterisks for bulleted lists as well. The regular expression you used here was incredibly naive. To get the results you're looking for, you'll want to search for *pairs* of asterisks. That requires being a little more specific about how you search for things.

When performing operations on streams of text, sed searches the whole file. But by providing more context, you can tell sed to zero in on a specific part of the file. sed calls this an *address*. An address can be a string of text, a line number, or a regular expression.

To explore this further, create a text file full of URLs. You'll fiddle around with this file for a bit:

```
$ cat << 'EOF' > urls.txt
> http://example.com
> http://facebook.com
> http://twitter.com
> https://pragprog.com
> EOF
```

Notice that the last entry uses https while the others use http. Try to use sed to replace all the instances of http with https by using what you've learned so far about replacing text.

Your first attempt might look like this:

```
$ sed -e 's/http/https/' urls.txt
https://example.com
https://facebook.com
https://twitter.com
httpss://pragprog.com
```

As you can see from the last entry in the output, this results in httpss, which isn't quite right. You'll need to be more specific. Including the colon in the match is good enough:

```
$ sed -e 's/http:/https:/' urls.txt
https://example.com
https://facebook.com
https://twitter.com
https://pragprog.com
```

The command s/http:/https:/ is an example of a command without an address, so it operates on every line of the file.

But you can target a specific line only. Use the following command to comment out the URL for Facebook by placing a hash mark in front:

```
$ sed -e '/facebook/s/^/#/' urls.txt
http://example.com
#http://facebook.com
http://twitter.com
https://pragprog.com
```

This command finds the line that contains the word facebook and replaces the beginning of the string with the text #. In this case, the string facebook is the address.

Remember that sed doesn't modify the original file, so redirect the output to a new file to save this new list of URLs with a commented-out Facebook URL:

```
$ sed -e '/facebook/s/^/#/' urls.txt > commented_urls.txt
```

Now, using the commented_urls.txt file, uncomment the Facebook URL. Use /facebook/ to find the line, then remove the comment like this:

```
$ sed -e '/facebook/s/^#//' commented_urls.txt
http://example.com
http://facebook.com
http://twitter.com
https://pragprog.com
```

This command finds the line containing the string facebook and replaces the # at the beginning of the line with nothing. While you're using the explicit string facebook here, you could use a more complex regular expression for the address.

And that's exactly what you have to do with your Markdown document to replace the asterisks with underscores. The easiest way to do that is to target lines of the file that contain the pairs of asterisks and only operate on those. Use a regular expression for the address, then use the substitution to replace the characters:

```
$ sed -e '/\*.*\*/s/\*/_/g' document.md
```
➤ This is _very_ important text with _very_ important words.

```
* These words are not important.
* Neither are these.
```

➤ You can _always_ tell very important text because it's in italics.

That's more like it. Addresses make it much easier to zero in on what you want to change, but you can be even more specific.

Operating on Lines by Number

In addition to finding a line with text or a regular expression, you can find it by its number. Let's go back to the urls.txt file and explore this further.

Let's comment out the first line of the file. Use the following command to target the first line and insert the comment character:

```
$ sed -e '1 {s/^/#/}' urls.txt
```
➤ #http://example.com
```
http://facebook.com
http://twitter.com
https://pragprog.com
```

To comment out lines 2 through 4 of the file, use this command which specifies a range:

```
$ sed -e '2,4 {s/^/#/}' urls.txt
http://example.com
```
➤ #http://facebook.com
➤ #http://twitter.com
➤ #https://pragprog.com

You can also manipulate the beginning and end of a file. Want to add a line to the top of the file? Use the number 1 to reference the first line of the file, followed by the letter i and a backslash to indicate the text to insert. Add the text "Bookmarks" to the top of the file:

```
$ sed -e '1i\Bookmarks' urls.txt
```
➤ Bookmarks
```
http://example.com
http://facebook.com
http://twitter.com
https://pragprog.com
```

To append a line to the end of the file, use a dollar sign instead of a number, followed by the letter a:

```
$ sed -e '$a\http://google.com' urls.txt
http://example.com
http://facebook.com
http://twitter.com
https://pragprog.com
➤ http://google.com
```

You can do multiple expressions in the same command too, which means you can prepend and append text to a file in a single command. Just specify both expressions:

```
$ sed -e '1i\Bookmarks' -e '$a\http://google.com' urls.txt
➤ Bookmarks
http://example.com
http://facebook.com
http://twitter.com
https://pragprog.com
➤ http://google.com
```

You can prepend i and a with a line number to prepend or append text anywhere in the file. If you use i\ or a\ without a location, sed applies the operation for every line of the file.

In addition, you can change a specific line of the file using c. Change example.com to github.com with this command:

```
$ sed -e '1c\https://github.com'  urls.txt
https://github.com
http://facebook.com
http://twitter.com
https://pragprog.com
```

You can delete a line with d:

```
$ sed -e '1d'  urls.txt
http://facebook.com
http://twitter.com
https://pragprog.com
```

Now, let's look at how to add content from other files.

Replacing Text with Content from Another File

Using sed, you can create a template file with some placeholder text, and then replace that text with text from another file. Let's create a new document and then use sed to inject our list of URLs inside of it.

First, create a new document with the placeholder LINKS where you want the links to appear:

```
$ cat << 'EOF' > useful_links.md
> Here are a few interesting links:
> LINKS
> I hope you find them useful.
> EOF
```

The r command tells sed to read text from an external file. So you'll search for LINKS in the file and then use r to place the contents of urls.txt below that line. Then you'll delete the line containing the LINKS placeholder. Try it out:

```
$ sed -e '/LINKS/r urls.txt' -e '/LINKS/d' useful_links.md
Here are a few interesting links:
➤ http://example.com
➤ http://facebook.com
➤ http://twitter.com
➤ https://pragprog.com
I hope you find them useful.
```

This worked nicely, but you can shorten the command by using braces to group the commands, like this:

```
$ sed -e '/LINKS/{r urls.txt' -e 'd}' useful_links.md
Here are a few interesting links:
➤ http://example.com
➤ http://facebook.com
➤ http://twitter.com
➤ https://pragprog.com
I hope you find them useful.
```

With sed, use regular expressions, text, and even external files to modify the contents of any stream of text, whether it comes from a file or another program. Let's look at another tool for parsing and manipulating files.

Advanced Processing with awk

awk lets you process text in a number of ways. You can use it to extract fields in a file, calculate totals, and even change the order of the output of a file. awk is a command-line utility, but it's also a scripting language with loops, variables, and conditionals.

Much like sed, awk works slightly differently depending on the version installed on your operating system. On Ubuntu, the awk command that ships out-of-the-box is missing a few features, so install a more full-featured version before moving on:

```
$ sudo apt install gawk
```

Let's explore awk by using some data from the 2010 U.S. Census that shows population by state. You can find the full dataset in the book's code download, but you'll use a subset for this exercise. Create the file population.txt with the following contents:

```
streams_of_text/population.txt
State,Population,Reps
Alabama,4802982,7
California,37341989,53
Florida,18900773,27
Hawaii,1366862,2
Illinois,12864380,18
New York,19421055,27
South Dakota,819761,1
Wisconsin,5698230,8
Wyoming,568300,1
```

Create this file with cat:

```
$ cat << 'EOF' > population.txt
> State,Population,Reps
> Alabama,4802982,7
> California,37341989,53
> Florida,18900773,27
> Hawaii,1366862,2
> Illinois,12864380,18
> New York,19421055,27
> South Dakota,819761,1
> Wisconsin,5698230,8
> Wyoming,568300,1
> EOF
```

The legislative branch of the United States government has two houses—the Senate and the House of Representatives. The Senate consists of 100 seats, with 2 members from each of the 50 states. The House of Representatives has 435 members, but the number from each state is based on the the state's population, as recorded by the most recent census. As you can see from the data you have here, the state of California has 53 members of the House of Representatives, and is the most populous state. By contrast, Wyoming has only 1 member.

We'll use awk to view, transform and manipulate this data.

First, let's look at how to print a specific line of the file. Use this command to print out the line associated with Wisconsin:

```
$ awk '/Wisconsin/' population.txt
Wisconsin,5698230,8
```

That is not that useful, since you already know you could have used grep to get the same results. However, you can use awk to manipulate the data further. Try this command, which will print out just the name of the state from that line:

```
$ awk -F ',' '/Wisconsin/ {print $1}' population.txt
Wisconsin
```

The -F switch lets you specify the field delimiter. By default, awk assumes fields are delimited by spaces. But since this is a CSV file, the fields are delimited by commas. The {print $1} directive tells awk to print the first field.

Using the same approach, you can find Wisconsin's population with this command:

```
$ awk -F ',' '/Wisconsin/ {print $2}' population.txt
5698230
```

You can pretty up that result by using the printf function and the formatter %'d. Unfortunately, because the ' character is the separator for specifying the program commands, you have to escape it, resulting in a somewhat gnarly bit of characters:

```
$ awk -F ',' '/Wisconsin/ { printf("%'"'"'d\n", $2) }' population.txt
5,698,230
```

That said, it's pretty cool that this works from the command line.

So, you can use awk to grab a line out of a file and format it. But what else can you do? Well, you can print only certain columns of the file. Run this command to print out the first and second columns:

```
$ awk -F ',' '{ print $1 $2 }' population.txt
StatePopulation
Alabama4802982
California37341989
Florida18900773
Hawaii1366862
Illinois12864380
New York19421055
South Dakota819761
Wisconsin5698230
Wyoming568300
```

That's a little difficult to read. If you separate the $1 and $2 in the print statement with commas, your output will have spaces between the fields when they're printed:

```
$ awk -F ',' '{ print $1, $2 }' population.txt
State Population
Alabama 4802982
California 37341989
...
Wyoming 568300
```

You can include other characters too. Separate each field with a hyphen with spaces on either side:

```
$ awk -F ',' '{ print $1 " - " $2 }' population.txt
State - Population
Alabama - 4802982
California - 37341989
...
Wyoming - 568300
```

In this case, you didn't separate the output fields with commas, but instead used literal space characters. You'd get the same result if you used { print $1, "-", $2 }, as the commas will insert the spaces for you.

Using a similar approach, you can convert the CSV file into a tab-delimited file by using \t in between the columns, although the output will look a little odd due to the way the terminal displays tabs:

```
$ awk -F ',' '{ print $1 "\t" $2 "\t" $3 }' population.txt
State    Population    Reps
Alabama 4802982 7
California    37341989    53
Florida 18900773    27
Hawaii  1366862 2
Illinois    12864380    18
New York    19421055    27
South Dakota    819761  1
Wisconsin    5698230 8
Wyoming 568300  1
```

This approach changes the delimiter to an actual tab character so another program can parse the output. If you're just looking to see the columns lined up onscreen, you probably want the column command, which formats text into columns:

```
$ column -t -s, population.txt
State         Population Reps
Alabama       4802982    7
California    37341989   53
...
Wyoming       568300     1
```

The -t switch states you want the output in a table, and the -s switch specifies what the original file uses for its delimiter. You can learn more about column with man column. Time to get back to awk.

The first line of the data file has headers. Sometimes you don't want to see the headers in the output, or you just want to work with certain parts of the file. You already saw how to read parts of a file with head and tail, but you can do it with awk too. To skip the first line of the file, add the expression NR>1, like this:

```
$ awk -F ',' 'NR>1 { print $1 " - " $2 }' population.txt
Alabama - 4802982
California - 37341989
...
Wyoming - 568300
```

NR is the record number. The statement NR>1 says to print the line if its row number is greater than 1. Increase the number to skip more lines, or flip the sign around to only print a few lines. This has a similar effect to using head and tail.

You might have figured out by now that you can change the order of the columns that print, too, by rearranging them in the print statement. Let's make the population field the first field in the output this time. You'll keep the first line in the output, though, so you can see the headers:

```
$ awk -F ',' '{ print $2, $1, $3 }' population.txt
Population State Reps
4802982 Alabama 7
37341989 California 53
18900773 Florida 27
1366862 Hawaii 2
12864380 Illinois 18
19421055 New York 27
819761 South Dakota 1
5698230 Wisconsin 8
568300 Wyoming 1
```

Now that the first field in the output is a number, you can use the sort command to sort the output numerically and find out which state has the highest population. Print the population column and the state name, skipping the first line of the file so the headings aren't included. Then, pipe the output to sort to sort population in descending order. Finally, pipe to head to show the first entry:

```
$ awk -F ',' 'NR>1 { print $2, $1 }' population.txt | sort -nr | head -n 1
37341989 California
```

While this works and illustrates how you can use individual programs together, it's not very efficient if you have a large dataset. As you explore more of awk's features, see if you can figure out how you can do this without piping results to sort and head.

awk supports conditional statements, which means you can compare values to other values and modify the output based on the results. To demonstrate this, you'll show only the states with less than three representatives. The representatives are in the third column, so use an if statement to see if the value in the third column is less than three and print the line if it is:

```
$ awk -F ',' '{if ($3 < 3) print $1 ": " $2 }' population.txt
Hawaii: 1366862
South Dakota: 819761
Wyoming: 568300
```

Notice that this time, the header doesn't show up since it doesn't match the condition.

Finally, you can create variables to hold data so you can perform operations like computing totals.

Try it out by using awk to sum up the representatives:

```
$ awk -F ',' '{ sum+=$3 } END { print sum }' population.txt
144
```

First, you declare a variable named sum and add up the values in the third column. You then use the END keyword, followed by a print statement.

An awk program can have the following structure:

```
BEGIN {
# some optional initialization stuff
}

optional search pattern {
  # steps
}

END {
# some final stuff
}
```

As you've seen so far, some of these sections aren't necessary. For example, you've never used the BEGIN section; you only used a search pattern once. You haven't always used the END section either, so your print statements executed once for each line in the file.

The program to sum up the number of representatives, formatted, could look like this:

```
BEGIN {
   sum=0
}
{
   sum+=$3
}
END {
   print sum
}
```

You only want to print *after* you have computed the total. You also don't need to initialize the sum variable, so you can omit the entire BEGIN section, giving you this:

```
{ sum+=3 } END { print sum }
```

Interestingly enough, awk ignores the header column when you sum up the data. It's doing some implicit coercion for us. But you can be more explicit by using the int function to make sure values get cast explicitly:

```
$ awk -F ',' '{ sum+=int($3) } END { print sum }' population.txt
144
```

So based on this, you can probably figure out how to show the most populous state. Instead of a sum variable, use a variable to track the population. Compare the value in the population column to the value stored in your variable. If the current value is higher, replace the variable and store the state name too. When you're done, print the result:

```
$ awk -F ',' '{if (pop < int($2)) {pop=$2; state=$1 }} END {print pop, state}'
population.txt
```

```
37341989 California
```

That's a little more efficient than formatting the entire dataset, sorting it, and grabbing the first record.

If you combine a few of the tricks you've learned so far, can you figure out how to use awk to find the total population of the states with less than three representatives and format the result?

```
$ awk -F ',' '{if ($3 < 3) {sum+=int($2)} } END {printf("%'"'"'d\n", sum)}' \
> population.txt
```

```
2,754,923
```

That's getting a little long and difficult to read. You can move the script to its own file and tell awk to use it.

Create the file population.awk with the following code:

streams_of_text/population.awk
```
{
  if ($3 < 3) {
    sum+=int($2)
  }
}

END {
  printf("%'d\n", sum)
}
```

Notice that you don't need to do any escaping of single quotes with the printf command. That's another nice advantage of using an external file for the script.

Use cat to create the population.awk script:

```
$ cat << 'EOF' > population.awk
> {
>   if ($3 < 3) {
>     sum+=int($2)
>   }
> }
>
> END {
>   printf("%'d\n", sum)
> }
> EOF
```

To run the script, use the -f switch and specify the file:

```
$ awk -F "," -f population.awk population.txt
2,754,923
```

This is a good place to stop. awk is complex enough to deserve its own book, but you have enough understanding of the basics that you can start to incorporate awk into your workflows where it makes sense.

Before wrapping up, let's explore how to take output and transform it into arguments to another program.

Using xargs

The xargs program takes data from standard input and lets you use it as arguments to another program. To understand how it works, let's do something incredibly trivial: print out the numbers 1 to 5 with echo, using xargs. You'll use the seq command, which prints out a sequence of numbers, each on its own line.

```
$ seq 5 | xargs echo
1 2 3 4 5
```

What actually happened here? The numbers 1 through 5 were passed as arguments to the echo command. You can see this for yourself with the -t argument:

```
$ seq 5 | xargs -t echo
echo 1 2 3 4 5
1 2 3 4 5
```

If you don't specify a command, xargs uses echo by default. Test it out:

```
$ seq 5 | xargs -t
echo 1 2 3 4 5
1 2 3 4 5
```

Printing a sequence of numbers like this is an incredibly contrived example, so let's do something more interesting—create a text file with a list of filenames in it and use that text file with xargs to create the files:

```
$ cat << 'EOF' > file_list.txt
> index.html
> about.html
> projects.html
> presentations.html
> EOF
```

Now, use xargs to pass the contents of that file to the touch command:

```
$ cat file_list.txt | xargs -t touch
touch index.html about.html projects.html presentations.html
```

Verify that the files now exist by using the ls command. To save time, use xargs to invoke ls:

```
$ cat file_list.txt | xargs ls -l
-rw-rw-r-- 1 brian brian 0 Mar  3 04:03 about.html
-rw-rw-r-- 1 brian brian 0 Mar  3 04:03 index.html
-rw-rw-r-- 1 brian brian 0 Mar  3 04:03 presentations.html
-rw-rw-r-- 1 brian brian 0 Mar  3 04:03 projects.html
```

Now, delete the files the same way:

```
$ cat file_list.txt | xargs rm
```

The xargs command can also read data directly from a file instead of standard input. Specify the file with the -a switch:

```
$ xargs -a file_list.txt touch
$ xargs -a file_list.txt ls -l
-rw-rw-r-- 1 brian brian 0 Mar  3 04:09 about.html
-rw-rw-r-- 1 brian brian 0 Mar  3 04:09 index.html
-rw-rw-r-- 1 brian brian 0 Mar  3 04:09 presentations.html
-rw-rw-r-- 1 brian brian 0 Mar  3 04:09 projects.html
$ xargs -a file_list.txt rm
```

---
xargs on macOS

 The -a option is only available on the GNU version of xargs. You can use Homebrew to install the GNU version of xargs by using brew install findutils. See Installing diffutils and findutils, on page 292, for more on how to set it up.

The possibilities of this are pretty interesting. You can feed xargs a list of files from a file listing, a data file you parse, or the results of another command.

In Finding Files, on page 46, you worked with the find command to locate files with certain attributes and learned about the -exec argument, which lets you perform a command on the results you found, like this command which finds any file in the /var/log directory that changed within the last 30 minutes and performs a long file listing on the results by sending all of the files it finds as the argument to the ls command:

```
$ find /var/log -mmin -30 -exec ls -ldh {} +
```

You can perform the same operation with xargs:

```
$ find /var/log -mmin -30 | xargs ls -ldh
```

Both of these commands give the same results. The xargs version is easier to read and remember. The -exec argument in find didn't always exist, and it's also somewhat cryptic, so many people prefer xargs instead. People also prefer xargs when working with a larger file set because the shell has a limit on the length of a command's arguments. xargs can split up the invocations so you don't hit the limit.

Like all of the commands you've used in this chapter, there's much more to explore. Be sure to look at the documentation for this command and others.

Your Turn

These exercises might help you understand how to use programs together to process text.

1. In Redirecting Streams of Text, on page 6, you used the ps command to see the list of all processes running on the machine. Use the ps -ef and

grep commands together to search for a process by name. Once you've found the result, use another tool you learned about in this chapter to extract just the process ID from the results. Although you can do this with the ps command itself, try to parse it out using a different method.

2. Use the sed and awk command to turn a directory listing into an HTML document. Ensure your document has a proper HTML header and footer as well.

3. In the streams_of_text folder, you'll find a file named awesome.log, which is part of an Apache log file. Use what you learned in this chapter to find the following:

    a. The most popular URL on the site.
    b. The least popular URL on the site.
    c. The most frequent visitor to the site by IP address.
    d. The most popular web browser used to access the site.

What You Learned

You now have a handful of important tools you can use to manipulate program output on the command-line interface. Take the results of commands and pipe them to other commands, transforming the data and extracting out what you need along the way. This chapter only covers the basic usage of these tools. Tools like sed and awk deserve their own proper books due to their depth and complexity. But what you learned here covers the most common cases.

Now let's shift gears a little and look at the command-line environment itself.

## CHAPTER 6

The Shell and Environment

The command-line interface is more than just a place to run commands. It's an environment for managing everything from your operating system to the code you write.

When you open a new shell session, some behind-the-scenes processes configure an environment for you to use by reading through various configuration files, running some scripts, and setting some variables you can access. Most of this is customizable. You can store data in variables for easy reuse, create configuration files for your shell session that set everything up just the way you want every time you log in, change the information your prompt displays, and even create your own shortcuts and keybindings. You'll do all of those things in this chapter, and you'll gain a better understanding of how you can leverage the shell for your own needs.

Exploring Environment and Shell Variables

The two types of variables are *environment variables* and *shell variables*. Environment variables are variables defined in the current shell session and are available to any programs executed within that session. Environment variables often control how programs work. For example, you might set a LANG environment variable that other programs can use to determine the language a program should use to communicate with you. Shell variables are similar, except they're not available to programs and subprocesses. You can think of environment variables as global variables, and shell variables as local ones.

The env command shows you all the environment variables that are set. A lot's there, so pipe the results to less:

```
$ env | less
```

In the output, you'll see many environment variables, including the following:

```
...
USER=brian
PWD=/home/brian
HOME=/home/brian
TERM=xterm-256color
SHELL=/bin/bash
...
LOGNAME=brian
PATH=/usr/local/sbin:/usr/local/bin:/usr/sbin:/usr/bin:/sbin:/bin:
/usr/games:/usr/local/games:/snap/bin
...
```

Here's what a few of these do:

- The USER and LOGNAME variables hold the username of the current user. The PWD variable holds the full path to the current working directory.

- The TERM variable defines the terminal output mode, which terminal software uses to determine what fonts, colors, and other features are available.

- The SHELL variable defines what shell you're using. In this case, it's the Bash shell, located at /bin/bash.

- The HOME variable holds the value of the current user's home directory. When you issue the cd command with no arguments, this value is used.

- The PATH variable holds a list of directories the OS uses to locate executable programs.

The env command shows only environment variables. To see shell variables in addition to environment variables, use the set command. In Bash, this command prints environment variables, shell variables, and functions, which may be a huge amount of output you might not want to see.

```
$ set -o posix; set; set +o posix
```

This configures the set command to run in POSIX mode, which doesn't display functions. It then runs the set command, and restores the original behavior. You can shorten this to:

```
$ (set -o posix; set)
```

The parentheses around the statement tells Bash to execute the command in a subshell, leaving the current shell's settings unchanged. This eliminates the need to restore the default behavior. You'll learn about subshells in Running Commands in Subshells, on page 164.

This command shows a lot more detail:

```
...
BASHOPTS=checkwinsize:cmdhist:complete_fullquote:expand_aliases:extglob:
extquote:force_fignore:histappend:interactive_comments:login_shell:progcomp:
promptvars:sourcepath
...
BASH_VERSION='4.4.19(1)-release'
COLUMNS=211
...
DIRSTACK=()
...
HISTCONTROL=ignoreboth
HISTFILE=/home/brian/.bash_history
HISTFILESIZE=2000
HISTSIZE=1000
...
HOSTNAME=puzzles
HOSTTYPE=x86_64
...
LINES=93
MACHTYPE=x86_64-pc-linux-gnu
...
OSTYPE=linux-gnu
PPID=3462
PS1='\[\e]0;\u@\h: \w\a\]${debian_chroot:+($debian_chroot)}\[\033[01;32m\]
\u@\h\[\033[00m\]:\[\033[01;34m\]\w\[\033[00m\]\$ '
PS2='> '
PS4='+ '
SHELLOPTS=braceexpand:emacs:hashall:histexpand:history:interactive-comments:
monitor:posix
UID=1000
```

Unfortunately, there's no easy way to show only the shell variables due to the way the env and set commands display output. You'd have to take the output of set and then subtract everything returned by env.

Using Variables

To print one of these environment variables to the screen, use the printenv command, followed by the variable name:

```
$ printenv HOME
/home/brian
```

This is good for checking the value, but you can also use these variables as values in your shell commands. To do so, prefix the variable with the dollar sign. For example, print out the HOME variable's value:

```
$ echo $HOME
/home/brian
```

If you omit the dollar sign, you'd only see the literal value HOME instead. The dollar sign tells the shell to expand the variable and use its value. This concept is called *parameter expansion*, or *variable expansion*.

You can use variable expansion in combination with other strings as well. Run this command to print out the current username in a longer string:

```
$ echo "The current user is ${USER}"
The current user is brian
```

Notice the curly braces around the variable? It's good practice to use these when mixing your variables with other strings. You can leave them off, but in some situations you'll get the wrong results. Here's an example of one of those situations.

You can create a text file that will hold your history, but use the value of the USER variable as part of the filename. Before you create the file, use echo to add _history.txt as a suffix to the value of USER to see what the filename would look like:

```
$ echo "$USER_history.txt"
.txt
```

All you see is .txt, because the shell thought the variable was USER_history rather than USER. It doesn't always know what the word boundaries are. Using braces makes it unambiguous. Try this:

```
$ echo "${USER}_history.txt"
brian_history.txt
```

This results in the filename you're looking for, so create the actual history file now that you know the target filename is correct:

```
$ history > "${USER}_history.txt"
$ ls "${USER}_history.txt"
brian_history.txt
```

Use braces like this when performing variable expansion when building strings. You won't be surprised by the results if you do this consistently. In addition, it's a really good idea to use double quotes around the strings you create when using variables. It's not always required, but like the braces, you can run into unexpected results. For example, variables may contain spaces or characters that the shell might interpret differently. The Bash manual explains the rules of how quotes work in more detail.[1]

---

1.   https://www.gnu.org/software/bash/manual/html_node/Quoting.html

One of the more important environment variables is PATH, which determines where the shell should look for executable programs. Let's explore that one in detail.

Locating Executables with PATH

When you type commands like cd or ls, you're executing a program. The PATH environment variable contains a colon-delimited list of directories the OS uses to look up executable programs.

Print out the value of the PATH variable with echo:

```
$ echo $PATH
/home/brian/bin:/home/brian/.local/bin:/usr/local/sbin:/usr/local/bin:
/usr/sbin:/usr/bin:/sbin:/bin:/usr/games:/usr/local/games:/snap/bin
```

The which command will tell you where an executable is located on your filesystem by looking through all the directories in the PATH and displaying the first instance it finds. Try it out with the ls command:

```
$ which ls
/bin/ls
```

According to this output, the ls command is located at bin/ls. That directory is one of the entries on your PATH of executable files, which is why you can execute it from anywhere on your filesystem. Many of the commands you've used so far are located somewhere on your PATH, either because they were installed there during the initial installation of the operating system or by an installation tool such as your package manager.

Sometimes you'll have to download programs or scripts yourself and place them on your PATH so you can run them system-wide. Let's create a little executable program so you can get more comfortable with the PATH.

First, create a new directory to hold the script, then navigate into that folder:

```
$ mkdir greeting_script
$ cd greeting_script
```

Instead of using a programming language like C, Ruby, Python, or Perl, you'll create a shell script and make it executable. You'll learn a lot more about how these scripts work in Chapter 9, Automation, on page 231.

Use cat to create the following shell script. This prints the text "Hello" to the screen:

```
$ cat << 'EOF' > greetings
> #!/usr/bin/env bash
> echo Hello
> EOF
```

The line #!/usr/bin/env bash tells the shell which program should run the script. In this case, we're stating we want Bash to run the script. The second line of the script is the echo statement you've seen many times before.

Use the chmod +x command to make this script executable:

```
$ chmod +x greetings
```

Now execute the greetings command:

```
$ greetings
greetings: command not found
```

The greetings command fails to run because the shell can't find it on the PATH. By default, the shell prevents you from running executable files in the current working directory without explicitly specifying the path to the executable. This prevents you from accidentally running a malicious script with the same name as a built-in command. Imagine if someone wrote a script called ls that deleted all the files in your home directory. That could be disastrous.

To run an executable file in the current directory, prefix it with ./:

```
$ ./greetings
Hello
```

You can now see the output. Switch your working directory to the /var folder and then run the greetings command. This time, since you are not in the same directory as the command, you will have to provide the path to the command:

```
$ cd /var
$ ~/greeting_script/greetings
Hello
```

To make the command available system-wide without having to specify the path, copy it to a location contained in your PATH variable, or modify the value of PATH to include a new directory. You'll do the former for now; you'll look at modifying the PATH later.

The /usr/local/bin path is a common location for user-added scripts that should be available system-wide. So move the greetings script from the ~/greeting_script directory to that folder:

```
$ sudo mv ~/greeting_script/greetings /usr/local/bin/greetings
```

Now that the file is in place, you can execute the greetings command from any location on your filesystem without specifying the full path:

```
$ greetings
Hello
$ cd
$ greetings
Hello
$ cd /tmp
$ greetings
Hello
```

Many programs and processes rely on the PATH variable. You can modify this variable or create your own variables to hold information you want to reference later.

You're not limited to the variables the shell provides for you. You can make your own.

Setting Your Own Variables

You can set your own environment or shell variables in addition to the ones that are set up for you. This is helpful when you have to store long strings like API keys, access tokens, or credentials. Many web frameworks and applications use environment variables to store database credentials and other sensitive information to keep it out of the code.

Try it out. Create a new shell variable named SHIELD_PASSWORD and assign it the value of 12345:

```
$ SHIELD_PASSWORD=12345
```

Now print out the value:

```
$ echo $SHIELD_PASSWORD
12345
```

This variable is available at the shell level, so it's not available to any subshells or any other programs. Use the env command to verify this, and use grep to filter for SHIELD_PASSWORD:

```
$ env | grep SHIELD_PASSWORD
```

You won't see any results.

To make SHIELD_PASSWORD an environment variable, use the export keyword:

```
$ export SHIELD_PASSWORD
```

Now use env and grep to check if it's part of the environment. This time you see it returned:

```
$ env | grep SHIELD_PASSWORD
SHIELD_PASSWORD=12345
```

The Bash shell offers a shortcut for creating an environment variable in a single step. Make an environment variable named SECRET_KEY using this method:

```
$ export SECRET_KEY=12345
```

Verify that it's set:

```
$ env | grep SECRET_KEY
SECRET_KEY=12345
```

Finally, use the unset command to remove it:

```
$ unset SECRET_KEY
$ env | grep SECRET_KEY
$
```

Beware of Secrets in History

 It's common to use environment variables to store sensitive information. However, remember that every command you enter gets saved to your shell history. Many shells are preconfigured to not record commands starting with a leading space. Later in this chapter you'll learn how to configure your shell history's options to enable that behavior.

Shell and environment variables give you control over how many pieces of your environment work. Many commands have environment variables you can set to change their default behavior. For example, if you plan to use grep a lot, and you want it to always show two lines around every result, you can export the GREP_OPTIONS variable:

```
$ export GREP_OPTIONS='-A 2 -B 2'
```

Now when you use grep, those options are applied.

Supplying Environment Variables to Specific Programs

Sometimes you'll have a script or program that needs some variables from the environment, but you don't need or want to set these values forever, or you need to override values in your environment temporarily. You can do this by prefixing the command with the variables you need.

To demonstrate this, you'll create a quick Perl script which grabs values from the environment and prints them out. Perl is great for this because it's already installed on macOS and Ubuntu, and it makes it easy to write a small program to illustrate this concept.

Create a file named variables that reads the variables HOME and API_KEY from the environment. You'll use the cat command to create this file quickly, using the heredoc method you've used throughout the book.

Variables in Perl start with a dollar sign, and that's how you get the values of shell and environment variables. That's why you've been placing single quotes around EOF when you've used cat to create files. Doing this instructs Bash to treat the contents of the heredoc literally rather than expanding the variables into their values.

First, switch to your home directory:

```
$ cd
```

Then execute this command to create the script:

```
$ cat << 'EOF' > variables
> #!/usr/bin/env perl
> $home =  $ENV{'HOME'};
> print "Home directory: $home\n";
>
> $apikey = $ENV{'API_KEY'};
> print "API key: $apikey\n";
> EOF
```

Then use chmod +x to make the script executable:

```
$ chmod +x variables
```

Now run the script. Remember that you have to prefix the script's name with ./ since it's in the current working directory:

```
$ ./variables
Home directory: /home/brian
API key:
```

The output shows a value for the home directory, but the API key is empty. The program is looking for an environment variable, so define the API_KEY environment variable and run the script again:

```
$ export API_KEY=12345
$ ./variables
Home directory: /home/brian
API key: 12345
```

If you're going to be using the API_KEY variable over and over, this is a fine way to do it. But if you only need it for a single run, it can be overkill; you'd have to set the variable, run the program, and, if you didn't want the variable lying around, you'd have to unset it:

```
$ export API_KEY=abcde
$ ./variables
Home directory: /home/brian
API key: abcde
$ unset API_KEY
```

A shorter way to accomplish this is to use the env command, which creates a new environment using the values you define.

```
$ env API_KEY=abcde ./variables
Home directory: /home/brian
API key: abcde
```

The value is set, the value is displayed, but the value of abcde doesn't persist. You can verify that with echo $API_KEY if you like.

The env command isn't necessary in Bash in most cases. Run the script again, but this time define the API_KEY variable by prefixing its definition to the command without using env:

```
$ API_KEY=12345 ./variables
Home directory: /home/brian
API key: 12345
```

You'll see people use both methods. The env method is more universal, while the method that doesn't use it is a Bash feature.

You can override the value of the HOME environment variable this way too. Give it a try:

```
$ API_KEY=abcde HOME=/var/www ./variables
Home directory: /var/www
API key: abcde
```

The HOME variable is overridden, but only for that command's run.

Shell and environment variables won't persist when you close your shell. To have things persist beyond your existing session, you need to add it to your shell initialization files. You'll get to that shortly. Before you do, let's look at a better way to create and edit files while you're working on the command line. That'll make it easier to create the shell initialization files you'll need.

Editing Text with GNU nano

Throughout this book, you've created files with echo, touch, and cat, and you've edited files with sed, but sometimes you need to make more substantial modifications to existing files. Or, to be more honest, sometimes it's just more comfortable to use a more familiar method of creating and editing text.

GNU nano[2] is a basic text editor that's great for beginners, and it's available in a lot of environments out of the box. Let's look at how to use nano to create and edit files, and how to configure it to enable more options.

> \|/   **Joe asks:**
> ɔ̃̈   **# Why not Vim or Emacs?**
>
> Both Vim and Emacs require a significant amount of time and effort to demonstrate. There are entire books devoted to each. Additionally, picking Vim over Emacs would upset Emacs fans, while using Emacs over Vim would upset Vim fans. So I decided it would be best to frustrate both and use nano instead.
>
> On a more serious note, nano is the default shell editor on macOS and Ubuntu, so it's worth learning, as you may encounter it. Once you outgrow it, explore Vim and Emacs and decide if they're worth the investment.

Let's use nano to create and edit a basic HTML file. Create the file nano.html using the nano command:

```
$ nano nano.html
```

The nano editor appears in your terminal:

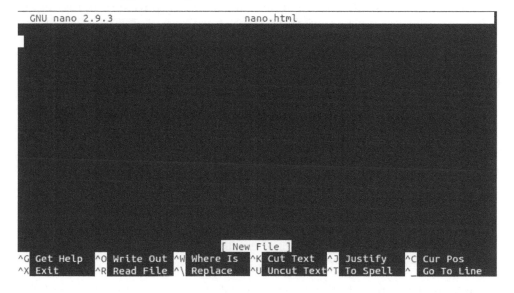

---

2.   https://www.nano-editor.org

Enter the following text in the editor:

```
environment/nano.html
<!DOCTYPE html>
<html lang="en-US">
  <head>
    <meta charset="utf-8">
    <title>Nano</title>
  </head>
  <body>
    <p>I made this in Nano</p>
  </body>
</html>
```

Once you've entered the text, save the file by exiting the editor with `Ctrl+x`. You'll be prompted to save the file. Press `y`, followed by `Enter` to accept.

To change the file later, open it again with `nano`.

`nano` looks like a basic editor when you first work with it, but it's quite capable. It has some handy features you'll want to turn on to make it more useful, like syntax highlighting. You can customize `nano` by creating a configuration file at ~/.nanorc.

On Ubuntu, `nano` already has syntax highlighting and some other features enabled by default. These settings are located in the file /etc/nanorc, which `nano` reads first. Changes in your local `nano` configuration will override these settings.

On macOS, the default version of nano does not support syntax highlighting, so you will need to install a newer version of `nano` using Homebrew to follow along:

```
$ brew install nano
```

This installs a more up-to-date version of nano at /usr/local/bin/nano. This directory is specified first in the default `PATH` variable on macOS, so when you use the nano command, it's the one that will be run. You can verify this with `which nano`.

Use `nano` to create and edit the configuration file. That's right—you're going to use nano to edit nano's configuration file. Good times.

```
$ nano ~/.nanorc
```

First, enable syntax highlighting by including `nano`'s syntax highlighters. You'll do this by including some additional configuration files, and the files you'll include depend on which OS you're using.

If you're on Ubuntu, add this line to load all of the syntax highlighter files:

```
environment/nanorc
include "/usr/share/nano/*.nanorc"
```

On macOS with nano installed via Homebrew, add this line instead:

```
include /usr/local/share/nano/*.nanorc
```

Next, add this line which will allow you to suspend nano as a background process, which is useful if you need to run a command while nano is running:

```
environment/nanorc
set suspend
```

You'll learn more about suspending programs in Running and Managing Jobs, on page 179.

Then add this line to turn off word-wrapping:

```
environment/nanorc
set nowrap
```

Finally, add this to make nano show line numbers on the left-hand side:

```
environment/nanorc
set linenumbers
```

Save the file and exit the editor (Ctrl+x, y, Enter.)

Now open your HTML file in nano again:

```
$ nano nano.html
```

You'll now see line numbers and a nicely colorized output:

Using nano, you can inspect and edit any file on your system without leaving your terminal. Let's use nano to create files to configure the environment.

Customizing Your Shell Session

When you open a new Bash shell session, your shell executes a series of configuration scripts. You can modify these scripts to customize your environment to your liking. You can set your default terminal editor, create shortcuts for commands, change the information displayed in your prompt, set environment variables, and more.

Shells are of two types: *login shells* and *non-login shells*. The type of shell determines which files you use to define the settings. If you put the settings in the wrong place, they won't apply. This can be a massive source of frustration when you're trying to set things like environment variables for certain processes, so let's walk through how each shell works.

When you connect to a machine remotely or physically and you provide your username and password, you're using a login shell. When you do this, Bash first looks at the file /etc/profile, which contains global settings shared by all users. It then looks for the files ~/.bash_profile, ~/.bash_login, or ~/.profile, in that order, and executes the first one it finds. The settings in that file are applied.

A non-login shell is the kind that you open when you've already logged into the machine and start a shell session. For example, on Ubuntu, you launch the terminal from a graphical desktop. This launches the ~/.bashrc file, but not the ~/.profile or ~/.bash_profile files.

Similarly, if you execute the command bash, which will launch a new instance of the Bash shell, the ~/.bashrc file is executed. Again, this is because you're already logged in, so you're running a non-login shell.

You can check whether you're running in a login shell or a non-login shell by looking at the value of the $0 shell variable:

```
$ echo $0
-bash
```

If you see a leading -, you're running in a login shell. If there's no leading -, you're in a non-login shell.

Unfortunately, macOS works a little differently. When you open a new terminal on macOS, it uses a login shell instead, so it loads ~/.bash_profile instead. You'd expect it to use ~/.bashrc since you're already logged in, but that's not the case.

Maintaining multiple configuration files is terrible, and while you could alter how the various terminal applications on systems work, the best approach is to use the ~/.bashrc file for everything that's common, and then load that file from ~/.bash_profile. This is similar to how Ubuntu's defaults work, and that's the approach you'll use in this book.

First, check to see if you have an existing ~/.bashrc file:

```
$ cat ~/.bashrc
```

If it has a bunch of content, you have two choices: you can back it up and start fresh, or you can work with what's there. For this exercise, back it up and start over.

Rename the existing file so you can refer to it later. You should explore on your own some good stuff in there.

```
$ mv ~/.bashrc ~/.bashrc_old
```

Now use nano to create and open a fresh ~/.bashrc file:

```
$ nano ~/.bashrc
```

The first thing to add to the file is a statement that ejects from the process if the shell is noninteractive. Shells are designed to be interactive, but some programs may fire up a shell session to execute commands noninteractively and so it's a good idea to avoid executing anything in this file if that's the case. This is common practice, and since you're starting your file from scratch, you should do this, too, so you don't break other programs that have expectations about noninteractive shells.

You could do this a few ways, but the easiest way is to check if the $PS1 variable is set. This variable holds the definition for the shell prompt. It's unset in a noninteractive shell. If it's unset, you stop processing the rest of the file.

Add this line to your file to do just that:

```
environment/bashrc
[ -z "$PS1" ] && return
```

The expression [-z "$PS1"] is a test that checks if the value of PS1 has a length of zero. The expression returns an exit code of 0 if it's true or 1 if it's false. The && return component of the statement only executes if the test is true. You'll learn more about exit codes and these boolean operators in Executing a Series of Commands, on page 162.

With this in place, you can start adding lines to this file to customize your environment. You can define environment variables, customize the prompt, and even create some shortcut commands. You'll start by setting some options to control how shell history works.

Controlling History

You can control which commands get stored in the history, as well as how many entries are preserved in the current session and across all sessions, all through a handful of shell variables. Let's add some to our .bashrc file.

The HISTCONTROL variable lets you ignore commands that start with a space. This can be really great to hide commands containing sensitive information from your history. It's often a default setting.

The HISTCONTROL variable also lets you ignore repeated duplicates. So if you type ls three times in a row, you can only have it saved once. This only checks the previous command for duplicates, but it's still a nice way to trim down the history a bit.

You can set one or both of these options like this:

```
HISTCONTROL=ignorespace:ignoredups
```

Better yet, to set both options, use the ignoreboth value instead:

```
environment/bashrc
HISTCONTROL=ignoreboth
```

If you want duplicates to go away entirely, add erasedups:

```
HISTCONTROL=ignoreboth:erasedups
```

This removes all previous instances of commands you've typed, only keeping the most recent command. I don't recommend this approach, as it makes it more difficult to see your actual linear history of commands.

History is saved to a file when you exit your session, If you'd like to append to the history file instead of starting with a fresh one each time you open your shell, add this line to your configuration:

```
environment/bashrc
shopt -s histappend
```

You can control the size of the history file. Add these lines to control the number of history lines saved in your current session (HISTSIZE) and how many lines you save in the file (HISTFILESIZE) when you exit your shell:

environment/bashrc
```
HISTSIZE=1000
HISTFILESIZE=2000
```

Finally, if there are commands you'd like the history command to ignore, add them to the HISTIGNORE command. For example, to stop recording exit and clear commands, add this line:

environment/bashrc
```
HISTIGNORE="exit:clear"
```

This keeps your history cleaner. Be careful what you ignore here too, especially if you want to use your history as a log of your session.

That's it for history management. Now let's set environment variables that control which text editor CLI programs should invoke.

Setting Your Shell Editor

In some situations, a CLI program will try to rely on a terminal text editor. For example, if you use Git and you don't specify a commit message when making a commit, Git will attempt to open a shell editor so you can create the message interactively. The default value for the editor might be Vim, which might not be what you'd expect, or want.

The EDITOR and VISUAL environment variables let you specify the shell editor other programs should use to edit text.

The EDITOR variable is for line editors like the classic ed program. The VISUAL variable is for full-screen editors like nano. You most likely only need VISUAL, but since people tend to get these confused, it's not a bad idea to set both. Add these two lines to your ~/.bashrc file to set both to use the nano editor:

environment/bashrc
```
export EDITOR=nano
export VISUAL=nano
```

You use the export option here because you need the value of these variables to be available to other programs as well as the shell itself.

Now let's look at modifying the PATH variable.

Modifying the PATH

As you learned earlier in the chapter, the PATH environment variable determines where the shell looks for executable programs. You may want to add additional directories to the list.

One common approach is to create a local bin folder in your home directory to hold executable scripts you create yourself. This way you don't have to move executable scripts to a directory like /usr/local/bin.

When modifying the PATH variable, you usually want to append or prepend a directory to the list. Rather than setting the entire PATH value, use the existing value. Add the following line to the ~/.bashrc file to prepend the ~/bin directory to the PATH variable's value:

environment/bashrc
```
export PATH="~/bin:$PATH"
```

Use double quotes around the value to ensure that any spaces in existing pathnames are preserved.

Each directory in the PATH value is separated by a colon. In this case, you put ~/bin first, followed by a colon, followed by the current value of PATH.

When you execute commands, the shell searches through directories in the PATH variable one at a time, executing the first command it finds. By prepending ~/bin, it's now possible to add your own commands in the ~/bin directory that override any built-in commands.

Try it out. Save the file with Ctrl+o, followed by Enter. The settings you added to this file won't be applied to the current shell session, and we want to keep the text editor open since we're not done changing this file yet. Open a new shell session instead.

In the new session, create the ~/bin directory:

```
$ mkdir ~/bin
```

Now create a new executable script in that directory. In Locating Executables with PATH, on page 129, you created a simple greetings script which you copied to /usr/local/bin. Let's create a new version of that script that displays a different message:

```
$ cat << 'EOF' > ~/bin/greetings
> #!/usr/bin/env bash
> echo Hi there
> EOF
```

Make the new script executable:

```
$ chmod +x ~/bin/greetings
```

Use the which command to verify that you're using the new file:

```
$ which greetings
/home/brian/bin/greetings
```

Because the ~/bin directory is the first entry in PATH, this will be the command executed, rather than the one in /usr/local/bin:

```
$ greetings
Hi there
```

You've modified the PATH variable and created a place for your own executable scripts. Close the new shell session and return to your editor.

Now let's customize the prompt.

Building Your Prompt

The value of the PS1 variable lets you specify what your prompt should look like. You can put lots of information in your prompt, including your username, your current working directory, and much more.

Let's start by creating a prompt that's nothing more than the dollar sign with a space after it. Add this line to your ~/.bashrc file:

```
PS1='\$ '
```

The \$ sequence displays a dollar sign for regular users and a pound sign (#) for root users. Using single quotes around the prompt value ensures that the value isn't expanded into a literal dollar sign.

Save the file with Ctrl+o, followed by Enter. Then open a new shell session to see your new prompt. Close the new shell session and return to your editor.

Let's add the current working directory to the prompt. Add the characters \w, which shows the full path to the current directory unless the directory is in your home directory, in which case it displays ~ instead:

```
PS1='\w \$ '
```

To add user@host: to the front of the path, so you can see the username and hostname, use \u for username, the literal @, and \h for the hostname, followed by a colon (:):

```
PS1='\u@\h:\w \$ '
```

You can use color codes in your prompt as well by using ANSI color codes within your prompt.

In a new terminal, try this command:

```
$ echo -e "\033[36mhello\033[0m world"
```

The word "hello" appears in cyan:

```
Hello world
```

The sequence \033[36m signifies where coloring should start. 36 is the color for cyan. The sequence \033[0m reverts formatting back to the original colors. Calling echo with the -e option tells it to interpret these sequences.

However, the tput command makes it much easier to set colors. The tput setaf command sets the foreground color, while the tput sgr0 command resets everything to normal again. Run this in your terminal:

```
$ echo "$(tput setaf 6)Hello $(tput sgr0)world"
```

You get the same results as before. tput setaf 6 is cyan. This example uses a feature called command substitution, which you'll explore more in Using Command Substitution, on page 187. Note that this time you don't need the -e switch, as there are no escape characters to interpret.

Close this terminal session and return to the one running nano.

You can use these in your prompt too, but you'll want to surround the color sequences in escaped square braces to ensure that Bash doesn't count those characters in its prompt length calculations. If you omit them, you might end up with things not lining up on the screen right or a previous command's text overflowing onto your prompt.

To color the username, alter the prompt like this:

```
PS1="\[\$(tput setaf 6)\]\u\[\$(tput sgr0)\]@\h:\w \\$ "
```

This time we have to switch the single quotes around the prompt to double quotes, because we need to execute the embedded tput commands to get the color codes in the prompt. That also means we need to add an extra backslash in front of the dollar sign at the end so it gets interpreted properly.

That prompt is pretty hard to read and will be difficult to manage later on. To make it more maintainable, store the colors you want in variables with the escaped braces already in place. Remove the existing PS1 value and replace it with these lines:

```
environment/bashrc
USERCOLOR='\[$(tput setaf 6)\]'  # cyan
RESET='\[$(tput sgr0)\]'

PS1="${USERCOLOR}\u${RESET}@\h:\w \\$ "
```

We use single quotes around the values for USERCOLOR and RESET because we do not want to evaluate the expressions when we assign them. The value stored in PS1 is evaluated before the prompt is displayed, so the expressions will be evaluated at that time. This gives us more flexibility when constructing complex prompts, which you'll explore in Using Command Substitution in Your Prompt, on page 189.

This code is easier to read and easier to maintain going forward. You could expand this to add additional colors too.

Save the file and exit your editor.

The changes you made to the file will apply to any new shells you open, but they don't affect the current shell. To apply the changes to your current shell, use the source command and specify the ~/.bashrc file. You'll see your new prompt displayed:

```
$ source ~/.bashrc
brian@puzzles:~ $
```

Using source to load or reload a configuration file is called *sourcing* a file. You will do this a few more times in the book as you make changes to your configuration files.

Now let's make sure all the changes you've made will work in both login and non-login shells.

Handling .bash_profile

As you learned earlier in this section, the .bashrc file isn't read by macOS and might not be read on other systems. The best solution is to tell ~/.bash_profile to load ~/.bashrc if it exists. On Ubuntu, the .profile file already does this for you, but let's walk through the process anyway so you understand how it works. In addition, the ~/.bash_profile will be used instead of ~/.profile if it exists.

Open ~/.bash_profile in your text editor:

```
$ nano ~/.bash_profile
```

Add this code to the file which checks to see if the file ~/.bashrc exists and loads it if it does.

```
environment/bash_profile
if [ -f ~/.bashrc ]; then
    source ~/.bashrc
fi
```

Save the file and exit the editor. Now the settings will be applied no matter which way you start a new shell session.

Now let's look at creating shortcuts to commands.

Creating Shortcuts with Aliases and Functions

Bash lets you define your own versions of commands, either through aliases or functions.

Aliases let you create shortcuts for commands or override the default options for existing commands. You define them with the alias command, but it's better to define them in your ~/.bashrc file. Let's define some aliases.

Open your ~/.bashrc file in nano:

```
$ nano ~/.bashrc
```

Let's create an alias for ls -alh so you can avoid typing it out. Add this line to the end of the ~/.bashrc file to define an alias called ll:

environment/bashrc
```
alias ll='ls -alh'
```

Save the file and exit the editor. Then source the file to apply the changes:

```
$ source ~/.bashrc
```

Try running the ll alias:

```
$ ll
total 124K
drwxr-xr-x 15 root root 4.0K Mar  3 11:34 .
drwxr-xr-x  4 root root 4.0K Mar  3 10:06 ..
...
```

You can use this any time you want a long listing.

You can make an alias for any command you'd like. Let's add an alias to display your public IP address quickly. Open the ~/.bashrc file again:

```
$ nano ~/.bashrc
```

Add this alias to the file which fetches your public IP address from an external website:

environment/bashrc
```
alias myip='curl icanhazip.com'
```

You'll learn how this command works in Making Web Requests with cURL, on page 208.

Save the file, exit the editor, and then source the file to apply the changes to the current shell:

```
$ source ~/.bashrc
```

Try out your new alias:

```
$ myip
203.0.113.24
```

Aliases you create won't be available if you use the sudo command.

Try it out:

```
$ sudo ll
sudo: ll: command not found
```

By default, Bash doesn't look beyond the first word for any aliases, but you can fix that by adding an alias for sudo. Open up the ~/.bashrc file again:

```
$ nano ~/.bashrc
```

Add this alias to the file:

environment/bashrc
```
alias sudo='sudo '
```

Note the space after sudo. By leaving a space as part of the command, Bash will look at the next word to see if it's an alias, which means the ll alias will now work.

Save the file, exit the editor, and then source the ~/.bashrc file to apply the changes. Then try the command again. This time it works:

```
$ sudo ll
total 96K
drwxr-xr-x 15 brian brian 4.0K Mar  2 16:05 .
drwxr-xr-x  3 root  root  4.0K Mar  2 17:59 ..
...
```

As you can see from the sudo alias, you can use an alias to override a command with new behavior. So if you always want a long listing when you run ls, you can do that. Just define the alias ls like this:

```
$ alias ls='ls -lh'
```

Now when you type ls, you'll get the long listing:

```
$ ls
total 36K
drwxr-xr-x 2 brian brian 4.0K Mar  2 11:59 Desktop
drwxr-xr-x 2 brian brian 4.0K Mar  2 11:59 Documents
...
```

But don't worry; the old behavior is still available. All you have to do is prefix the command with \:

```
$ \ls
Desktop          Documents      Downloads
examples.desktop                Music
Pictures         Public         Videos
```

And you can remove the alias with the unalias command:

```
$ unalias ls
```

Aliases have some limitations. First, they're really only designed to either redefine or point to a different command. Arguments you pass to an alias get forwarded along.

If you need more flexibility, you can define functions. Let's explore this by creating a new function called mcd that creates a directory and navigates to it in a single command. You've probably wanted something like this every time you've created a new folder and had to navigate to it. Open the ~/.bashrc file in nano:

```
$ nano ~/.bashrc
```

To declare a function, use the function keyword, followed by the name of the function and the function body, similar to how you'd define a function in many other programming languages. Add this to the file to define the mcd function:

```
environment/bashrc
function mcd () {
  mkdir -p "$1" && cd "$1"
}
```

The $1 variable is a reference to the argument passed to the mcd function when it's called. It'll be the name of the directory we want to create and switch to.

If you're defining a small function like this, you can write it in only one line of code:

```
mcd () { mkdir -p "$1" && cd "$1"; }
```

Note the semicolon after the cd command. That's necessary if you're creating a one-line function. Another difference here is that this definition doesn't use the function keyword. You don't actually need the function keyword when defining a function. whether it's simple or complex, but it's easier for others to follow what you're doing if you use it, so I recommend including it.

Save the file, exit the editor, and source the file with source ~/.bashrc. Then try it out:

```
$ mcd ~/testdir
$ pwd
/home/brian/testdir
$ cd
```

You can make more complex functions than this. Let's create a function that displays info about your environment. You'll use the uname -a command to get OS info, the free command to display available memory, and you'll use curl icanhazip.com to fetch your public IP address. You'll then use echo with the -e flag to preserve new lines so you get a nice-looking output.

Open your .bashrc file:

```
$ nano ~/.bashrc
```

Add this function to the file:

environment/bashrc
```
function showme () {
  echo "OS:"
  uname -a
  echo -e "\nUptime:"
  uptime
  echo -e "\nMemory:"
  free
  echo -e "\nWAN IP :"
  curl -s icanhazip.com
}
```

If you want to try this on macOS, replace the free command in this function with top -l 1 -s 0 | grep PhysMem, as macOS doesn't have the free command.

Save the file, exit the editor, source your .bashrc file, and run the command:

```
$ showme
OS:
Linux puzzles 4.18.0-15-generic #16~18.04.1-Ubuntu SMP Sun Mar 3 14:06:04
UTC 2019 x86_64 x86_64 x86_64 GNU/Linux

Uptime:
 17:46:48 up 18:13,  1 user,  load average: 0.08, 0.02, 0.01

Memory:
          total      used       free     shared  buff/cache   available
Mem:    2041112   1059040     241124      47652      740948      775436
Swap:    483800      5388     478412

WAN IP :
203.0.113.24
```

You can put all sorts of logic inside of these functions, including conditional statements.

Let's make a function named less that overrides the real less command. When you call less and pass it a file, you'll display the file with line numbers. If you pipe data to the less command from another program, you'll keep the original behavior. It sounds a little like an alias, but by using a function, you can add logic to see how the function was invoked and specify different options depending on whether it's called directly or if it's receiving data from standard input.

To do this in a somewhat naive way, you'll check to see if the standard input stream is connected to a terminal. In other words, you'll check to see if the input is coming from a command the user typed, rather than from another program.

The expression [-t 0] is how you test that file descriptor 0, or standard input, is connected to your terminal. You can use if-else statements in your functions to evaluate boolean expressions like this. Here's how that looks:

```
if [ -t 0 ]; then
  # input is interactive
else
  # input is coming from a pipe
fi
```

So, to make the less command show line numbers unless you pipe data, add this function declaration to your ~/.bashrc file:

environment/bashrc
```
function less() {
  if [ -t 0 ]; then
    command less -N "$@"
  else
    command less "$@"
  fi
}
```

Now, when you call less, you're not calling the actual less program; you're calling this function. This function will then test to see if the input came from the connected terminal or from a pipe. If it came from a connected terminal, it calls the actual less command with the -N option, enabling line numbers. $@ refers to all of the arguments you passed to less when you invoked it. Notice that we use command less inside the function. This ensures that we're calling the actual less command. This is a safe way to wrap built-in commands with your own functions to extend their behavior.

Save your ~/.bashrc file and apply the changes using source ~/.bashrc. Now try it out by using less to view a file. You'll have it display the nano.html file you created earlier in this chapter:

```
$ less nano.html
     1 <!DOCTYPE html>
     2 <html lang="en-US">
     3   <head>
     4     <meta charset="utf-8">
     5     <title>Nano</title>
     6   </head>
     7   <body>
     8     <p>I made this in nano</p>
     9   </body>
    10 </html>
```

Press q to quit less and return to the prompt.

Now invoke less by sending data to your less function through standard input:

```
$ less <nano.html
<!DOCTYPE html>
<html lang="en-US">
  <head>
    <meta charset="utf-8">
    <title>Nano</title>
  </head>
  <body>
    <p>I made this in nano</p>
  </body>
</html>
```

This function demonstrates how you can add conditional logic, but it's not a perfect test. In some situations it won't give you the behavior you want because the test will think you are using a pipe, such as when used in command substitution.

You'll learn about command substitution in the next chapter.

Since this function has some side effects, you should remove it from your ~/.bashrc file before moving forward, or rename it so it doesn't conflict with the built-in less command and surprise you later.

Using Symlinks for Configuration Files

You may not want to keep your configuration files in your home directory for a number of reasons. If you have multiple computers, you may want to share your configuration files across systems. Or you may just want to put your configuration files on GitHub to share them with the world. In many cases, it's easier to manage your configuration files if you put them in a separate directory and then use symlinks to those files in your home directory.

Try it out. Create a new directory named dotfiles in your home directory:

```
$ mkdir dotfiles
```

Then move your .bashrc file into that directory:

```
$ mv ~/.bashrc dotfiles/bashrc
```

Notice that the destination name no longer has a leading dot. This way the file isn't a hidden file.

Now create a symlink in your home directory that points to ~/dotfiles/bashrc:

```
$ ln -s ~/dotfiles/bashrc ~/.bashrc
```

Now close and reopen your terminal. Your shell settings are still preserved, but the files are in their own separate directory. You can then use Git[a] to manage changes you make or share them with the world. And if you have multiple machines with Dropbox or Google Drive installed, you can place your dotfiles directory in the location where these apps look for files, and adjust your symlinks to point there. Then a change on one system automatically propagates to others. Best of all, using nano ~/.bashrc opens the correct file, as it follows the symlink to the actual file.

---

a.   https://git-scm.com/

Creating Keyboard Shortcuts

A number of keyboard shortcuts are at your disposal. You learned about several of them in Useful Shortcuts, on page 13. For example you learned that Ctrl+l clears the screen, and Ctrl+a jumps to the beginning of the line. Use the bind -p command to see a list of all the defined commands available. It's a long list, so use less:

```
$ bind -p | less
"\C-g": abort
"\C-x\C-g": abort
"\e\C-g": abort
"\C-j": accept-line
"\C-m": accept-line
...
```

In addition to the ones already defined, you can make your own. Try it out by using the bind command to map Ctrl+t to execute the pwd command:

```
$ bind '"\C-t": "pwd\n"'
```

Note a couple things about this. First, you need single quotes around the keybinding definition. This prevents any shell expansion or evaluation. Second, you need quotes around the keybinding and the printed value. Single quotes around the pair, double quotes around each part, with a colon separating the pair.

Press Ctrl+t and you'll see the current working directory printed to the screen.

The bind command takes the key combination and maps it to a string of characters. In this case, we used pwd\n because you want the line break included so the command executes. Without the \n, it would just put pwd on the same line. That's useful though. Remember that to redirect the standard error stream to the standard output stream, you use the sequence 2>&1. You can make a keybinding to add this quickly. Let's make Ctrl+t insert those characters instead. The command is similar; you just don't include the \n at the end:

```
$ bind '"\C-t": " 2>&1"'
```

Note the space that is in front of the 2>&1 bit. It is a literal space, so when you trigger this keyboard shortcut, it will put that space in. This way you can just type a command, press Ctrl+t, and it will insert all of the characters, including the space.

You do have to be careful you don't override built-in shortcuts you rely on, though. For example, you know that Ctrl+l clears the screen. But if you bind another keystroke to that key combo, your new one takes over. In addition to the Ctrl key, you have a few other options for defining shortcuts.

Let's create a keybinding which sets the F1 key to insert the 2>&1 sequence. To do that, you need the character sequence for the F1 key. Terminal software doesn't send keys to the shell; it sends character data, and each keystroke sends different data depending on the configuration of your terminal. Some keys, like F1, send a sequence of characters, starting with an *escape character*.

At the prompt, press Ctrl+v, followed by the F1 key to view the character sequence for F1. The characters ^[OP appear on the screen. The first two characters, ^[represent the escape character. The rest of the sequence is the value for F1.

For the keybinding, replace ^[with \e. Define the new keystroke like this:

```
$ bind '"\eOP": " 2>&1"'
```

Now press F1 and you'll see the results on the screen.

Use Ctrl+v to view the character sequence for any special key so you can create your own bindings. Some keys, like F12, show results like ^[[24~. Note the two opening square braces in a row. In this case, ^[is the escape character and [24~ is the value.

> ## The Meta Key
>
> Bash, and some other programs, occasionally refers to the Meta key, but you won't find this key on modern keyboards. It comes from the Symbolics Space-Cadet keyboard.[a] On modern terminals, this key is emulated by the Esc key, and other terminals let you use the Alt or Option key.
>
> The Bash manual lists \M as the option to create keybindings using the Meta key, but it doesn't work in practice due to how terminal programs and modern keyboards are configured. To define a keybinding that works with the Esc or Alt keys, use the \e escape sequence instead.
>
> For example, to map the Alt+z key sequence to change to the previous directory you used, you'd use this keybinding:
>
> ```
> $ bind '"\ez": "cd -\n"'
> ```
>
> For the Alt key to work properly, your terminal software has to support it. macOS has an option in the built-in Terminal app for this. On Ubuntu, the default Terminal app has this configured already. The popular iTerm2 app[b] has a similar option which is enabled by default.
>
> ---
>
> a. https://en.wikipedia.org/wiki/Space-cadet_keyboard
> b. https://iterm2.com/

In addition to using Ctrl and other special keys, you can create a shortcut that starts with one of these options:

- \\ for a backslash.
- \" for a double quote.
- \' for a single quote.

Instead of using a keybinding for 2>&1, you'll create a shortcut that looks for the characters \eout and converts them to 2>&1. It's the same number of characters, but easier to remember. Here's how you do it:

```
$ bind '"\\eout": " 2>&1"'
```

Test it out. Type \eout and the text appears. When you type the backslash, you won't see the rest of the characters. You also have a limited amount of time to type the characters following the backslash before the shell just assumes you want a literal backslash.

One downside to these prefixes is that it does cause a slight delay when typing the prefix character. For that reason, I don't recommend using double or single quotes, since you'll want to use those often.

All the commands you've entered so far will go away as soon as you close your session. To persist them, add them to your .bashrc file like you would with aliases or environment settings.

Now, let's add a keybinding to the environment permanently. Open your ~/.bashrc file:

```
$ nano ~/.bashrc
```

In the file, add this keybinding that inserts the text >> output.txt when you press Ctrl+x Ctrl+o.

environment/bashrc
```
bind '"\C-x\C-o": " >> output.txt'
```

This keybinding requires a little more work to use, but it demonstrates that you can create more complex keybindings.

Finally, let's add one more keybinding you might find useful. If you're in the middle of typing a command, and you realize you need to prefix it with sudo, you could press Ctrl+a to jump to the beginning of the line, type sudo, a space, and then press Ctrl+e to jump to the end.

Or you can create a keybinding to do that for you when you press Alt+s. Add this to your .bashrc file:

environment/bashrc
```
bind '"\es": "\C-asudo \C-e"'
```

This keybinding illustrates that it's possible to have one binding activate other keybindings, which means you can compose more complex macros from smaller ones.

Save the file, exit the editor, and source the ~/.bashrc file to apply the changes to your current session. Then try it out. Type the ls command, and then press Alt+s or Esc+s and the command will be prefixed with sudo.

You can customize your environment in another place, and it will affect more than just your shell.

Modifying Readline Behavior

The Bash shell uses the GNU Readline library[3] to process command input. Other tools you'll encounter also use this library, including the MySQL console, interactive shells for Python, Node.js, and Ruby, and many other tools. Many of the keyboard shortcuts and behaviors you've learned about so far are available in any tool that uses this library.

The .inputrc file lets you define options that affect any program that uses the Readline library. It lets you control how tab completion works, and lets you define additional keyboard shortcuts for working with text and how some aspects of command history behave.

On some systems, the file /etc/inputrc contains a bunch of default settings. Check to see if this file exists on your system:

```
$ ls -l /etc/inputrc
-rw-r--r-- 1 root root 1748 May 15  2017 /etc/inputrc
```

This file contains system-wide Readline configuration settings shared by all users. Let's create a local .inputrc file which overrides the one in /etc/inputrc. If the /etc/inputrc file exists on your system, you'll want to include it in your own local .inputrc file so you don't lose any existing functionality. Create your local file with nano:

```
$ nano ~/.inputrc
```

If the /etc/inputrc file exists on your system, its contents will no longer be read now that you have an .inputrc file in your home directory. Add this line to include it so it gets read anyway:

environment/inputrc
```
$include /etc/inputrc
```

Let's start the customization by defining some keybindings. Defining keybindings in ~/.inputrc instead of in ~/.bashrc means that these bindings are available wherever Readline is supported.

First, configure how the Up and Down arrows work. Typically, these keys cycle through your command history. But let's make them more useful by telling them to filter the search using characters we've already typed.

The syntax for creating keybindings in ~/.inputrc is similar to the bind commands you used in the previous section and in your ~/.bashrc file. The difference is that you don't need to explicitly call bind, and you don't need to wrap the definition in single quotes.

---

3.   https://tiswww.case.edu/php/chet/readline/rltop.html

Add these lines to the file, which rebind the Up and Down keys:

```
environment/inputrc
"\e[A": history-search-backward
"\e[B": history-search-forward
```

Now create a keybinding that binds Alt+" to wrap the contents of the line with double quotes:

```
environment/inputrc
"\e\"": "\C-a\"\C-e\""
```

To make this work, we use an approach similar to the keybinding in the previous section that inserted sudo at the front of the line.

The binding executes commands that jump to the beginning of the line, inserts the literal double quote, jumps to the end of the line, and inserts the closing double quote. Note that you have to escape all of the literal double quotes, including both the double quote in the trigger, as well as the quotes in the output.

Save the file. To test out the results, exit your editor and use the bind command to load the .inputrc file so these changes are applied to your current session:

```
$ bind -f ~/.inputrc
```

Now test out the changes you made. When you press the Up arrow, it'll fill the line with the previous bind command. But type ls, then press the Up arrow, and the line fills with the most recent ls command you typed. Don't forget to try out your keybinding that wraps the line with quotes too.

Let's add some additional settings to the file. You can test each one as you go, or add them all and test them out at the end. Open the file for editing:

```
$ nano ~/.inputrc
```

When you press Tab to complete file or directory names, you may run into times where you stumble because the completion is case-sensitive. If you'd rather ignore case when you use tab completion, add this line:

```
environment/inputrc
set completion-ignore-case On
```

When you're using tab completion, you may want to see a little more information about the file, such as whether the file is a symlink or a regular file. The stat -F command prints a forward slash (/) after directories, an asterisk (*) after executable files, and an "at" sign (@) after symlinks. Add the following line to get these symbols to show up when you do tab completion:

```
environment/inputrc
set visible-stats On
```

Usually, you have to press Tab multiple times if the characters you've typed are ambiguous. Add this line to see results right away when you press Tab, even if there are multiple files that can match:

environment/inputrc
```
set show-all-if-ambiguous on
```

If you've been bothered by an annoying beep when you've pressed the Backspace key, it's because you've triggered the *bell*—an audible indication of a problem. When you press Backspace and there's nothing to delete, Bash rings the bell. You might hear the bell go off when you try tab completion too. And other programs can ring the bell in an attempt to get your attention. If you find it obnoxious, add this line to silence the audible bell:

environment/inputrc
```
set bell-style none
```

That may be too aggressive; other programs can ring the bell to let you know they encountered a problem or need your attention. Modern terminal emulators have a *visual bell*, where they'll display a visual indicator instead of an audible one. Instead of disabling the bell, you can specify you want just the visual bell with this line:

```
set bell-style visible
```

With these settings in place, save the file and exit your editor. Then, apply the changes with bind -f ~/.inputrc and try them out. These settings apply anywhere Readline works.

Change Editing Mode to Vi

The shortcut keys supported in the Readline library are modeled after the ones in the Emacs editor. If you happen to know Vim and want to enable Vim-like behavior on the command line, add this to your .inputrc file:

environment/inputrc
```
set editing-mode vi
```

This applies the changes to any program that uses the Readline library. If you want to restrict this to Bash only, add this line to ~/.bashrc instead:

environment/bashrc
```
set -o vi
```

Reload the configuration files. To move around the line or edit a command, press the Esc key, and then use Vim navigation keys. For example, use $ to jump to the end of the line, ^ to jump to the beginning, w to jump forward one word, and b to move backward. You can look at the Bash man page to review other shortcuts.

Your Turn

In this chapter, you explored a few ways to customize your environment. Take a shot at these challenges to stretch your thinking before moving on.

1. For each of the following variables, identify what the variable is for and whether it's an environment variable or a shell variable:

    -   HOME
    -   LANG
    -   OLDPWD
    -   CDPATH

2. Create the following aliases:

    -   An alias called ep which opens your ~/.bashrc file in nano so you can make changes quickly.

    -   An alias called sp which sources your ~/.bashrc file so you can apply those changes.

    -   An alias that displays the shell and environment variables, without displaying functions, that displays the results one page at a time.

3. Modify your showme function to display a calendar. Use the cal or ncal command you explored in the exercises in Chapter 1, Getting Your Feet Wet, on page 1.

4. You can use the source command inside of your .bashrc file to load other files. This lets you create a more organized and modular configuration. Try this out:

    a. Create a new file called ~/.aliases and move your alias definitions to that file.

    b. Modify the ~/.bashrc file to load the ~/.aliases file using source ~/.aliases.

    c. For extra safety, research how to only include the file if it exists.

5. Add these keybindings in your ~/.inputrc file:

    a. Create a binding that wraps a line with opening and closing parentheses.

    b. Create a binding similar to the binding that wraps the line with quotes, but instead of adding a quote to the beginning of the line, add it after the first word. This way, you can convert echo hello world to echo "hello world" with a keystroke. Hint: \ef jumps forward one word and \eb jumps back one word.

What You Learned

You can now customize your command-line interface instead of just living with the defaults. You know how to use environment and shell variables, you can create a configuration file for your shell with various settings, and you know how to make shortcuts using aliases and functions.

With your environment customized, it's time to dig in to some different ways to run commands. While you're there, you'll also explore process management.

## CHAPTER 7

Running and Managing Programs

Throughout this book, you've run various commands one at a time or in a pipeline, but there are more advanced ways to run commands you should know. In this chapter, you'll explore some additional ways to run commands and programs. You'll chain separate commands together, run long-running commands in the background, and even suspend a program temporarily so you can do something else. You'll also look at how to manage the processes running on your computer and terminate programs that don't respond, and you'll explore subshells and command substitution.

Let's start by looking at a few ways to issue and reuse commands.

Working with Commands

By now, you're already pretty comfortable running commands in your shell. You've redirected program output, and you've used the command history to recall previous commands. But you can also chain commands together, execute them in different environments, and much more.

Running Multiline Commands

As soon as you press the Enter key, the shell executes the command. Some commands have a lot of options or are just very long and might not fit on your screen, and you'd like to be able to break the command into multiple lines. You can do this by typing the \ character before pressing Enter.

In Creating Pipelines of Data, on page 94, you saw this example which lets you see the most-used commands in your history:

```
$ history | awk '{c[$2]++}END{for(i in c){print c[i] " " i}}' | sort -rn | head
```

You can break this command onto multiple lines by using the \ character, like this:

```
$ history \
> | awk '{c[$2]++}END{for(i in c){print c[i] " " i}}' \
> | sort -rn \
> | head
```

After you enter the first line, the prompt changes to a > to indicate the command isn't finished yet. Once you press Enter on a line that doesn't end in the \ character, the command runs.

The command will execute as if it were all typed on a single line. This is a great way to share commands with others, as it improves the readability.

Executing a Series of Commands

One common pattern you'll find yourself doing repeatedly is creating a directory and then switching to the directory you just created, like this:

```
$ mkdir workstuff
$ cd workstuff
```

You even created your own function to speed this up in Creating Shortcuts with Aliases and Functions, on page 146.

You can execute multiple commands at once by placing two ampersands (&&) or a semicolon between the commands. Let's explore both methods, as they work differently.

Using two ampersands requires that the first command completes successfully. Try to create the directory /tmp/websites/awesomeco using the mkdir command, but omit the -p switch so it won't attempt to create parent folders that don't exist. Then use two ampersands, followed by the cd command to switch to the new directory:

```
$ mkdir /tmp/websites/awesomeco && cd /tmp/websites/awesomeco
mkdir: cannot create directory '/tmp/websites/awesomeco':
No such file or directory
```

The mkdir command fails because the /tmp/websites folder doesn't exist, so it can't create the awesomeco directory. The cd command never executes because the first command failed. How does the shell know it failed though? Let's take a deeper look.

Try running the mkdir command by itself:

```
$ mkdir /tmp/websites/awesomeco
mkdir: cannot create directory '/tmp/websites/awesomeco':
No such file or directory
```

It displays an error message to the screen to tell you that it didn't work, but it also returns an *error code* to the shell. You can see that by printing the value of $? to the screen. Try it:

```
$ echo $?
1
```

According to the output, the previous command returns an exit code of 1. If a command-line program returns any exit code other than 0, the shell interprets this as a failure. The && sequence is an AND condition, and so anything to the right of the && only executes if the previous commands executed successfully.

Run the same command with a semicolon instead of two ampersands:

```
$ mkdir /tmp/websites/awesomeco;cd /tmp/websites/awesomeco
mkdir: cannot create directory '/tmp/websites/awesomeco':
No such file or directory
bash: cd: /tmp/websites/awesomeco: No such file or directory
```

This time both the mkdir and cd commands execute. The semicolon is just a separator between commands. It's as if you pressed Enter between each command.

This is a subtle difference, but an important one, especially if you only want to run subsequent commands if the previous commands were successful.

You can use the || characters to do something if a command fails. This is a boolean OR operation. Give this a try:

```
$ mkdir /tmp/websites/awesomeco || echo "Unable to create directory"
mkdir: cannot create directory '/tmp/websites/awesomeco':
No such file or directory
Unable to create directory
```

You can combine this with && too. Try to create the directory and switch to it, but print a message if it fails:

```
$ mkdir /tmp/websites/awesomeco && cd /tmp/websites/awesomeco \
> || echo "Unable to create directory"
mkdir: cannot create directory '/tmp/websites/awesomeco':
No such file or directory
Unable to create directory
```

Finally, use mkdir -p instead, which will create the parent directory, resulting in a successful execution. Your working directory will change:

```
$ mkdir -p /tmp/websites/awesomeco && cd /tmp/websites/awesomeco \
> || echo "Unable to create directory"
$ pwd
/tmp/websites/awesomeco
```

Unfortunately, some developers don't send proper exit codes from their programs. For example, on macOS, the built-in file command still returns an exit code of 0 when you pass it a file that doesn't exist. In cases like that, you'll have to rely on more robust error handling mechanisms, such as parsing the program's output.

You will get a chance to do more advanced command automation in Chapter 9, Automation, on page 231.

Before moving on, switch back to your home directory:

```
$ cd
```

Sometimes, you need a different environment when you run commands. Subshells are great for that.

Running Commands in Subshells

When you run commands in your shell, they execute in the current shell and have access to shell and environment variables you've set. Sometimes you want to run commands with different variables temporarily or run a series of commands without affecting your current shell. Subshells let you do that.

To run a command in a subshell, wrap it in parentheses:

```
$ (echo "Hello ${USER}")
Hello brian
```

The command executes in the subshell and prints out the results. The current shell and environment variables are passed on to the subshell, which is why you can access the USER variable.

That example doesn't demonstrate anything terribly useful, but using a subshell, you can create variables that only exist in the subshell. Try this out:

```
$ (API_KEY=1234; echo $API_KEY)
1234
$ echo $API_KEY

$
```

Within the parentheses, we define API_KEY and then print out its value with echo. The API_KEY variable was only defined in the subshell, so attempting to print it out later doesn't work.

This is a contrived example, but you'll find situations where you do want to alter some shell settings for a single command. In the previous chapter, you used this technique to alter how the set command worked:

```
$ (set -o posix; set)
```

This means you can use subshells to create temporary environments for programs or scripts that don't affect your main shell. Try this out by using a subshell to create a WORKDIR environment variable and use it to create a directory. Then, switch to that directory, download the companion files for this book using curl, unzip the files, and then remove the zip file:

```
$ (
> WORKDIR=/tmp
> mkdir "${WORKDIR}/project"
> cd "${WORKDIR}/project"
> curl -O https://media.pragprog.com/titles/bhcldev/code/bhcldev-code.zip
> unzip bhcldev-code.zip
> rm bhcldev-code.zip
> )
```

The commands execute and you see the results, but when you return to the prompt you're still in the original directory. The cd commands in the subshell don't affect your current environment, and the WORKDIR variable isn't set either:

```
$ pwd
/home/brian
$ printenv WORKDIR

$
```

This approach is great for situations you'll encounter when a program must be run in a specific directory because the program can only operate on files in that directory.

Typing out complex commands can be difficult, especially if they happen to span multiple lines. Thankfully, you can lean on a text editor for assistance.

Using Your Editor to Create and Modify Commands

Sometimes you have a complex multiline command or a series of commands you need to run, but you're concerned that you might goof them up. You can use your default text editor to edit and create these complex commands. It's a lifesaver.

Invoke this by pressing Ctrl+x followed by Ctrl+e. This opens nano, or whichever editor you've configured as your default through the VISUAL environment variable in your shell configuration.

Type the following command into the editor:

```
ls -alh /var/
```

Save the file and exit the editor. The command executes and displays the results as if you typed out the command directly. This isn't that useful with short commands, but it's very helpful when typing out longer and more complex commands. For example, it's incredibly handy for building up long pipelines like this:

```
history \
| awk '{c[$2]++}END{for(i in c){print c[i] " " i}}' \
| sort -rn \
| head
```

And it's very useful when constructing long multiline commands you'll run in a subshell.

You can also use your editor to edit or modify anything in your command history. You can use your Up arrow key to recall a previous command, then use Ctrl+x Ctrl+e to edit the command. When you save the changes in the editor, the command executes.

The fc command, short for "fix command," lets you edit any previous command. Use the history command to find the number of the command you want to fix. Then use fc followed by the number to open the command in your editor:

```
$ history
...
    53  find /var/log -mmin -30
    54  find /var/log -mmin -60
    55  find /var/ -mmin -60
    56  find /var/ -mmin -5
$ fc 56
```

The command opens in your editor and you can modify it much more easily. When you save and exit the editor, the command is executed. If you decide you don't want to execute the command, the safest method is to delete the command from the editor and then exit the editor, saving the blank file.

In addition to running commands, you can also measure how long they take.

Timing Program Execution

Sometimes it's helpful to know how long a process takes. Maybe you're seeing how long it takes to build a program from source, or maybe you're comparing program execution on different machines. The time command tracks how long a process takes to complete.

To use it, prefix your command with time. Execute this command to search for all of the files on your hard drive that changed in the last 30 minutes and time how long it takes:

```
$ time find / -mmin -30
```

Launching GUI Apps from the Terminal

On macOS, the open command lets you open directories, URLs, and applications from your terminal. And on Ubuntu, the xdg-open does the same thing.

For example, on macOS, you can open the current working directory in Finder with this command:

```
$ open .
```

You can open the file index.html in the default browser with this one:

```
$ open index.html
```

Use xdg-open on Ubuntu to get the same results.

On macOS, you use the open command to launch an application by name:

```
$ open -a "Google Chrome"
```

On Linux systems, you can launch the GUI application directly like any other command.

These commands are a great way to integrate the command-line interface with the GUI.

You'll see the results of the find command trickle in, but once it's done, you'll see output like this:

```
real    0m49.082s
user    0m0.716s
sys     0m6.349s
```

The real time is the amount of total time the program took to run. The user time is how much time the program spent running on the CPU, and the sys time is how much time the program spent waiting for the operating system to perform tasks for the program.

The time program displays all of these numbers so you can see how things break down.

It's important to note that the real time isn't necessarily the sum of the user and sys times. For example, the user and sys times only count the CPU time actually dedicated to the program by the operating system. It doesn't count time where the program was idle because there were no resources available to it.

In this example, the find command spent around 6 seconds in Kernel mode, which makes sense because Kernel mode can access the hard drive. It took a total of 49 seconds for the find command to finish though, because other programs needed to use the CPU. There are hundreds of other programs all fighting for your CPU's attention.

In Bash, the time command is a built-in command with limited options. Some distributions of Linux have a more fully featured time command which can show more detailed statistics. To use it, specify the full path, which is usually located at /usr/bin/time. The GNU version of time and the BSD version found on macOS have different options which you can explore through the man time command.

Next, you'll look at how to record a log of your shell session.

Recording Program Interaction

You've seen that the shell records the history of the commands you run on your system, but you can also record the output of those commands, thanks to the script command. This is incredibly handy for logging a shell session to share with others to get debugging help, or for demonstrating how you did things. The official description in the documentation for script even states that one of the uses is for students who "need a hardcopy record of an interactive session as proof of an assignment." The resulting log becomes a text file you can edit or reformat, so it makes a great documentation tool as well. To use it, execute the script command, followed by a filename for the output:

```
$ script myscript.txt
Script started, file is myscript.txt
```

If you don't specify a default file, the script command creates one called typescript, which should not be confused with the TypeScript programming language. From this point on, every command and every piece of output on your terminal is logged to the file myscript.txt.

Execute these commands to create a directory structure, list its contents, and then remove it:

```
$ mkdir -p test_site/{images,js,css}
$ cat << 'EOF' > test_site/index.html
> <!DOCTYPE html>
> <html lang="en">
>   <head><title>Test page</title></head>
> </html>
> EOF
$ ls -l test_site
total 16
drwxrwxr-x 2 brianhogan brianhogan 4096 Mar  3 14:34 css
drwxrwxr-x 2 brianhogan brianhogan 4096 Mar  3 14:34 images
-rw-rw-r-- 1 brianhogan brianhogan  154 Mar  3 14:34 index.html
drwxrwxr-x 2 brianhogan brianhogan 4096 Mar  3 14:34 js
$ rm -r test_site
```

To stop recording, type exit and press `Enter`:

```
$ exit
exit
Script done, file is myscript.txt
```

The script program stopped recording. View the log with less:

```
$ less myscript.txt
Script started on Sun 03 Mar 2019 09:30:35 PM CST
$ mkdir -p test_site/{images,js,css}

...
exit

Script done on Sun 03 Mar 2019 09:32:16 PM CST
```

The script command shows all of the commands, as well as datestamps for when it started and stopped recording. You can take this text file and annotate it for documentation purposes, or even remove the output and use it as the basis for an automated script.

If you want to append to the script, execute the command script -a myscript.txt. You can then run additional commands and they, along with their output, will be appended to the file until you type exit.

The script command does record almost everything you do, so it may capture passwords you type. And launching programs like nano or top won't work very well, so keep those things in mind as you use it.

You've looked at several ways to run and construct commands so far. You can use your shell's command history to reduce the amount of typing you have to do.

Reusing Previous Commands and Arguments

By now, you're likely familiar with the history command, and you've probably used the Up arrow key to recall a previous command you've typed. And, way back in Chapter 1, Getting Your Feet Wet, on page 1, you saw the !! command, which lets you run the previous command again. This works because of a feature called *history expansion*, which you can use to rerun previous commands, extract arguments, or even fix typos.

Let's review the !! command before you get into the more advanced features. Use the ls -lh command to get a list of your home directory:

```
$ ls -lh
total 44K
drwxr-xr-x 2 brian brian 4.0K Oct 26 10:09 Desktop
drwxr-xr-x 2 brian brian 4.0K Oct 26 10:07 Documents
...
```

Use the !! command to execute the command again:

```
$ !!
total 44K
drwxr-xr-x 2 brian brian 4.0K Oct 26 10:09 Desktop
drwxr-xr-x 2 brian brian 4.0K Oct 26 10:07 Documents
...
```

The ! symbol is an *event designator*. It refers to some event in your history. !! is a shortcut for "the last command," but ! followed by a number refers to the specific command in your history. When you execute the history command, you'll see numbers next to each entry, like this:

```
$ history
    14  ls
    15  cd ..
    16  ls /var
```

In this example, ls /var is the sixteenth entry in the history. It's also the last entry. To run it again, you could use !16, or you could just use !!.

The most common use for !! is with the sudo command if you've accidentally left it off. Try creating a directory structure in the /var folder which is owned by the root user:

```
$ mkdir -p /var/testing/commands
mkdir: cannot create directory '/var/testing': Permission denied
```

Since you didn't use sudo, the command failed. Run it again and it will execute the command:

```
$ sudo !!
sudo mkdir -p /var/testing/commands
```

Notice that when you execute the command, the shell prints out the command it ran in addition to running it. To see the last command instead of executing it, you can add :p to the end:

```
$ !!:p
sudo mkdir -p /var/testing/commands
```

Change the working directory to /var/testing/commands. Typing that path out again isn't terribly difficult if you use tab completion, but you can save some time by making use of your history. The sequence !$ will grab the last argument of the previous command, which was the path you just created. Use that sequence as the argument to the cd command:

```
$ cd !$
cd /var/testing/commands
```

The full cd command prints to the screen and your current working directory changes.

Sometimes, you want to work with specific arguments of the previous command, rather than just the last one. You can do this using *word designators* in addition to event designators.

For example, you can use !:0 to grab the first argument from the last command, !:1 to grab the second, and so on. The arguments include the commands as well, though, so sometimes you'll have to give it a little more thought, like when you use sudo in front of another command. Let's see how this all works in practice.

You should still be in the /var/testing/commands directory. Create three files named file1.txt, file2.txt, and file3.txt:

```
$ sudo touch file1.txt file2.txt file3.txt
```

Use the previous command and extract the arguments to create a new touch command that reverses the filenames. The sudo and touch commands are the first two arguments here, so to get to the files themselves, you have to start at position 2:

```
$ sudo touch !:4 !:3 !:2
sudo touch file3.txt file2.txt file1.txt
```

What if you wanted all of the arguments? The sequence !* takes all of the arguments of the previous command, excluding the command itself. This is an extremely handy shortcut when you need to reuse all the arguments. This won't work right if the previous command used sudo though, because sudo is a command of its own, so the !* sequence will include touch as one of the arguments. Try to use the rm command with the previous command's arguments to remove the three text files:

```
$ sudo touch file1.txt file2.txt file3.txt
$ sudo rm !*
sudo rm touch file3.txt file2.txt file1.txt
rm: cannot remove 'touch': No such file or directory
```

You'll get an error message. The !* sequence technically did exactly what you asked: it used all of the arguments from the previous command. But the previous command was sudo, not touch, so you'll want keep that in mind.

You can grab the arguments of any previous command. Create the text files again, and then in a separate command, create three more files:

```
$ sudo touch file1.txt file2.txt file3.txt
$ sudo touch file4.txt file5.txt file6.txt
```

Now, use the ls command to display file1.txt, but do it by using the sequence !-2:2:

```
$ ls !-2:2
ls file1.txt
file1.txt
```

!-2 gets the second-to-last command you typed, and :2 fetches the third argument from that command.

You can use this method to save yourself a lot of time. Use the history command to get your command list, find the number you want, and use it to snag that really long path you don't want to type again. Here's an example:

```
$ history
...
   21  sudo mkdir -p /var/testing/commands
   22  cd /var/testing/commands
...
$ cd !22:1
cd /var/testing/commands
```

If you don't want to work with numbers when referencing a previous command, you can also use search strings. Use a string instead of the number, like this:

```
$ !cd
cd /var/testing/commands
```

In this case, you just used cd as the search string. But you can also recall a previous command based on a string anywhere in the command. Try changing to a few different directories:

```
$ cd /
$ cd /usr/local/
$ cd
```

Your history now contains a few additional cd commands. To change to the /var/testing/commands folder, use !? and part of the string:

```
$ !?var/te
cd /var/testing/commands
```

Before moving on, switch back to your home directory:

```
$ cd
```

Now let's look more closely at history expansion modifiers.

Extracting Data with Modifiers

History expansion supports modifiers, which are suffixes you add to the command. For example, you saw that adding :p to a history expansion prints the result of the change, but doesn't execute the altered command. But other modifiers let you alter the path of the results.

Here's a trivial example to see how this works. Use the ls command to list the ~/.bashrc file:

```
$ ls ~/.bashrc
/home/brian/.bashrc
```

Use echo to print out the previous command's first argument, but then use the :h modifier which will extract the path up to the last segment:

```
$ echo !^:h
echo ~
/home/brian
```

The :t modifier lets you grab the end of the path. Try it by listing the ~/.bashrc file and then using echo with the previous argument, but this time use the :t modifier:

```
$ ls ~/.bashrc
/home/brian/.bashrc
$ echo !^:t
echo .bashrc
.bashrc
```

This turns out to be useful when copying a file from another directory to your current one.

Execute the following command to create a file in /tmp/some/long/directory:

```
$ mkdir -p /tmp/some/long/directory
$ touch !$/data.csv
touch /tmp/some/long/directory/data.csv
```

The mkdir command creates the structure, and then the touch command uses the last argument of the previous command to specify the path to the file. So now copy the file to the current directory using history expansion to grab the source and specify the target filename:

```
$ cp !$ !$:t
cp /tmp/some/long/directory/data.csv data.csv
```

It's a little cryptic at first, but if you practice this enough, it becomes something you can do quickly.

The :r modifier can chop off the file extension on a file. Use echo to try it out:

```
$ echo !$:r
echo data
data
```

You can use this modifier to change a file extension when you copy or move it.

Use the ls -l command to get the details of the /tmp/some/long/directory/data.csv file:

```
$ ls -l /tmp/some/long/directory/data.csv
-rw-rw-r-- 1 brian brian 0 Mar  3 12:17 /tmp/some/long/directory/data.csv
```

Copy that file to the current directory with a new name using modifiers:

```
$ cp !$ !$:t:r.txt
cp /tmp/some/long/directory/data.csv data.txt
```

That's pretty handy, but you're not limited to using arguments in previous commands; you can access the arguments in the current command as well. This is an incredibly powerful trick that saves a lot of typing once you have mastered it.

Rename the /tmp/some/long/directory/data.csv file to /tmp/some/long/directory/data.txt using the # event designator, which lets you reference the entire command typed so far, and the ^ word designator which extracts the first argument:

```
$ mv /tmp/some/long/directory/data.csv !#^:r.txt
mv /tmp/some/long/directory/data.csv /tmp/some/long/directory/data.txt
```

The sequence !#^ extracts the first argument, /tmp/some/long/directory/data.csv, and :r.txt changes data.csv to data.txt.

Extracting previous commands and arguments is handy, but it might be overkill. Sometimes you will just want to run the previous command with a minor change.

Correcting Mistakes and Altering Previous Commands

You'll occasionally come across times where you make a mistake when typing a command. There's a syntax to address that.

Type the following (intentionally wrong) command:

```
$ mdkir secret_files
mdkir: command not found
```

Of course, there's no mdkir command, but rather than retyping the command, you can fix it with the notation ^old^new. Type the following to fix the command:

```
$ ^dk^kd
mkdir secret_files
```

This replaces dk with kd in the previous command and executes it again. It also prints the corrected command to the screen.

You can use this again to list the new directory to make sure it exists:

```
$ ^mkdir^ls -ld
ls -ld secret_files
drwxrwxr-x 2 brian brian 4096 Mar  3 23:00 secret_files
```

You might see some people use the form !!:s/old/new. This works exactly like ^old^new, but it also supports using the :p modifier which prints the command but doesn't execute it, and they both have a limitation: they only change the first occurrence. If you need to do this more globally and you're on a more recent version of Bash, you can use the syntax !!:gs/old/new, which will change all instances of the old text to the new text.

Let's explore how to manage the programs and processes running on your computer.

Managing Processes and Jobs

The ps command, short for Process Status, shows you the running processes on your computer, as well as information about who's running them. It's good for finding out what's currently running and for identifying a process ID with a program so you can stop it.

The ps command takes different options based on which OS you're using. In this book, we'll cover the Linux options, which also work on macOS.

When you execute the ps command without any arguments, you see the processes running in your current session:

```
$ ps
  PID TTY          TIME CMD
 3927 pts/1    00:00:00 bash
 7139 pts/1    00:00:00 ps
```

The output shows the PID, or Process ID, the terminal session that's running the command, how long it's been running, and the command itself. In this case, the only results you see are the Bash shell itself and the ps command you just ran, since it's only showing you what's running in this particular session.

Use the -f flag to get a more detailed output:

```
$ ps -f
UID         PID  PPID  C STIME TTY          TIME CMD
brian      3927  3926  0 20:35 pts/1     00:00:00 -bash
brian      7264  3927  0 23:09 pts/1     00:00:00 ps -f
```

The UID column shows the user that started the process. The PPID is the ID of the parent process. Some processes spawn child processes, so it's often helpful to know what process is responsible for creating the process you're looking at. The C column shows the CPU usage of the process, and STIME shows the time the process was started.

To see all of the processes running on the system, use ps -e. This generates a very long list, as your OS has a lot of background processes running.

Pipe the output to the less command to make it easier to read:

```
$ ps -e | less
  PID TTY          TIME CMD
    1 ?        00:00:01 systemd
    2 ?        00:00:00 kthreadd
    4 ?        00:00:00 kworker/0:0H
    6 ?        00:00:00 mm_percpu_wq
    7 ?        00:00:00 ksoftirqd/0
  ...
```

Some of the processes aren't attached to a terminal session, so you see a question mark (?) in the TTY column.

You can combine the -e and -f flags to get a very detailed view of all processes:

```
$ ps -ef | less
UID         PID  PPID  C STIME TTY          TIME CMD
root          1     0  0 10:33 ?        00:00:01 /sbin/init splash
root          2     0  0 10:33 ?        00:00:00 [kthreadd]
  ...
```

This is a rather long list, so you might want to pare it down to only the processes you're running.

To see only the processes started by your user, use the -x flag instead.

This list may still be pretty big, depending on what programs you currently have running:

```
$ ps -x | less
```

Using the -u flag, you can list the processes running as another user on your system. Use this to list things running as the root user:

```
$ ps -u root
  PID TTY          TIME CMD
    1 ?        00:00:00 systemd
    2 ?        00:00:00 kthreadd
    4 ?        00:00:00 kworker/0:0H
...
```

If you know the name of the process, you can use the -C flag to look up its details.

Use this to search for all the bash processes on your machine:

```
$ ps -C bash
  PID TTY          TIME CMD
 2001 pts/0    00:00:00 bash
 3927 pts/1    00:00:00 bash
```

Unfortunately, this option only works on the Linux versions of ps. One solution that works on all platforms is to pipe the output to grep, like this:

```
$ ps -e | grep bash
 2001 pts/0    00:00:00 bash
 3927 pts/1    00:00:00 bash
```

Finally, you can control the output fields with the -o flag. Execute this command to show the process ID, the command, and the user:

```
$ ps -o pid,command,user
  PID COMMAND                   USER
 3927 -bash                     brian
 7295 ps -o pid,command,user    brian
```

When using this option with other flags, make sure it comes last. For example, to list all of your processes, but only show the PID and command, execute this command:

```
$ ps -xo pid,command
```

The ps command is just one way to look at processes on your machine. The top command offers a more interactive look at what's going on.

Execute the top command:

```
$ top
```

Your terminal is replaced with a window that shows all of the running processes on your machine, similar to the following image:

```
top - 23:28:31 up 1 day,  2:52,  2 users,  load average: 3.41, 1.16, 0.41
Tasks: 214 total,   1 running, 180 sleeping,   0 stopped,   0 zombie
%Cpu(s):  0.7 us,  0.3 sy,  0.0 ni, 99.0 id,  0.0 wa,  0.0 hi,  0.0 si,  0.0 st
KiB Mem :  1009116 total,    64844 free,   655964 used,   288308 buff/cache
KiB Swap:  1557568 total,   877632 free,   679936 used.   184792 avail Mem

  PID USER      PR  NI    VIRT    RES    SHR S %CPU %MEM     TIME+ COMMAND
 1253 brian     20   0 3052536 210480  35092 S  0.3 20.9   0:45.94 gnome-shell
 7334 brian     20   0   48884   3824   3240 R  0.3  0.4   0:00.06 top
    1 root      20   0  225644   5712   3404 S  0.0  0.6   0:02.01 systemd
    2 root      20   0       0      0      0 S  0.0  0.0   0:00.00 kthreadd
    4 root       0 -20       0      0      0 I  0.0  0.0   0:00.00 kworker/0:0H
    6 root       0 -20       0      0      0 I  0.0  0.0   0:00.00 mm_percpu_wq
    7 root      20   0       0      0      0 S  0.0  0.0   0:00.53 ksoftirqd/0
    8 root      20   0       0      0      0 I  0.0  0.0   0:01.69 rcu_sched
    9 root      20   0       0      0      0 I  0.0  0.0   0:00.00 rcu_bh
   10 root      rt   0       0      0      0 S  0.0  0.0   0:00.00 migration/0
   11 root      rt   0       0      0      0 S  0.0  0.0   0:00.20 watchdog/0
   12 root      20   0       0      0      0 S  0.0  0.0   0:00.00 cpuhp/0
   13 root      20   0       0      0      0 S  0.0  0.0   0:00.00 kdevtmpfs
   14 root       0 -20       0      0      0 I  0.0  0.0   0:00.00 netns
   15 root      20   0       0      0      0 S  0.0  0.0   0:00.00 rcu_tasks_k+
   16 root      20   0       0      0      0 S  0.0  0.0   0:00.00 kauditd
   17 root      20   0       0      0      0 S  0.0  0.0   0:00.05 khungtaskd
```

This shows a real-time view of the processes on your system, their memory
consumption, and CPU usage. Like ps, the Linux version works a little differently than the macOS and BSD versions, so we'll focus on the Linux version.

You can change how the results sort. Use Shift+m to sort the results by
memory usage, and use Shift+p to sort by CPU usage.

Press c to show the full path to each command. Press it again to hide the full path.

To sort by any other field, or to control the fields displayed, press Shift+f to
display the Field Management screen.

```
top - 23:28:31 up 1 day,  2:52,  2 users,  load average: 3.41, 1.16, 0.41
Tasks: 214 total,   1 running, 180 sleeping,   0 stopped,   0 zombie
%Cpu(s):  0.7 us,  0.3 sy,  0.0 ni, 99.0 id,  0.0 wa,  0.0 hi,  0.0 si,  0.0 st
KiB Mem :  1009116 total,    64844 free,   655964 used,   288308 buff/cache
KiB Swap:  1557568 total,   877632 free,   679936 used.   184792 avail Mem

  PID USER      PR  NI    VIRT    RES    SHR S %CPU %MEM     TIME+ COMMAND
 1253 brian     20   0 3052536 210480  35092 S  0.3 20.9   0:45.94 gnome-shell
 7334 brian     20   0   48884   3824   3240 R  0.3  0.4   0:00.06 top
    1 root      20   0  225644   5712   3404 S  0.0  0.6   0:02.01 systemd
    2 root      20   0       0      0      0 S  0.0  0.0   0:00.00 kthreadd
    4 root       0 -20       0      0      0 I  0.0  0.0   0:00.00 kworker/0:0H
    6 root       0 -20       0      0      0 I  0.0  0.0   0:00.00 mm_percpu_wq
    7 root      20   0       0      0      0 S  0.0  0.0   0:00.53 ksoftirqd/0
    8 root      20   0       0      0      0 I  0.0  0.0   0:01.69 rcu_sched
    9 root      20   0       0      0      0 I  0.0  0.0   0:00.00 rcu_bh
   10 root      rt   0       0      0      0 S  0.0  0.0   0:00.00 migration/0
   11 root      rt   0       0      0      0 S  0.0  0.0   0:00.20 watchdog/0
   12 root      20   0       0      0      0 S  0.0  0.0   0:00.00 cpuhp/0
   13 root      20   0       0      0      0 S  0.0  0.0   0:00.00 kdevtmpfs
   14 root       0 -20       0      0      0 I  0.0  0.0   0:00.00 netns
   15 root      20   0       0      0      0 S  0.0  0.0   0:00.00 rcu_tasks_k+
   16 root      20   0       0      0      0 S  0.0  0.0   0:00.00 kauditd
   17 root      20   0       0      0      0 S  0.0  0.0   0:00.05 khungtaskd
```

To add or remove fields from the display, use the arrow keys to select the field you want to add and press `Spacebar` to toggle the field. Fields with an asterisk (*) will be displayed.

To sort on a specific field, use the arrow keys to select the field you want to sort on and press `s` on the field.

Try this: enable only the `PID`, `USER`, `%CPU`, `%MEM`, and `COMMAND` fields. Then select the `PID` field again and press `s` to tell `top` to sort on the PID.

Press `q` to return to the processes window. The results are sorted by what you selected.

Press `?` to see a help screen that will give you a quick overview of the various options you can use. If you're on a Mac, this screen will show you how to sort the output.

Press `q` to exit and return to your prompt.

Now that you've got a feel for how `top` works, let's explore how to make processes run in the background.

Running and Managing Jobs

Many of the commands you've run in this book returned their results in a reasonable amount of time. But sometimes commands take a long time to run, or take over your terminal entirely. `nano`, `top`, and even development servers completely take over your terminal, forcing you to open another terminal window to interact.

Instead of running tasks in the foreground, you can run them in the background. Or you can suspend them so you can do other work and then resume the original command to pick up where you left off. Let's look at how this works with a few different examples.

The following command looks for all files on the filesystem that have changed within the last half hour, writes them to the file results.txt, and throws away any error messages:

```
$ find / -mmin -30 2> /dev/null > results.txt
```

Depending on the size of the filesystem, that may take considerable time to run. Add an ampersand (&) to the end of the command to make the command run in the background instead:

```
$ find / -mmin -30 2> /dev/null > results.txt &
[1] 23170
$
```

You're immediately returned to your prompt, and the job number and process ID appear.

Run the jobs command to see the status of the command:

```
$ jobs
[1]+  Running                 find / -mmin -30 2> /dev/null > results.txt &
```

The find command is running. Wait a minute or so and run the jobs command again:

```
$ jobs
[1]+  Exit 1                  find / -mmin -30 2> /dev/null > results.txt
```

The Exit 1 output lets you know the job has finished. The 1 is the exit status of the command. In this example, find returned some errors which we didn't see because we suppressed them for this example. But they're related to some temporary files that were deleted during the run, or issues with access permissions. When you see an exit status of anything other than zero, you should assume something went wrong.

Let's try this a different way. You'll often kick off a command and then wish you'd run it in the background. You can suspend the running command and then tell it to run in the background.

Run the command without the ampersand. Then press Ctrl+z once it starts:

```
$ find / -mmin -30 2> /dev/null > results.txt
^z
[1]+  Stopped                 find / -mmin -30 2> /dev/null > results.txt
```

The command is now stopped. If you run jobs again, you see the same thing:

```
$ jobs
[1]+  Stopped                 find / -mmin -30 2> /dev/null > results.txt
```

The bg command takes a stopped job and runs it in the background. Pass it the ID of the job:

```
$ bg 1
[1]+ find / -mmin -30 2> /dev/null > results.txt &
```

Notice the resulting command now has the ampersand appended. Run jobs again to see the status:

```
$ jobs
[1]+  Running                 find / -mmin -30 2> /dev/null > results.txt &
```

Eventually the task finishes like before.

This approach comes in really handy when you're working with nano or another full-screen text editor. In Customizing Your Shell Session, on page 138, you built up a shell configuration file one piece at a time. To test things out, you had to exit your editor, test out the changes, and then open the file again. Instead, you could suspend the editor with Ctrl+z, test out your changes, and then resume the command. Let's try this out by adding another change to the .bashrc command by adding a handful of aliases for changing directories.

Open up the ~/.bashrc file in nano:

```
$ nano ~/.bashrc
```

At the bottom of the file, add an alias named .. that executes the cd .. command:

```
alias ..='cd ..'
```

Save the file with Ctrl+o. Now, suspend nano with Ctrl+z. You're returned to your prompt and the job ID for nano appears:

```
Use "fg" to return to `nano`.

[1]+  Stopped                 nano ~/.bashrc
```

nano also helpfully tells you how you can get back to your editor. But before doing so, apply the changes you made to the configuration:

```
$ source ~/.bashrc
```

Try out the new .. command and use pwd to ensure it worked:

```
$ pwd
/home/brian
$ ..
$ pwd
/home
```

Now that you've verified it worked, use fg to return to nano and you can pick up where you left off.

Add an alias named ... which goes up two directories:

```
alias ...='cd ../../'
```

Save the file with Ctrl+o, then test it out by suspending nano with Ctrl+z. Source the command, test it out, and use fg to return to nano.

When you're done, press Ctrl+x to exit nano.

Let's try juggling a couple of jobs. Run the top command:

```
$ top
```

Press Ctrl+z to suspend it. Then, run man top to view the manual for top. Suspend it with Ctrl+z as well. Finally, run the jobs command:

```
$ jobs
[1]-  Stopped                top
[2]+  Stopped                man top
```

You now have two suspended jobs. To bring top to the foreground, use the fg command, followed by the job number. In this case, it's fg 1.

Next, suspend it and bring the manual to the foreground with fg 2. Exit the manual with q. Then, bring top to the foreground and exit it with q as well.

This is an incredibly powerful technique. You'll often find yourself in the middle of something and need to switch back to a shell to run a command, whether you need to test something out, get more information, or just look at another file. Instead of juggling two terminal windows, just suspend the process that's running in the background.

Sometimes processes that do not behave properly or stop responding—and sometimes you just want to stop them yourself quickly. Let's look at how.

Terminating Processes

Every so often, a program misbehaves. Sometimes it's due to something you configured incorrectly. Other times it's because the program has a bug. You've probably experienced a stuck program before and figured out a way to kill the task using a graphical task manager. You can manage tasks from the command-line interface as well. All you need is the process ID.

Let's start a long-running task in the background. In your terminal, execute this command:

```
$ sleep 9999999 &
[1] 23841
```

This process is now running. Use the jobs -l command to list the running background jobs and show the process ID in addition to the job ID:

```
$ jobs -l
[1]+ 23841 Running                sleep 999999 &
```

The kill command terminates processes by sending the process a signal. A well-behaved program listens for these signals and responds appropriately. To terminate a process, you specify the kill command, followed by the signal you want to send, followed by the process ID.

The SIGHUP signal, or "hang up," is the disconnection signal. It's the signal that gets sent when you press Ctrl+d, or when you close a terminal session. Programs have to be designed to respond to this signal and can choose to ignore it.

Use kill -SIGHUP, followed by the process ID to send the signal to the program. Be sure to use the process ID on *your* computer, not the one in this book, as it will be different:

```
$ kill -SIGHUP 23841
$ jobs -l
[1]+ 23841 Hangup                sleep 999999
```

Sometimes the program doesn't respond to the hangup signal, so you'll have to be a little more aggressive. Let's use the nohup program to start this job. nohup is a utility that will start a program and ignore hangup signals. It's useful for spawning some job that persists even after you log out.

Execute the sleep command with nohup:

```
$ nohup sleep 999999 &
[1] 23909
nohup: ignoring input and appending output to '/home/brian/nohup.out'
```

Now, try sending the SIGHUP signal to this program:

```
$ kill -SIGHUP 23909
```

Then, review the list of jobs:

```
$ jobs -l
[1]+ 23909 Running               nohup sleep 999999 &
```

The program ignores the hangup signal.

Now, let's try sending the SIGINT, or "interrupt" signal, which is equivalent to pressing Ctrl+c:

```
$ kill -SIGINT 23909
$ jobs -l
[1]+ 23909 Interrupt             nohup sleep 999999
```

This time the program stops. Like SIGHUP, the program has to be able to respond to the SIGINT signal for that to happen. Well-behaved programs handle these signals.

Next, let's look at the SIGTERM, or "terminate" signal, which is the default signal the kill command uses. This signal is designed to terminate a process quickly, but programs still get the opportunity to shut down gracefully, provided that the developer has written the program that way.

Fire up the sleep command again. This time, there's no need for nohup:

```
$ sleep 999999 &
[1] 23949
```

Then stop the process using SIGTERM:

```
$ kill -SIGTERM 23949
$ jobs -l
[1]+ 23949 Terminated          sleep 999999
```

The process terminates successfully.

Try the same thing again, but don't specify the signal at all. You'll see the same result:

```
$ sleep 999999 &
[1] 24101
$ kill 24101
[1]+ 24101 Terminated          sleep 999999
```

While SIGTERM is the default signal for kill, it's best to try to use SIGHUP or SIGINT signals first if you can.

So far, you've used a few options to get programs to stop gracefully, but sometimes things go sideways and a program or process just becomes unresponsive. In these cases, the only way to make it stop is to terminate the process by telling the OS to pull the rug out from under it. Unlike the other signals, the program can't ignore this signal. The OS cuts it off entirely. You should use this as a last resort.

In Downloading Files, on page 11, and in the exercises in Chapter 2, Creating an Ubuntu Virtual Machine with VirtualBox, on page 17, you downloaded the book's companion files and extracted the files to the ~/sharptools/code directory in your home directory. Those files contain a small command-line utility named responder which you'll use to explore signals. The responder program ignores the SIGINT, SIGHUP, and SIGTERM signals, as well as the SIGQUIT signal which causes a program to halt and dump its core.

The responder Program

 The responder program is written in the Go programming language, and I've included the source code in that directory so you can verify I'm not asking you to run some sketchy malware.

Run the program and send it to the background:

```
$ ~/sharptools/code/responder/linux/responder start &
[1] 24269
```

If you want to try this on a Mac, you'll find a Mac version of this program as well.

Try sending the SIGHUP signal:

```
$ kill -SIGHUP 24269
hangup
```

The responder program intercepted the signal and printed hangup to your screen. If you look at the running jobs, you'll see it's still running:

```
$ jobs -l
[1]+ 24269 Running        ~/sharptools/code/responder/linux/responder start &
```

Try SIGINT or SIGTERM and you'll see similar messages. The program won't die.

```
$ kill -SIGINT 24269
interrupt
$ kill -SIGTERM 24269
terminated
$ jobs -l
[1]+ 24269 Running        ~/sharptools/code/responder/linux/responder start &
```

No matter what you've tried, the program refuses to quit, so use the SIGKILL signal:

```
$ kill -SIGKILL 24269
$ jobs -l
[1]+ 24269 Killed         ~/sharptools/code/responder/linux/responder start
```

The program stops. The program can't respond to SIGKILL because the operating system pulled the plug. This also means that the program had no way of performing any cleanup tasks.

You may have seen suggestions from others to use the command kill -9 to forcibly kill a process. This is the same thing as kill -SIGKILL. You can specify the signal by name or number. Use the kill -l command to see all available signals and their corresponding number:

```
$ kill -l
 1) SIGHUP       2) SIGINT       3) SIGQUIT      4) SIGILL       5) SIGTRAP
 6) SIGABRT      7) SIGBUS       8) SIGFPE       9) SIGKILL     10) SIGUSR1
11) SIGSEGV     12) SIGUSR2     13) SIGPIPE     14) SIGALRM     15) SIGTERM
16) SIGSTKFLT   17) SIGCHLD     18) SIGCONT     19) SIGSTOP     20) SIGTSTP
21) SIGTTIN     22) SIGTTOU     23) SIGURG      24) SIGXCPU     25) SIGXFSZ
26) SIGVTALRM   27) SIGPROF     28) SIGWINCH    29) SIGIO       30) SIGPWR
31) SIGSYS      34) SIGRTMIN    35) SIGRTMIN+1  36) SIGRTMIN+2  37) SIGRTMIN+3
38) SIGRTMIN+4  39) SIGRTMIN+5  40) SIGRTMIN+6  41) SIGRTMIN+7  42) SIGRTMIN+8
43) SIGRTMIN+9  44) SIGRTMIN+10 45) SIGRTMIN+11 46) SIGRTMIN+12 47) SIGRTMIN+13
48) SIGRTMIN+14 49) SIGRTMIN+15 50) SIGRTMAX-14 51) SIGRTMAX-13 52) SIGRTMAX-12
53) SIGRTMAX-11 54) SIGRTMAX-10 55) SIGRTMAX-9  56) SIGRTMAX-8  57) SIGRTMAX-7
58) SIGRTMAX-6  59) SIGRTMAX-5  60) SIGRTMAX-4  61) SIGRTMAX-3  62) SIGRTMAX-2
63) SIGRTMAX-1  64) SIGRTMAX
```

That's a lot of signals. Most people new to the CLI tend to try kill with no arguments first, which sends SIGTERM, and if that doesn't work, they go right to kill -9. While it doesn't matter whether you use signal names or numbers, you should consider using SIGHUP and SIGINT first and see if they work. This gives your programs a better chance of shutting down gracefully. They may want to delete some temporary files or finish writing entries to logs first. If you go right for kill -9, you could lose data. Think of kill -9 as the last resort when nothing else you've tried works.

The process that's misbehaving might not always be available through the job control system, so you'll have to find the program's corresponding process ID and then plug it in. Fire up the responder program again:

```
$ ~/sharptools/code/responder/linux/responder start &
[1] 24279
```

Then use ps and grep to look up the ID:

```
$ ps -e | grep responder
24279 pts/1    00:00:00 responder
```

You can whittle that down further by passing the result to awk:

```
$ ps -e | grep responder | awk '{print $1}'
24279
```

Once you have the ID, you can use it to kill the process:

```
$ kill -9 24279
```

The pgrep and pkill commands, available on macOS and Ubuntu, make it a lot easier to do this work. pgrep lets you grab the ID for a process by name quickly:

Fire up the responder program again:

```
$ ~/sharptools/code/responder/linux/responder start &
[1] 12944
```

pgrep lets you find the process ID for the program by its name:

```
$ pgrep responder
12944
```

If you fired up multiple processes with the same name, pgrep would return multiple process IDs.

Similarly, pkill will look up the process ID by name and kill it:

```
$ pkill -9 responder
[1]+  Killed                  ~/sharptools/code/responder/linux/responder start
```

You need to be careful with pkill. It kills all of the processes it finds that match, so if you have multiple processes with the same name, and you only want to stop one, you might be better off specifying the PID with kill instead.

Now you know how to stop processes that get away from you or become unresponsive, and you know how to do it several ways.

Limiting Program Execution

The timeout utility lets you run a program and kill it if it doesn't complete within a certain time frame. To use it, specify the timeout command, followed by the duration and the command you want to run. For example, to run the top command for five seconds, type this command:

```
$ timeout 5s top
```

After five seconds, top exits. The timeout command sends the TERM signal by default, allowing the program to attempt a graceful shutdown. You can send other signals too. Just look at the documentation for the timeout command.

The timeout command doesn't come with macOS, but you can install it with Homebrew. It's part of the coreutils package. Install it with brew install coreutils and use the gtimeout command.

So far you have run some compound commands, managed jobs, and killed processes. Next, you will use the results of commands *within* other commands.

Using Command Substitution

You can use the output of one command when invoking another command. This is handy when a program's argument needs to be generated from another program's output. You can do this with a feature called command substitution. You've already seen variable expansion with curly braces, like ${variable}, where the variable's value is expanded. Command substitution works in a similar way. With command substitution, the output of the command replaces the command itself. To define a command substitution, you wrap the command in parentheses instead of curly braces.

You saw an example of command substitution in Building Your Prompt, on page 143, when you used the tput command to emit color codes:

```
$ echo -e "$(tput setaf 6)Hello $(tput sgr0)world"
```

Let's look at another example and explore how command substitution works in more detail.

The date command prints the current date and time. You can use the result of this command in conjunction with the echo command to print out a message displaying the date and time as part of a string:

```
$ echo "The curent date and time is $(date)."
The current date and time is Sat Mar  3 00:10:43 CST 2019
```

The $(date) expression is evaluated in a subshell, and the standard output is returned.

Command substitution has another interesting use; instead of printing the result to the screen, you can save it to a shell variable you can use later:

```
$ startTime=$(date)
$ echo "The start time was ${startTime}"
The start time was Sat Mar  3 00:12:09 CST 2019
```

You can use more complex pipelines in command substitution as well. The ls command doesn't print out the number of entries, but you can get that quickly enough by using ls -A1 (that's the number 1, by the way), which will show a single-column listing of all files except the . and .. entries, and piping the result to the wc command and telling it to count the lines. Try it out. Create a new directory named substitution and create a few files and directories in that folder. Then, switch to the folder:

```
$ mkdir -p substitution/{one,two,three}
$ touch substitution/{four,five,six}.txt
```

Print out the number of entries in the substitution directory using echo and command substitution:

```
$ echo "There are $(ls -A1 substitution | wc -l) entries"
There are 6 entries.
```

The BSD version of wc, found on macOS, includes extra spaces in the output. If you're on a Mac, use sed to remove those spaces:

```
$ echo "There are $(ls -A1 substitution | wc -l | sed -e 's/^ *//') entries"
There are 6 entries.
```

For good measure, remove the directory you just created, since you don't need it anymore:

```
$ rm -r substitition
```

One of the most common uses for command substitution is to take the result of a command or series of commands and use it as the argument for another command. Earlier in the chapter, you learned about pgrep, which lets you look up the process ID of a program, and the pkill command, which kills a process by name. You can achieve the same results using process substitution if those commands aren't available.

Launch the responder program again:

```
$ ~/sharptools/code/responder/linux/responder start &
```

You know you can get the ID with ps, grep, and awk:

```
$ ps -e | grep responder | awk '{print $1}'
27208
```

Use command substitution to send the process ID right to the kill command and skip the manual intermediate step of retyping the process ID:

```
$ kill -9 $(ps -e | grep responder | awk '{print $1}')
```

Use the jobs command to verify it's been killed:

```
$ jobs
[1]+  Killed                  ~/sharptools/code/responder/linux/responder start
```

Command substitution is especially useful when you want to display information programmatically.

Using Command Substitution in Your Prompt

Command substitution gives you the ability to put useful information in your shell prompt, and lots of utilities and scripts leverage this approach.

The only tricky part about doing this is that you want the command substitution to occur every time the prompt is displayed, rather than when you first define the prompt. To do this, you escape the dollar sign for the command substitution.

For example, to use the date command to print the current time in your prompt, you'd define the prompt like this:

```
PS1="${USERCOLOR}\u${RESET}@\h:\w - \$(date '+%I:%M %P') \\$ "
```

Escaping the dollar sign in front of the command substitution ensures that the current time will always be displayed. If you left it off, the prompt would display the time it was when you defined the PS1 variable.

This results in a prompt that looks like this:

```
brian@puzzles:~ - 08:15 pm $
```

Let's explore this further by displaying the error code for the previous command, so you know immediately if the previous command executed with errors. Remember that you can retrieve the previous error with $?.

> \|/   **Joe asks:**
> ≈ƒ   # What's eval?
>
> The eval command lets you execute a string of text as a command. Many people use eval to construct commands programatically. It's dangerous, but you'll see it from time to time, so it's good to understand what it's for.
>
> In its simplest form, you call eval and pass it a string of text, which it evaluates:
>
> ```
> $ eval "ls -alh"
> ```
>
> One of the more common recent uses of eval is with the docker-machine[a] tool, which makes it easy to manage remote Docker hosts to run containers. Take the following docker-machine command, which unsets all of the environment variables docker-machine might have set up:
>
> ```
> $ docker-machine env -u
> unset DOCKER_TLS_VERIFY
> unset DOCKER_HOST
> unset DOCKER_CERT_PATH
> unset DOCKER_MACHINE_NAME
> # Run this command to configure your shell:
> # eval $(docker-machine env -u)
> ```
>
> This command prints a bunch of unset statements to the screen, along with some commented-out instructions telling you to run eval $(docker-machine env -u). This statement uses command substitution to execute the docker-machine env -u command, and eval then executes the statements the command emitted. It's an interesting way of programmatically building up a command.
>
> The biggest issue with eval is that there's nothing that sanitizes the data. It's going to run whatever you send it, which can lead to arbitrary code execution if what you tell it to evaluate is dangerous. It's why you'll find many people who say "eval is another way to spell evil." While it's useful in some edge cases, it should be your last resort.
>
> ──────────
> a.   https://docs.docker.com/machine/

The simplest way to do this is to display the error code with a command substitution as the first element in the prompt:

```
PS1="\$(echo \$?) - ${USERCOLOR}\u${RESET}@\h:\w\\$ "
```

This results in a prompt like this:

```
0 - brian@puzzles:~$
```

To make this work, you will have to get the error code right away so that nothing else alters it, and you have to escape the dollar sign for the command substitution, as well as the dollar sign inside of the command substitution, so the shell doesn't evaluate these substitutions when you define the prompt.

If you want to put the error code elsewhere in the prompt, things get a lot more complicated because you need to retain the previous command's error code, in case something else you use in the prompt executes another program.

One approach is to use command substitution to create the entire prompt, like this:

```
PS1="\$(err=\$?; echo "${USERCOLOR}\u${RESET}@\h:\w\ - $err - \\$) "
```

Within the substitution, you save the result of the previous command to the variable err, again escaping the dollar sign so the command doesn't execute when you set the prompt. Saving the error code ensures that it won't be altered by any other commands you might want to call and inject into the prompt later. Then, you use echo to build the prompt like normal. The only change you make here is to once again escape the dollar sign for err so you don't accidentally write out its value when defining the prompt. The dollar signs for $USERCOLOR and $RESET aren't escaped because you do want to embed the actual values here when constructing the prompt.

This results in a prompt that looks like this:

```
brian@puzzles:~ - 0 - $
```

Another way you can embed the output of programs in your prompt is by defining a function to build the prompt and then assigning the name of the function to the PROMPT_COMMAND variable. The function gets executed every time the shell shows the prompt. This is a much cleaner method.

Try it out. Add the following to your ~/.bashrc file:

```
running_commands/bashrc
function setPrompt() {
  let error_code=$?
  PS1="${USERCOLOR}\u${RESET}@\h:\w - ${error_code} - \\$ "
}
PROMPT_COMMAND=setPrompt
```

In this case, the setPrompt function stores the previous error code in the error_code variable and then assigns the PS1 variable.

Save the file and source it, and your prompt shows the error code in the prompt as before:

```
brian@puzzles:~ - 0 - $
```

This approach is a more manageable solution for custom prompts, as it doesn't require any odd escaping or other hacks. However, other scripts that add information to your prompt might not work with this as they also rely on this approach to customize the prompt. If you notice these conflicts, you'll need to modify your customized version to invoke those other scripts in addition to your own logic.

Process Substitution

Process Substitution is similar to command substitution, except that it lets you treat the output of a program as if it were a file. It's useful in situations where you might otherwise need to use a temporary file.

For example, if you have two directories, you might want to compare them to see which files are unique to the first directory, which are unique to the second, and which files exist in both. The comm command compares files and shows the differences. So you could redirect the output of each directory listing to temporary files and then use comm to compare them, but by using process substitution, you can use comm to compare the results of two commands.

Try it out by creating two directories with some similar files:

```
$ mkdir dir1 && touch dir1/{index,about,contact}.html
$ mkdir dir2 && touch dir2/{index,about,resume}.html
```

Then, use the comm command and process substitution to invoke the ls command on both directories:

```
$ comm <(ls dir1/) <( ls dir2)
                about.html
contact.html
                index.html
        resume.html
```

The ls commands are wrapped in parentheses and preceded by the < symbol. At first glance, you might confuse this with input redirection when reading it. The shell might too, so make sure you don't put a space after the < symbol. The results show that about.html and index.html files exist in both directories, while contact.html only appears in the first directory and resume.html only appears in the second.

You may encounter some programs that don't support reading data from standard input, meaning you can't pipe data to them. If they can read data from files, you can use process substitution instead of using temporary files. You'll also find process substitution used in some Bash scripts, as people use it to capture the output of programs and iterate over the output.

Keeping Commands Running with GNU Screen

You may occasionally find yourself in situations where you'll want to keep something running for a longer period of time, even when you close your shell session. You might need a file to download, a program to compile, or a complex installation process to finish. You've already seen how to background tasks, but often this isn't enough.

Of a few methods you can use to keep long-running tasks going, the GNU Screen program is one of the easiest and most flexible options. screen is a terminal multiplexer, meaning that it creates virtual terminal sessions on top of your actual terminal session. You can start tasks in these sessions, "detach" from them, and they'll run in the background, even if you log out. You can also use screen to run multiple programs simultaneously, and even split your terminal window into multiple panes so you can run programs side-by-side.

On macOS, screen is already installed. Depending on the version of Ubuntu you're using, you may need to install it. Use which screen to see if screen is installed. If you get no response from the command, install screen with sudo apt install screen.

> ## tmux
>
> tmux[a] is a popular alternative to screen. It offers the same features as screen, along with many additional features that make it great for creating a powerful development environment. You'll focus on screen in this chapter because it's either already installed on your operating system or easily available in your package manager and doesn't require any configuration. You can learn all about tmux and how you can put it to work for you in *tmux 2: Productive Mouse-free Development [Hog16]*.
>
> ---
>
> a.   https://github.com/tmux/tmux/wiki

Let's explore a couple of uses for screen. The most basic usage is to use screen to run a long-running process in the background and have it persist even when you close your terminal window. To see how this works, run this command to run the top command with screen:

```
$ screen top
```

The top command runs, but it's actually running in a screen session. Programs launched this way will keep running even if you accidentally close your terminal window.

Let's get back to the shell prompt but leave top running. When screen is running, it listens for special keystrokes which it can interpret and act upon. Press Ctrl+a, then press d. This "detaches" from your session, drops you back at your prompt, and displays the following message:

```
[detached from 20757.pts-0.puzzles]
```

If you look through your process list, you'll see that top is still running:

```
$ ps -e | grep top
20758 pts/2    00:00:02 top
```

Use the command screen -ls to list the screen sessions:

```
$ screen -ls
There is a screen on:
        20757.pts-0.puzzles  (03/03/2019 08:22:11 PM)        (Detached)
1 Socket in /run/screen/S-brian.
```

The output shows the session 20757.pts-0.puzzles is active but detached. The number is the process ID of the screen process.

Use screen -r to "reattach" your terminal to the session:

```
$ screen -r
```

You see top again. Press q to quit top and screen closes too.

```
[screen is terminating]
```

screen exits when the program you told it to run exits.

You can use the options -d and -m to create a new screen session and immediately detach:

```
$ screen -d -m top
```

When you execute it this way, you don't see any output. But use screen -ls to see the list of screen sessions:

```
$ screen -ls
There is a screen on:
        21802..puzzles  (03/03/2019 08:25:31 PM)        (Detached)
1 Socket in /run/screen/S-brian.
```

This is the quickest way to use screen to run a long-running process in the background, since it doesn't require any interaction from you.

When you only have one screen session listed, you can reattach to the session using screen -r like you did before. But when you have multiple sessions running, you'll have to specify which one you want.

Use screen to launch nano in a detached session:

```
$ screen -d -m nano
```

List the sessions:

```
$ screen -ls
There are screens on:
        21812..puzzles  (03/03/2019 08:26:15 PM)        (Detached)
        21802..puzzles  (03/03/2019 08:25:31 PM)        (Detached)
2 Sockets in /run/screen/S-brian.
```

You have two detached sessions. You can see the times they were started. The most recent session should be at the top of the list. To attach to it, use screen -x followed by the session name. You don't need to use the whole name; the number is enough. In the preceding example, the screen session running nano is named 21812..puzzles, so you can attach to it like this:

```
$ screen -x 21812
```

Exit nano and the screen session exits.

Use the same approach to connect to the other session running top and shut it down as well.

You can also start screen up without running any commands at all. This gives you an environment where you can run multiple commands in a single session. Unlike the previous examples, screen will not close automatically when you do this.

Try it out. Start a new screen session, but this time use the -S flag to create a session called work instead of letting screen generate the name for you. This makes it easier to locate your session when looking at the list of sessions:

```
$ screen -S work
```

The screen will clear and you will see your prompt. Now, execute the top command:

```
$ top
```

top starts like before. Press q to quit top. This time, screen doesn't exit. You can run additional commands, detach from the session with Ctrl+a d, or type exit to exit the session and close screen. But before you shut things down, try running two programs at the same time.

Fire up top again:

```
$ top
```

Now, press Ctrl+a followed by c to create a new window in screen. The screen clears and you see a new prompt. Press Ctrl+a followed by Ctrl+a again to toggle back to the window containing the top command. Press Ctrl+a Ctrl+a again to flip back to the second window with the prompt.

Detach from this session with Ctrl+a d:

Then, look at the screens:

```
$ screen -ls
There is a screen on:
        21597.work        (03/03/2019 08:28:31 PM)        (Detached)
1 Socket in /run/screen/S-brian.
```

Reattach to the session with screen -x, but this time use its name:

```
$ screen -x work
```

Your session is restored, and you can toggle between the two windows with Ctrl+a Ctrl+a. Navigate to the window containing your prompt and type exit. This closes the window and then switches to the original window running top.

screen lets you run programs side-by-side too. Try running nano and top on the same screen.

With top visible, split the window horizontally so you can run a second command in the lower half of your screen. Press Ctrl+a followed by Shift+s. The window splits horizontally, leaving the lower half of your screen blank:

```
top - 03:35:47 up 15:34,  2 users,  load average: 0.09, 0.27, 0.18
Tasks: 217 total,   2 running, 183 sleeping,   0 stopped,   0 zombie
%Cpu(s):  1.7 us,  0.7 sy,  0.0 ni, 97.7 id,  0.0 wa,  0.0 hi,  0.0 si,  0.0 st
KiB Mem :  1009112 total,   123856 free,   793360 used,    91896 buff/cache
KiB Swap:  1557568 total,  1107008 free,   450560 used.    96960 avail Mem

  PID USER      PR  NI    VIRT    RES    SHR S %CPU %MEM     TIME+ COMMAND
 4086 brian     20   0 3138272 324664  21328 S  1.3 32.2   0:37.16 gnome-shell
 3918 brian     20   0  390012  42688   3844 S  0.3  4.2   0:06.70 Xorg
 4046 brian     20   0  125764      0      0 S  0.3  0.0   0:32.35 VBoxClient
 6600 brian     20   0   48884   2264   1668 R  0.3  0.2   0:00.99 top
    1 root      20   0  225700   3692   1436 S  0.0  0.4   0:02.89 systemd
  0 bash



 - -
```

Press Ctrl+a, followed by Tab to move to the lower region. Then, press Ctrl+a followed by c to start a new shell in that region.

When the prompt appears, run nano:

```
$ nano
```

You now have a session running both top and nano simultaneously.

```
top - 03:33:59 up 15:32,  3 users,  load average: 0.17, 0.37, 0.21
Tasks: 219 total,   1 running, 185 sleeping,   0 stopped,   0 zombie
%Cpu(s):  0.7 us,  0.0 sy,  0.0 ni, 99.3 id,  0.0 wa,  0.0 hi,  0.0 si,  0.0 st
KiB Mem :  1009112 total,   130352 free,   796052 used,    82708 buff/cache
KiB Swap:  1557568 total,  1106752 free,   450816 used.    98856 avail Mem

  PID USER      PR  NI    VIRT    RES    SHR S %CPU %MEM     TIME+ COMMAND
 3918 brian     20   0  390012  42680   3844 S  0.3  4.2   0:06.14 Xorg
 4046 brian     20   0  125764      0      0 S  0.3  0.0   0:32.17 VBoxClient
 4086 brian     20   0 3138272 325808  21100 S  0.3 32.3   0:35.21 gnome-shell
 6600 brian     20   0   48884   2264   1668 R  0.3  0.2   0:00.74 top
    1 root      20   0  225700   3692   1436 S  0.0  0.4   0:07.89 systemd
  0 bash
  GNU nano 2.9.3                              New Buffer

1

^G Get Help   ^O Write Out  ^W Where Is   ^K Cut Text   ^J Justify    ^C Cur Pos    M-U Undo
^X Exit       ^R Read File  ^\ Replace    ^U Uncut Text ^T To Spell   ^  Go To Line M-E Redo
  1 bash
```

Unfortunately, splits don't persist once you detach from your session. When you reattach, they'll each be an individual full-screen window. Modern versions of screen support the layout option which lets you save a window layout which you can then restore later, so if you're interested in that, consult the screen documentation.

screen is a solid choice for running programs in the background, and it's especially useful for running long-running processes on a remote server where you might be worried about a dropped connection interrupting your work. It's also good for those cases where you accidentally close your terminal window. screen sessions persist until you stop them or if you reboot the machine.

To exit this screen session, exit nano. Type exit, and then press Ctrl+a, followed by Shift+x to close the lower pane. Then press q to close top. Finally, type exit to exit screen.

Your Turn

You worked through a lot of different ways to run programs in this chapter, but you'll probably need a little more practice to commit some of the things you learned to memory. These exercises should help.

1. Create the following directory structure using the command line, but only press the `Enter` key once:

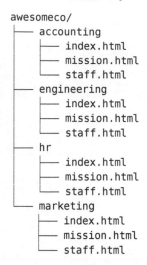

```
awesomeco/
├── accounting
│   ├── index.html
│   ├── mission.html
│   └── staff.html
├── engineering
│   ├── index.html
│   ├── mission.html
│   └── staff.html
├── hr
│   ├── index.html
│   ├── mission.html
│   └── staff.html
└── marketing
    ├── index.html
    ├── mission.html
    └── staff.html
```

2. Use what you learned about history and substitution to create the same directory structure again, but use amazingtek instead of awesomeco.

3. Launch the Firefox web browser in your GUI and then use the command line to gracefully terminate the process.

4. Use top to identify the programs using the most memory and CPU usage.

5. Use the uptime command to display the hours and minutes of uptime on your system in your prompt. You may need to use additional text-processing commands to do this.

What You Learned

You now have a better understanding of how to use the command history, how to reuse arguments from previous commands, how to run one command conditionally after another, and how to use your editor to edit the current or previous command.

You also know how to monitor your CPU and memory usage, shut down programs that may have become unresponsive, and how to suspend a program and resume it later or run programs in the background.

Next, you'll look at tools for communicating over the Internet.

## CHAPTER 8

Networking Tools

Whether you're making websites or mobile applications, you'll probably be doing something with other computers. You'll want to know how to talk to remote systems, fetch data from APIs, and do some diagnostics to ensure that there are no communication errors.

In this chapter, you'll use tools to do network detection and diagnostics and access remote sites. You'll look up IP addresses and domain names, fetch files and make API calls, transfer files between computers, scan networks, and do low-level network communications with netcat.

To follow along with the exercises in this chapter, you'll need an active Internet connection and an additional computer on your network you can access. I'll use the virtual machine configured in Chapter 2, Creating an Ubuntu Virtual Machine with VirtualBox, on page 17, in this chapter.

Let's get started by exploring information about your computer's network devices and connection.

Getting Your Connection Information

Every computer connected to the Internet or a TCP/IP network has an IP address, and there are several methods you can use to determine yours from the command line.

The ifconfig command is a legacy command that displays information about your network devices. While there are newer tools available, you're going to start by exploring this tool because it's universally available on Mac and Linux. On Ubuntu 18.04, you'll need to install the net-tools package to use it:

```
$ sudo apt install net-tools
```

Once it's installed, run ifconfig:

```
$ ifconfig
```

You'll see a bunch of output appear on the screen, starting with something that looks like this:

```
enp0s3: flags=4163<UP,BROADCAST,RUNNING,MULTICAST>  mtu 1500
        inet 10.0.2.15  netmask 255.255.255.0  broadcast 10.0.2.255
        inet6 fe80::9d31:775f:e1e7:8bf8  prefixlen 64  scopeid 0x20<link>
        ether 08:00:27:d2:c9:77  txqueuelen 1000  (Ethernet)
        RX packets 1214  bytes 864477 (864.4 KB)
        RX errors 0  dropped 0  overruns 0  frame 0
        TX packets 784  bytes 66085 (66.0 KB)
        TX errors 0  dropped 0 overruns 0  carrier 0  collisions 0
...
```

The ifconfig command displays information about each network adapter available on the computer, along with its connection information and other relevant details. Each adapter has a name, like en0, eth0, or in this case, enp0s3. The ifconfig command shows each adapter, along with its IPv4 address, denoted by the inet field, the netmask, and broadcast address for that network. It also shows the IPv6 address associated with each adapter, denoted by the inet6 field.

The ether field displays the MAC address of the network hardware. This string of hexadecimal characters uniquely identifies a network device.

The names and number of adapters may be different on various computers, but you'll always see an entry for the local loopback device with the inet address of 127.0.0.1:

```
...
lo: flags=73<UP,LOOPBACK,RUNNING>  mtu 65536
        inet 127.0.0.1  netmask 255.0.0.0
        inet6 ::1  prefixlen 128  scopeid 0x10<host>
        loop  txqueuelen 1000  (Local Loopback)
        RX packets 137  bytes 10557 (10.5 KB)
        RX errors 0  dropped 0  overruns 0  frame 0
        TX packets 137  bytes 10557 (10.5 KB)
        TX errors 0  dropped 0 overruns 0  carrier 0  collisions 0
```

This is a virtual networking device your machine uses to talk to itself. When the Wi-Fi is down, or your ethernet cable is unplugged, or you're on a plane, this is the network device that lets local services talk to each other. When you run a development server and connect to localhost, you're using this loop-back device.

If you configured another network adapter, such as a VirtualBox Host-only Adapter like the one you configured in Configuring a Network, on page 21, you'll also see something like this listed:

```
➤ enp0s8: flags=4163<UP,BROADCAST,RUNNING,MULTICAST>  mtu 1500
➤        inet 192.168.99.100  netmask 255.255.255.0  broadcast 192.168.99.255
➤        inet6 fe80::b30f:d1ae:9d08:5df5  prefixlen 64  scopeid 0x20<link>
➤        ether 08:00:27:22:64:d8  txqueuelen 1000  (Ethernet)
         RX packets 114  bytes 32395 (32.3 KB)
         RX errors 0  dropped 0  overruns 0  frame 0
         TX packets 95  bytes 11277 (11.2 KB)
         TX errors 0  dropped 0 overruns 0  carrier 0  collisions 0
```

The ifconfig command shows all of the adapters on your system. You can instruct it to show a specific adapter by providing the adapter name as an argument. To show only the enp0s8 adapter, run the command ifconfig enp0s8.

Learning to read the output of the ifconfig command is important, because while there are other tools that give you clearer details, those may not be installed or available for your platform.

Look at the first few lines of the output of the ifconfig command again:

```
enp0s3: flags=4163<UP,BROADCAST,RUNNING,MULTICAST>  mtu 1500
➤        inet 10.0.2.15  netmask 255.255.255.0  broadcast 10.0.2.255
```

In this case, the IPv4 address associated with the enp0s3 adapter is 10.0.2.15. This isn't a publicly accessible IP address. You can tell just by looking at the IP address that this computer is running behind some kind of router. How do you know? IP addresses are segmented into various ranges, with some of those ranges reserved for specific things.[1]

- Addresses from 127.0.0.0 to 127.255.255.255 are reserved for the local loopback device.

- Addresses from 10.0.0.0 to 10.255.255.255, 172.16.0.0 to 172.31.255.255, and from 192.168.0.0 to 192.168.255.255 are all reserved for local communications within a private network.

- Addresses from 169.254.0.0 to 169.254.255.255 are used to communicate between hosts when an IP address can't be automatically assigned. This is an indication that your computer couldn't get a proper IP address from your network.

Most routers assign your computer an IPv4 address starting with 192.168 or 10. The router uses Network Address Translation, or NAT, to share an external

---

1. https://en.wikipedia.org/wiki/Reserved_IP_addresses

IPv4 address with multiple computers. IPv4 addresses are very limited, so sharing an IP address with many computers using NAT is one way to meet the demand.

But this makes it more difficult to find your real public IP address if you're trying to let people outside of your network connect with you. To get your public IP address, you'll need to use an external service.

As you saw in Creating Shortcuts with Aliases and Functions, on page 146, you can use this command to find your public IPv4 address from the command line:

```
$ curl icanhazip.com
```

This uses the curl command to make a request to http://icanhazip.com which displays your IP address. You'll learn about the curl command in more detail later in this chapter.

Joe asks:
What's the difference between IPv4 and IPv6?

Internet Protocol version 4, or IPv4, is firmly established in the industry. Unfortunately, the biggest issue with IPv4 is that we have used up all of the IPv4 addresses because IPv4 uses a 32-bit address scheme. IPv6, the latest version of the Internet Protocol, has been in development since the late 1990s and is incredibly beneficial. IPv6 uses a 128-bit addressing scheme which allows for a lot more available addresses. The benefits go beyond just making more addresses available. It's a more efficient scheme for sending data around the Internet, and it has better performance.

Despite the advantages, adoption is slow. IPv4 is deeply entrenched in enterprise systems, consumer electronics, and other areas, and it's difficult to adopt new technology while maintaining backward compatibility. To alleviate some of the issues, commercial and consumer routers let multiple computers share an IP address through NAT, or Network Address Translation, so this lets the industry kick the can down the road a little. Since this isn't a book about networking, we are going to stick to covering IPv4 addresses since it's more likely that you will encounter them right now. But do keep IPv6 in mind, because adoption is increasing.

The ifconfig command is technically deprecated; it hasn't received an upgrade in years. Many Linux systems provide the ip command, which has more features and presents a different output:

```
$ ip addr show
1: lo: <LOOPBACK,UP,LOWER_UP> mtu 65536 qdisc noqueue state UNKNOWN
group default qlen 1000
    link/loopback 00:00:00:00:00:00 brd 00:00:00:00:00:00
    inet 127.0.0.1/8 scope host lo
      valid_lft forever preferred_lft forever
    inet6 ::1/128 scope host
      valid_lft forever preferred_lft forever
2: enp0s3: <BROADCAST,MULTICAST,UP,LOWER_UP> mtu 1500 qdisc fq_codel state UP
group default qlen 1000
    link/ether 08:00:27:d2:c9:77 brd ff:ff:ff:ff:ff:ff
    inet 10.0.2.15/24 brd 10.0.2.255 scope global dynamic noprefixroute enp0s3
      valid_lft 82320sec preferred_lft 82320sec
    inet6 fe80::9d31:775f:e1e7:8bf8/64 scope link noprefixroute
      valid_lft forever preferred_lft forever
...
```

This shows much of the same information as the ifconfig command but in a slightly different format. For example, it displays the IPv4 addresses using CIDR notation. CIDR, or Classless Inter-Domain Routing, is a method that allows IPv4 addresses to be allocated without as much waste.[2] Before CIDR, IP addresses were assigned to different classes of addresses which determined how many hosts a network could have.[3] This classification system has resulted in a lot of IP addresses that were allocated but then never used. CIDR corrects that.

In this case, the ip command shows that the IPv4 address is 10.0.2.15/24. The IPv4 address itself is 10.0.2.15, and the /24 says that the subnet mask is made up of 24 bits, making it 255.255.255.0, which you saw when you ran the ifconfig command. From this, you can determine that all IP addresses that start with 10.0.2. are on the same network.

The ifconfig command is universal, but it's deprecated and doesn't show you CIDR information. However, because ip isn't available everywhere, you should be comfortable using both ip and ifconfig.

You've spent some time looking at IP addresses; it's time to take a look at a few tools that make working with domains easier.

Finding Information About Domain Names

When you make a request to facebook.com, your computer looks up the domain name to translate that domain name into an IP address so your computer can make that connection. An IP address points to a computer on the Internet,

---

2.   https://en.wikipedia.org/wiki/Classless_Inter-Domain_Routing
3.   https://en.wikipedia.org/wiki/Classful_network

but a domain name is easier to remember than a group of numbers. Domain Name System (DNS) servers store the mappings of IP addresses, along with other information. There are several command-line tools you can use to query these servers.

Use the dig command to "dig" through domain name records and find the IP addresses associated with those. It's a reliable way to get information about a domain:

```
$ dig facebook.com

; <<>> DiG 9.11.3-1ubuntu1.2-Ubuntu <<>> facebook.com
;; global options: +cmd
;; Got answer:
;; ->>HEADER<<- opcode: QUERY, status: NOERROR, id: 30501
;; flags: qr rd ra; QUERY: 1, ANSWER: 1, AUTHORITY: 0, ADDITIONAL: 1

;; OPT PSEUDOSECTION:
; EDNS: version: 0, flags:; udp: 65494
;; QUESTION SECTION:
;facebook.com.                  IN      A

;; ANSWER SECTION:
facebook.com.           1       IN      A       157.240.18.35

;; Query time: 22 msec
;; SERVER: 127.0.0.53#53(127.0.0.53)
;; WHEN: Sun Mar 03 21:06:17 CDT 2019
;; MSG SIZE  rcvd: 57
```

Look at the *Answer Section* to see the IP addresses. In this example, only one IP address is associated with this domain name. But use the dig command with google.com and you'll see that they've associated more than one IP address. This is what sites do that need high availability. If one IP goes down, the others can answer.

Sometimes you need to find out who owns a domain name so you can contact them. Or you want to check if a domain name exists so you can purchase it. Some unscrupulous companies offer online domain searches, and when you search for a domain you want, they purchase it automatically so that when you go to pay for it, they can charge you more.

The whois command is a quick way to see if a domain name exists. If it does exist, you can see who owns it, along with contact information. The whois command uses domain name servers to query the registration information of a domain.

On Ubuntu, you may have to install the whois command with apt:

```
$ sudo apt install whois
```

Now use it to look at the registration information for the pragprog.com domain:

```
$ whois pragprog.com
```

When you run that, you'll be greeted with a wall of information, including when the domain name expires and who to contact about it.

Based on this information:

1. Who would you contact about technical issues?
2. When was the domain first registered?
3. Why do you think there are so many name servers associated?

You can learn a lot about a domain with the whois command.

Sometimes you don't know the domain name. Sometimes you only have the IP address. The host command makes it easy to look up a domain name from an IP. If you're looking through security logs and you're getting hits from a certain IP address, try using the host command to look up the domain name of the request:

```
$ host 8.8.8.8
```

This command tells you a lot about this IP address:

```
8.8.8.8.in-addr.arpa domain name pointer google-public-dns-a.google.com.
```

It looks like this IP belongs to Google. Try running this command with your own IP address. You might see a result like this:

```
113.6.in-addr.arpa domain name pointer 113-7.dhcp.eucl.wi.charter.com.
```

A lot of residential internet providers register IP addresses in their own DNS servers just like this, which makes it easy to tell who's the ISP. In this example, it looks like this IP address is associated with an ISP in Eau Claire, Wisconsin. With this knowledge, you can then get more information by contacting the ISP. Of course, you can't guarantee this information, and you really can't accurately tie an IP to a geographic region unless the owner of the IP helps you along like the ISP did in this example. Still, this is one tool of many that you can use to learn more about the IP addresses you're communicating with.

Now, let's look at how to test network connectivity.

Testing Network Connectivity

We've all been there. You open a browser and are immediately greeted with a message stating that there's no Internet access. Maybe you can't access anything else, or maybe you can access other servers on your network, but you can't reach the greater Internet. You've probably opened a command prompt or a terminal session and typed ping to see if you can reach another machine.

The ping command is the standard tool for testing connections between other computers. It sends a request to a remote machine and waits for a reply. It then displays the reply, along with some useful statistics about the connection. On Unix-like systems, ping sends these requests forever until you press Ctrl+c:

```
$ ping google.com
```

Let it run and receive four requests, then press Ctrl+c. You'll see a response like this:

```
PING google.com (216.58.192.206) 56(84) bytes of data.
64 bytes from ord3...1e100.net (216.58.192.206): icmp_seq=1 ttl=63 time=140 ms
64 bytes from ord3...1e100.net (216.58.192.206): icmp_seq=2 ttl=63 time=136 ms
64 bytes from ord3...1e100.net (216.58.192.206): icmp_seq=3 ttl=63 time=120 ms
64 bytes from ord3...1e100.net (216.58.192.206): icmp_seq=4 ttl=63 time=109 ms
^C
--- google.com ping statistics ---
4 packets transmitted, 4 received, 0% packet loss, time 3003ms
rtt min/avg/max/mdev = 109.646/126.776/140.527/12.448 ms
```

To tell ping to stop after four requests, use the -c switch:

```
$ ping -c 4 google.com
PING google.com (216.58.192.206) 56(84) bytes of data.
64 bytes from ord3...1e100.net (216.58.192.206): icmp_seq=1 ttl=63 time=140 ms
64 bytes from ord3...1e100.net (216.58.192.206): icmp_seq=2 ttl=63 time=136 ms
64 bytes from ord3...1e100.net (216.58.192.206): icmp_seq=3 ttl=63 time=120 ms
64 bytes from ord3...1e100.net (216.58.192.206): icmp_seq=4 ttl=63 time=109 ms
--- google.com ping statistics ---
4 packets transmitted, 4 received, 0% packet loss, time 3003ms
rtt min/avg/max/mdev = 109.646/126.776/140.527/12.448 ms
```

If you don't have an active connection, you'll see a message like this:

```
ping: unknown host google.com
```

When you use ping with a domain name, it tries to look up the IP address for that domain name. If there's no DNS service available, either due to a DNS outage, or more likely, a problem with your network's connection to a DNS resolution server, it can't continue.

However, if your computer is able to resolve the domain name but the other side isn't responding, you'll see something like this instead:

```
PING google.com (216.58.192.206) 56(84) bytes of data.
From 10.0.2.2 icmp_seq=1 Destination Net Unreachable
From 10.0.2.2 icmp_seq=2 Destination Net Unreachable
From 10.0.2.2 icmp_seq=3 Destination Net Unreachable
From 10.0.2.2 icmp_seq=4 Destination Net Unreachable
^C
--- 8.8.8.8 ping statistics ---
4 packets transmitted, 0 received, +4 errors, 100% packet loss, time 3065ms
```

Some firewalls and routers are programmed to ignore ECHO requests from the ping command, so they could also appear unreachable. The ping command is great when it works, but let's look at some other ways you can diagnose connection problems.

The traceroute tool is short for "trace route," and it'll tell you exactly how the request you make on your computer gets around your network. It's great for diagnosing those troublesome connections. Using traceroute is the quickest way to figuring out if the problem is on your end or somewhere else on the Internet.

Unfortunately, the traceroute tool isn't installed on some systems, but you should be able to install it with your package manager. On Ubuntu, install it with:

```
$ sudo apt install traceroute
```

Once it's installed, run it like this:

```
$ traceroute www.google.com
```

The command displays output which shows the "hops," or steps it takes for traffic to reach the destination:

```
traceroute to www.google.com (216.58.192.196), 30 hops max, 60 byte packets
 1  10.0.2.2 (10.0.2.2)  0.695 ms  0.610 ms  0.578 ms
 2  192.168.1.1 (192.168.1.1)  6.800 ms  6.727 ms  6.670 ms
 3  * * *
 4  dtr02euclwi-tge-0-4-0-15.eucl...  91.269 ms  95.517 ms  91.202 ms
 5  crr02euclwi-hge-0-0-0-4.eucl... 91.146 ms  91.128 ms  95.382 ms
 6  crr01sgnwmi-tge-0-0-0-4.sgnw.mi... 91.061 ms  89.390 ms  89.332 ms
 7  bbr01chcgil-bue-1.chcg.il...  110.649 ms  111.520 ms  111.441 ms
 8  prr01chcgil-bue-2.chcg.il...  104.027 ms  132.220 ms  132.104 ms
 9  72.14.195.76 (72.14.195.76)...  128.719 ms 131.978 ms
10  108.170.243.193 (108.170.243.193)  128.002 ms * *
11  ord30s25-in-f4.1e100.net (216.58.192.196)
138.802 ms 108.170.238.136 (108.170.238.136)  330.047 ms
216.239.42.109 (216.239.42.109)  140.450 ms
```

To get to Google, this connection had to go through eleven steps, or *hops*. First, it goes to my router (192.168.1.1), and then out to the local ISP, where it then connects with the ISP's other connected nodes. It eventually connects to some place in Michigan, then on to Chicago. (Thankfully, my ISP makes it easy to see where a lot of this traffic goes because they name their routers using city and state names). Then it goes on to some other places before it makes it to the final destination.

On step 10, you see two stars. This is where it had to make multiple attempts to get through because the connection timed out. If I ran this command again and it always timed out at the same step, this might indicate some network trouble there.

The traceroute tool is helpful when you're trying to figure out if there's an issue with your local network or trying to figure out why requests you're sending aren't coming back.

So far, you've looked at tools to diagnose some basic networking issues and get some information about hosts. Let's look at some more specific tools, starting with a powerful tool that can grab web pages and make web requests from the command line.

Making Web Requests with cURL

cURL is a powerful command-line tool for interacting with web servers. Using cURL, you can make requests and view the responses, download files, grab information about remote servers, or interact with remote APIs. cURL does exactly what your web browser does, except that it doesn't render the HTML. Let's explore how it works.

You'll use cURL to make a request to a URL. Execute this command in your terminal to make a request to Google's home page:

```
$ curl http://google.com
```

Responses from web servers come in two parts: the response header and the response body. cURL shows the response body by default:

```
<HTML><HEAD><meta http-equiv="content-type" content="text/html;charset=utf-8">
<TITLE>301 Moved</TITLE></HEAD><BODY>
<H1>301 Moved</H1>
The document has moved
<A HREF="http://www.google.com/">here</A>.
</BODY></HTML>
```

In this case, the response body contains some HTML, and it looks like the Google homepage exists at a different address.

You can use the -I switch to request only the headers from a web server. You can use this to see the kind of HTTP response you got, as well as more information about the server's response.

```
$ curl -I http://google.com
```

The response headers tell us a ton about the web server that hosts the page. You can see when the page was last modified, the character set of the response, and even the server that was used:

```
HTTP/1.1 301 Moved Permanently
Location: http://www.google.com/
Content-Type: text/html; charset=UTF-8
Date: Sun, 03 Mar 2019 14:46:24 GMT
Expires: Sun, 03 Mar 2019 14:46:24 GMT
Cache-Control: public, max-age=2592000
Server: gws
Content-Length: 219
X-XSS-Protection: 1; mode=block
X-Frame-Options: SAMEORIGIN
```

The first line shows you the HTTP status code. The code 200 means it was a successful request. The status code 404 means the page wasn't found. You've probably seen that message before.

If you saw 500 then there was a problem with the server, perhaps caused by a misconfiguration on the server or an error in the server-side programming language powering the application on the server you've connected to. And if you see the codes 301 or 302, someone moved the page to a new URL.

In this case, you see HTTP/1.1 301 Moved Permanently. When a server sends that response back, it also sends another header named location, which specifies where you should find the page now—sure enough, that's the second line of the response:

```
Location: http://www.google.com/
```

From this, you can see that Google has set up a permanent redirection from http://google.com to http://www.google.com.

Many websites redirect requests from one page to another. Sometimes it's to redirect people to the new location of some content when the URL changed. Other times it's to redirect a request for an insecure resource to a secure resource. Web browsers take care of following those redirects for you automatically so you barely notice. Visit http://google.com/ in your browser and you'll see that the URL does indeed change from http://google.com to http://www.google.com. Your browser inspected the headers and used the value of the location header.

You can make curl do this too, if you use the -L switch. Try it out:

```
$ curl -I -L http://google.com
```

You'll see the first request like before, followed by a second request:

```
HTTP/1.1 301 Moved Permanently
Location: http://www.google.com/
...
HTTP/1.1 200 OK
Date: Sun, 03 Mar 2019 19:19:47 GMT
```

curl is great for inspecting headers and making requests. It's also good for fetching files.

Downloading Files

Instead of displaying the response to the screen, you can use the redirection symbol (>) to push that content into a text file. You can grab a copy of the HTML response from Google this way:

```
$ curl http://google.com > google.html
```

The output now exists in the file google.html. You can verify this by using the cat command to view the file's contents.

You can also directly download that file. The -o switch lets you specify the filename you want to save the file to:

```
$ curl -o google.html http://google.com
```

As you saw in Downloading Files, on page 11, you can use cURL to download any file you want if you know the URL of the file. For example, if you needed Ubuntu 16.04 for a project, you could use cURL to download it like this:

```
$ curl -O -L http://releases.ubuntu.com/16.04/ubuntu-16.04.6-desktop-amd64.iso
```

You're using the -O switch this time. That's a capital letter O, not a zero. This tells cURL to use the remote filename so you don't have to specify your own. You also use the -L switch, just in case you encounter any redirects.

You probably wouldn't type that out yourself, but you might save it to a script and run it later.

You can use cURL for a lot more than just downloading and reading files though.

Working with Web APIs

An API, or Application Programming Interface, lets developers interface with data without having to access the data directly. Web APIs let you do this by making requests to servers. APIs can let you see current weather conditions, stock prices, sports scores, social media feeds, and pretty much any data you're looking to consume.

If you're writing software that interfaces with a third-party web API, or if you're developing your own, you can use cURL to explore and test that API. You can set headers, define request types, and send data payloads.

To explore this, you'll need an API you can work with. Instead of using a live API for testing, you'll use json-server,[4] a Node.js package that provides an API for these types of situations. Let's set it up inside of the Ubuntu virtual machine.

First, install Node.js on your Ubuntu virtual machine. You'll need Node.js to run json-server. The Node.js package available through Ubuntu's packages is out of date, but you can use the NodeSource repository[5] to get a more recent version.

First, use curl to download an installation script from Nodesource that adds their repository to your system and updates the list of available packages.

cURL and Bash: A Convenient but Dangerous Combination

The official installation documentation for Node.js says to use this command:

```
$ curl -sL https://deb.nodesource.com/setup_11.x | sudo -E bash -
```

This is a fairly common pattern. It downloads the script from NodeSource, then pipes the output to the sudo command which executes the script with bash. In other words, you're downloading an unknown script from the Internet and running it as your root account. If you trust the source of the script, you might not worry about this too much. But if the original server is compromised by hackers, you could be running arbitrary code on your servers. Security-minded folks frown on this approach, so the best approach is to download the file with cURL and then view its contents to ensure it's only doing what it says it's doing. Once you're comfortable with the contents, then you'd execute the script. That's what you'll do in this book.

---

4. https://github.com/typicode/json-server
5. https://nodesource.com/

First, download the installation script:

```
$ curl -L -O https://deb.nodesource.com/setup_11.x
```

Then, review the script to learn what it does and how it works. Never run scripts that you download from the Internet until you have inspected their contents:

```
$ less ./setup_11.x
```

Now execute the installation script and install the nodejs package:

```
$ sudo bash ./setup_11.x
$ sudo apt install nodejs
```

This installs Node.js, along with npm, a command for installing Node.js libraries and programs, and npx, a command which downloads and then executes applications.

Now, create a JSON file in your home directory called data.json with the following content:

networking/data.json
```
{
  "notes": [
    { "id": 1, "title": "Hello" }
  ]
}
```

json-server will use this as its data and turn it into a REST API you can query. You can use nano to create it, or create it with cat:

```
$ cat << 'EOF' > ~/data.json
> {
>   "notes": [
>     { "id": 1, "title": "Hello" }
>   ]
> }
> EOF
```

With the file created, use the npx command to run json-server and tell it to watch the data.json file for changes:

```
$ npx json-server -w ~/data.json
```

The files download and the server starts, displaying information about how to connect to the web API:

```
\{^_^}/ hi!

Loading data.json
Done

Resources
http://localhost:3000/notes

Home
http://localhost:3000

Type s + enter at any time to create a snapshot of the database
Watching...
```

Open a new terminal window so you can make some requests to the server with cURL.

In your new terminal window, make a request to http://localhost:3000/notes and you'll see the notes you created in the data.json file appear on the screen:

```
$ curl http://localhost:3000/notes
[
  {
    "id": 1,
    "title": "Hello"
  }
]
```

Now that you know the API is responding, and that you can use cURL to fetch data, let's use cURL to add a new record to this API. To do that, you'll need to make a POST request, specify headers, and specify the data you want to send:

```
$ curl -X POST http://localhost:3000/notes \
> -H 'Content-type: application/json' \
> -d '{"title": "This is another note"}'
```

The -X POST argument specifies that you want a POST request. The -H flag sets a request header that tells the server that you are sending JSON data. The -d argument specifies the data that you are sending, which is the JSON for the new note.

You'll see the new record returned from the API, letting you know you added the record:

```
{
  "title": "This is another note",
  "id": 2
}
```

Verify this by requesting the notes resource again:

```
$ curl http://localhost:3000/notes
[
  {
    "id": 1,
    "title": "Hello"
  },
  {
    "title": "This is another note",
    "id": 2
  }
]
```

You can delete that note with cURL as well:

```
$ curl -X DELETE http://localhost:3000/notes/2
```

To stop json-server, switch back to its terminal window and press Ctrl+c.

cURL is an invaluable tool in your tool belt as a developer. You can use it to drive the development of your API before you write the client, and you can use it to document how others can use your API.

Ready to look at connecting to servers or other machines using SSH?

Using Secure Shell to Connect to Remote Machines

Secure Shell, or SSH, is an encrypted and secure method for logging in to remote machines. You can also use it to execute commands remotely, and use related tools to copy files securely.

This is the standard way to log into remote Linux servers, either in your own data center or in the cloud. In this section, you'll use your local machine to connect to your Ubuntu virtual machine.

First, on your Ubuntu machine, install the openssh-server package and enable SSH connections:

```
(ubuntu)$ sudo apt install openssh-server
```

This installs and activates the SSH server on port 22.

Identify the IP address of your Ubuntu machine using the ip addr command, and use grep to look for inet in the output, filtering out inet6 so you don't see the IPv6 addresses:

```
(ubuntu)$ ip addr | grep inet | grep -v inet6
    inet 127.0.0.1/8 scope host lo
    inet 10.0.2.15/24 brd 10.0.2.255 scope global dynamic enp0s3
    inet 192.168.99.100/24 brd 192.168.99.255 scope global dynamic enp0s8
```

If you followed the steps in Configuring a Network, on page 21, then you're looking for the IP address that starts with 192.168.99. In this case, the IP to connect to the server is 192.168.99.100, the private Host-only IP address.

Then, on your local machine, you'll use the ssh command-line tool to connect. This tool is already installed on macOS and the Windows Subsystem for Linux.

To use it, specify the username and server address to which you wish to connect:

```
(local)$ ssh brian@192.168.99.100
The authenticity of host '192.168.99.100 (192.168.99.100)' can't be established.
ECDSA key fingerprint is SHA256:CDDYS4MsIVrWehucVVwaBpbRKD8Xs9ON5rkjm/U5/Qc.
Are you sure you want to continue connecting (yes/no)? yes
Warning: Permanently added '192.168.99.100' (ECDSA) to the list of known hosts.
```

The first time you connect to a remote host, SSH asks you to verify the authenticity of the host. Answering yes saves the fingerprint of the remote server to a file named ~/.ssh/known-hosts. If the server's fingerprint changes, you won't be able to connect to it because SSH will assume the machine has either been compromised or it's a different machine. It's just an extra security precaution; the fingerprint shouldn't change without you expecting it.

Once you add the server to the list of known hosts, you'll be prompted for your remote user's password. Once you enter it, you'll be logged in:

```
brian@192.168.99.100's password:
Welcome to Ubuntu 18.04.1 LTS (GNU/Linux 4.15.0-45-generic x86_64)

...

brian@puzzles:~$
```

Your prompt changes, indicating that you're now executing commands against the remote server instead of your local machine.

Execute the ls command to see the contents of your home directory:

```
brian@puzzles:~$ ls
data.json  Desktop  Documents  Downloads  examples.desktop
Music  Pictures  Public  setup_11.x  Templates  Videos
```

Type exit or press Ctrl+d to log out of the remote machine and return to your local prompt.

Now let's set up public key authentication so that you can log in without a password.

Connecting with Public Keys Instead of Passwords

If you are going to log in to a remote machine with SSH, you can increase your security by using a public key instead of a password. You generate a public and private keypair on your local machine, and then copy the public key to the ~/.ssh/authorized_keys file on the remote machine. When you connect, SSH will perform authentication using the key and won't prompt you for a password.

First, check if you already have a public key on your local machine. The default filename is id_rsa.pub and it's located in the .ssh folder of your home directory. Use the ls command to see if it exists:

```
(local)$ ls ~/.ssh/id_rsa.pub
```

If you don't see any results, generate a new RSA keypair using the ssh-keygen command and press Enter for each prompt to accept the defaults:

```
(local)$ ssh-keygen -t rsa
Generating public/private rsa key pair.
Enter file in which to save the key (/Users/brian/.ssh/id_rsa):
Enter passphrase (empty for no passphrase):
Enter same passphrase again:
Your identification has been saved in /Users/brian/.ssh/id_rsa.
Your public key has been saved in /Users/brian/.ssh/id_rsa.pub.
...
```

This creates the private key, located in ~/.ssh/id_rsa, which you should never provide to anyone. The public key, located in .ssh/id_rsa.pub, is something you can provide to any other service that supports public keys.

To use your public key to log in to your Ubuntu server, you have to place the contents of the public key on the server in a file named authorized_keys, which is located in the .ssh directory inside the home directory of the user you want to log in as. Additionally, the .ssh directory and the authorized_keys file need to have specific permissions set so that only that user can access them.

The command ssh-copy-id can perform all of these tasks. On macOS, you'll have to install it with brew install ssh-copy-id.

To use it, execute this command:

```
(local)$ ssh-copy-id brian@192.168.99.100
```

You will be prompted for the password for your user. Enter the password and your key will copy.

If you don't have ssh-copy-id, you can still copy the key manually with this command:

```
(local)$ cat ~/.ssh/id_rsa.pub \
> | ssh brian@192.168.99.100 "mkdir -p ~/.ssh && cat >>  ~/.ssh/authorized_keys"
```

This command connects to the server, creates the directory, and pushes the content of the key into the file.

Then, log in to the server again:

```
(local)$ ssh brian@192.168.99.100
```

If you are still prompted for a password, you will need to fix the permissions on the .ssh directory and the authorized_keys file. Enter your password so you can proceed. Then, once logged in, execute these commands to tighten up permissions:

```
brian@puzzles:~$ chmod go-w ~/
brian@puzzles:~$ chmod 700 ~/.ssh
brian@puzzles:~$ chmod 600 ~/.ssh/authorized_keys
```

Log out with exit, and then connect again. This time, you'll be logged in without being prompted for your password.

You can follow this procedure with any remote machine, including a shell account on a shared web host, a virtual private server, or a cloud server.

Let's look at how to copy files from your local machine to a server.

Transferring Files

The scp and rsync commands can copy files to and from a remote server. The scp command, short for "secure copy," works almost like the SSH command. You'll look at that one first.

Copying Files with scp

You can copy the data.json file you created previously from the server to your local machine using the scp command.

Specify the source path first, followed by the destination path. The source is on the remote server, so you'd specify the username and server address, followed by the path to the file on the server, using a colon to separate the host from the remote path:

```
(local)$ scp brian@192.168.99.100:~/data.json data.json
data.json                              100%  162    172.7KB/s   00:00
```

To transfer the file back, reverse the source and destination paths:

```
(local)$ scp data.json brian@192.168.99.100:~/data.json
data.json                          100%  162    172.7KB/s   00:00
```

You can also transfer multiple files to a server using scp. On your local machine, execute these commands to create a directory structure for a website:

```
(local)$ mkdir -p testsite/{css,js}
(local)$ touch testsite/{index.html,css/style.css}
```

This generates the following structure, which you can view with the tree command:

```
(local)$ tree testsite
testsite/
├── css
│   └── style.css
├── index.html
└── js
```

Now copy testsite to the server:

```
(local)$ scp -r testsite brian@192.168.99.100:~/testsite
style.css         100%   0     0.0KB/s   00:00
index.html        100%   0     0.0KB/s   00:00
```

Verify that those files are there by using the tree command on your server. You can also use the ssh command to execute the command:

```
(local)$ ssh brian@192.168.99.100 'tree ~/testsite'
/home/brian/testsite
├── css
│   └── style.css
├── index.html
└── js
```

You've just transferred a bunch of files and directories to a remote machine, and you can download them from the remote machine by switching the source and destination paths.

But if you've updated the files and want to transfer them again, you might run into a problem if you use the same command again. Try this out:

```
(local)$ scp -r testsite brian@192.168.99.100:~/testsite
```

The command completes, but when you use the tree command to view the directory structure on the remote machine again, you'll find a new testsite directory inside of the existing one:

```
(local)$ ssh brian@192.168.99.100 'tree ~/testsite'
testsite
├── css
│   └── style.css
├── index.html
├── js
└── testsite
    ├── css
    │   └── style.css
    ├── index.html
    └── js
```

The command created a new testsite directory inside of the original testsite directory instead of replacing the existing directory's contents. But that's not what you wanted. The command you used creates the testsite directory. It worked fine the first time because your remote server did not have a testsite directory yet. This problem has a few solutions, but the simplest is to tell scp to copy the *contents* of the testsite directory, rather than the directory itself.

First, remove the extra testsite folder on the server. Use the ssh command to delete it:

```
(local)$ ssh brian@192.168.99.100 'rm -rf ~/testsite/testsite'
```

Then, copy the contents of the testsite folder to the server:

```
(local)$ scp -r testsite/* brian@192.168.99.100:~/testsite
```

Finally, verify the remote directory structure is correct:

```
(local)$ ssh brian@192.168.99.100 'tree ~/testsite'
/home/brian/testsite
├── css
│   └── style.css
├── index.html
└── js
```

To review, the first time you copied the directory over, it worked fine because the destination directory didn't exist. The second time, since the destination directory existed, things didn't copy right. You fixed it by copying the *contents* of the testsite directory, not the directory itself.

The scp command is good for transferring files to a remote system, but it does have some limitations. It's not easy to remove files, for example. The rsync command gives you more options.

Transferring and Synchronizing Files with rsync

The rsync program can copy files and folders between two locations on the same system, and it can also transfer files between local and remote locations.

Let's use rsync to transfer the testsite directory you created on the local machine to your Ubuntu machine. This time, you will copy it to a new folder named testsite2.

Execute this command to perform the copy:

```
(local)$ rsync -v -r testsite/ brian@192.168.99.100:~/testsite2
building file list ... done
created directory /home/brian/testsite2
./
index.html
css/
css/style.css
js/

sent 210 bytes  received 82 bytes  194.67 bytes/sec
total size is 0  speedup is 0.00
```

Notice the trailing slash for the source. This tells rsync to copy the directory contents to the destination, rather than the directory itself. Unlike the scp command, you can use this for the first transfer as well as subsequent transfers; the destination directory is created if it doesn't exist.

Try it out. Run the command again and then use tree to view the files on the remote machine:

```
(local)$ rsync -v -r testsite/ brian@192.168.99.100:~/testsite2
...
(local)$ ssh brian@192.168.99.100 'tree ~/testsite2'
/home/brian/testsite2
├── css
│   └── style.css
├── index.html
└── js
```

rsync can also keep directories synchronized. For example, if you rename css/style.css to css/styles.css and run the command again, it would copy the new file to the server, but it would leave the old one in place. But if you add the --delete flag, then rsync will remove files at the destination if they no longer exist in the source location:

```
(local)$ mv testsite/css/style.css testsite/css/styles.css

(local)$ rsync -v -r --delete testsite/ brian@192.168.99.100:~/testsite2
building file list ... done
```
➤ `deleting css/style.css`
```
index.html
css/styles.css

sent 197 bytes  received 64 bytes  174.00 bytes/sec
total size is 0  speedup is 0.00
```

You can also use the --update argument to tell rsync to only transfer files that have changed. This can save a ton of time if you have a lot of files. Want to test it out?

First, add some text to the index.html file, then use rsync to send it to the server:

```
(local)$ echo "<h1>Hello</h1>" > testsite/index.html

(local)$ rsync -v -r --update testsite/ brian@192.168.99.100:~/testsite2
building file list ... done
```
➤ `index.html`
```
sent 174 bytes  received 42 bytes  432.00 bytes/sec
total size is 15  speedup is 0.07
```

This time, only the index.html file transferred over.

rsync is a good way to perform backups of data to a remote server. With the --delete and --update arguments, you can synchronize data from one source to another easily, and if you add the -z argument, you can compress the data before sending it over the network, improving transfer time. Finally, check out the -n option which performs a "dry run" so you can see what rsync will do without actually doing any transfers.

Both scp and rsync make it easy for you to transfer files between your systems, either manually or as part of scripts.

Next, you'll look at how to detect network connections. This is useful for discovering which computers on the network you're talking to and which ones are talking back.

Exploring Network Connections

Computers connect to other computers using an IP address and a port. Ports allow multiple network connections from a single machine. Imagine that the IP address is the street address to an apartment complex, and each port is an apartment number in the building.

For example, when you make a request to google.com with your web browser, your browser uses port 80, the default port for web traffic. To complete that request, your browser needs to figure out which IP address google.com resolved to, so it makes a request to a DNS server using port 53, the default port for DNS queries.

When you installed the openssh-server package, your Ubuntu machine started listening for incoming connections on port 22. When you connected to the server, your client made an outgoing connection on port 22.

Your OS makes all kinds of network connections to remote systems, and programs you install do as well. Unfortunately, so do malicious programs. It's not a bad idea to keep tabs on your computer's communication.

A handful of tools will let you see which ports are in use. The two you'll look at are netstat and ss.

netstat is older and more universally available on servers and Linux operating systems. Like ifconfig, it's also not supported anymore. You'll explore it first and then look at other options. On your Ubuntu virtual machine, stop the SSH server:

```
(ubuntu)$ sudo systemctl stop sshd
```

Now, you'll use netstat to look at what's listening for incoming TCP connections. Execute this command on your Ubuntu virtual machine:

```
(ubuntu)$ netstat -lt
Active Internet connections (only servers)
Proto Recv-Q Send-Q Local Address           Foreign Address         State
tcp        0      0 puzzles:domain          *:*                     LISTEN
tcp        0      0 localhost:ipp           *:*                     LISTEN
tcp6       0      0 ip6-localhost:ipp       [::]:*
```

The -l flag only displays servers or programs that are listening for connections. The -t flag only shows TCP connections.

netstat shows the protocol, the number of bytes queued up for receiving and sending, the local address, the remote address, and the state. In this example, everything is normal. Three entries are listening for connections, but there's no data in either the receive queue or the send queue. The Foreign Address field shows *:*, which indicates there's no remote connection, and the LISTEN state shows there's no connection established yet.

If you're wondering what those things are, hold tight; you'll explore that in a bit. But first, start up the SSH server again:

```
(ubuntu)$ sudo systemctl start sshd
```

Then, look at the connections again:

```
(ubuntu)$ netstat -lt
Active Internet connections (only servers)
Proto Recv-Q Send-Q Local Address           Foreign Address         State
tcp        0      0 puzzles:domain          *:*                     LISTEN
tcp        0      0 *:ssh                   *:*                     LISTEN
tcp        0      0 localhost:ipp           *:*                     LISTEN
tcp6       0      0 [::]:ssh                [::]:*                  LISTEN
tcp6       0      0 ip6-localhost:ipp       [::]:*                  LISTEN
```

This time you see two new entries in the output related to SSH.

Now, you can connect from your local machine to your Ubuntu virtual machine via SSH:

```
(local)$ ssh brian@192.168.99.100
```

Then, on the Ubuntu virtual machine, look at the connections again, but this time use netstat -at. The -a switch looks at active connections as well as ones that are waiting:

```
(ubuntu)$ netstat -at
Active Internet connections (servers and established)
Proto Recv-Q Send-Q Local Address           Foreign Address         State
tcp        0      0 puzzles:domain          *:*                     LISTEN
tcp        0      0 *:ssh                   *:*                     LISTEN
tcp        0      0 localhost:ipp           *:*                     LISTEN
tcp        0      0 puzzles:ssh             192.168.99.1:61809      ESTABLISHED
tcp6       0      0 [::]:ssh                [::]:*                  LISTEN
tcp6       0      0 ip6-localhost:ipp       [::]:*                  LISTEN
```

You can see the connection between the machines now.

So what are those other entries in the list? On Linux systems like Ubuntu, you can see which program or process owns the connection by executing netstat with sudo and adding the -p switch. You'll need sudo to see information about ports lower than 1024:

```
(ubuntu)$ sudo netstat -atp
Active Internet connections (servers and established)
Proto ... Local Address      Foreign Address       State        PID/Program name
tcp   ... puzzles:domain     *:*                   LISTEN       837/systemd-resolve
tcp   ... *:ssh              *:*                   LISTEN       14317/sshd
tcp   ... localhost:ipp      *:*                   LISTEN       7024/cupsd
tcp   ... puzzles:ssh        192.168.99.1:61809    ESTABLISHED  14363/sshd: brian...
tcp6  ... [::]:ssh           [::]:*                LISTEN       14317/sshd
tcp6  ... ip6-localhost:ipp  [::]:*                LISTEN       7024/cupsd
```

This output shows that the systemd-resolve and cups services are listening for connections. systemd-resolve is a service for resolving hostnames, and cups is a service for printing. These are built-in services configured by default when you installed Ubuntu. But the output also shows which user is connected to the SSH server, which can be very helpful.

Unfortunately, not all versions of netstat support this option. For example, the BSD version on macOS won't show you this information. Thankfully, some workarounds turn out to be a little better than netstat.

The lsof command lets you see which files are associated with processes. On a Linux-based system, everything is represented as a file, including network connections. This means you can use lsof to perform the same tasks that netstat performs.

To list all services listening for connections over TCP, execute this command:

```
(ubuntu)$ sudo lsof -nP -iTCP -sTCP:LISTEN

COMMAND      PID     USER    FD    TYPE DEVICE SIZE/OFF NODE NAME
systemd-r    321 systemd.. 13u   IPv4  16300       0t0  TCP 127.0.0.53:53 (LISTEN)
cupsd       7024     root   10u   IPv6 118530      0t0  TCP [::1]:631 (LISTEN)
cupsd       7024     root   11u   IPv4 118531      0t0  TCP 127.0.0.1:631 (LISTEN)
sshd       15866     root    3u   IPv4 169492      0t0  TCP *:22 (LISTEN)
sshd       15866     root    4u   IPv6 169508      0t0  TCP *:22 (LISTEN)
```

The -n switch tells lsof not to resolve domain names, which makes it run a lot faster. The -iTCP switch selects files associated with Internet addresses using the TCP protocol. The -sTCP:LISTEN selects only files in a listening state. From the results, you can see that the SSH server is running, as well as the systemd-resolver and cups services.

If you switch -sTCP:LISTEN with -sTCP:ESTABLISHED, you will see active network connections:

```
(ubuntu)$ sudo lsof -nP -iTCP -sTCP:ESTABLISHED
COMMAND    PID  USER ... NODE NAME
sshd     15879  root ...  TCP 192.168.99.100:22->192.168.99.1:64220 (ESTABLISHED)
sshd     15905 brian ...  TCP 192.168.99.100:22->192.168.99.1:64220 (ESTABLISHED)
```

In this case, you see two listings for the open SSH connection. One represents the SSH server itself, running as root, and the other represents the established client connection.

Before you finish up, let's look at the ss command, which is the modern replacement for netstat. It's part of the iproute2 package on Linux systems.

To see listening TCP connections along with which user and process, execute ss with the -ltp switches:

```
(ubuntu)$ sudo ss -ltp
State   Recv-Q Send-Q  Local Address:Port    Peer Address:Port
LISTEN  0      5              127.0.1.1:domain           *:*
  users:(("systemd-resolve",pid=837,fd=5))
LISTEN  0      128                    *:ssh              *:*
  users:(("sshd",pid=15866,fd=3))
LISTEN  0      5              127.0.0.1:ipp              *:*
  users:(("cupsd",pid=7024,fd=11))
LISTEN  0      128                  :::ssh             :::*
  users:(("sshd",pid=15866,fd=4))
LISTEN  0      5                    ::1:ipp             :::*
  users:(("cupsd",pid=7024,fd=10))
```

The -l switch shows listening sockets, -t shows TCP only, and -p shows the associated process information.

Unfortunately, macOS doesn't support ss, so you'll have to stick with lsof.

These tools are essential for quickly identifying either open ports or ports that are already in use by a development server. They're also helpful to identify which ports you need to open in your firewall.

Let's look at another versatile tool you should get to know when working with networks.

Using Netcat

The netcat program, or nc, is the "Swiss Army Knife" of networking tools. With this one tool, you can connect to remote systems, transfer files, and even scan ports to see what connections are available.

Determining Open Ports

You can use nc to determine if certain services are running by scanning the ports associated with those services. This is great for troubleshooting your own servers, but you don't want to just go around scanning anyone's machines. It sends them traffic, and some systems might think you're trying to find security vulnerabilities to exploit. For those reasons, you should only scan ports on servers you control.

Still, if you're attempting to see if you can connect to a server from another machine, or looking to see what ports are listening for connections so you can close them to improve security, you'll find this useful.

For example, you can scan a domain name or IP address to see if a web server is listening for connections by scanning for port 80, the default port for web servers:

```
$ nc -z -v your_domain_or_ip 80
```

If a web server is running, you'll see this:

```
Connection to your_domain_or_ip 80 port [tcp/http] succeeded!
```

You can also scan ranges of ports. For example, to scan for all ports from 22 (SSH) to 80 (Web), you would execute this command:

```
$ nc -z -v your_domain_or_ip 22-80
```

This command takes an incredibly long time to run, as it scans every port sequentially, attempting to connect. Scanning ranges of ports is usually something you'd do on one of your own machines to see if some ports are open that shouldn't be. Once you know what's open, you can explore how to shut them down or block access to them using firewalls.

Making Web Requests

You already used cURL to grab web pages, but netcat can do that too. However, netcat makes you do it a little more interactively.

First, type this command:

```
$ nc www.google.com 80
```

You'll be greeted by a blank line; netcat is expecting some input. You're going to craft your own HTTP request by hand. Type the following two lines:

```
GET / HTTP/1.1
HOST: google.com
```

Then, press the ENTER key once more to send a blank line, and you'll see the response from the server, including the headers and source code for the Google home page stream out to your screen.

You can add more data to the request. For example, when you send a request to a web server, the browser identifies itself, and oftentime sends along the URL of the page the request came from, also known as the referer (which is actually spelled incorrectly, believe it or not.) You can use nc to specify those headers, or even make them up.

Try it out. Make a new request:

```
$ nc www.google.com 80
```

Then, type the following lines in, pressing ENTER after each line:

```
GET / HTTP/1.1
Host: google.com
User-Agent: Internet Explorer
Referer: awesomeco.com
```

Press the ENTER key twice to send the request.

This makes a request with your own crafted request headers, which let you pretend to use Internet Explorer for the request. Why would we do this? Sometimes web developers write code to prevent people from using certain browsers, so you can use the User-Agent header to pretend to be something you're not and bypass these kinds of restrictions. Of course, a more legitimate usage is to correctly identify the program you're using.

Serving Files with Netcat

You can use netcat to serve files if you combine it with a little bit of shell scripting. Create a file called hello.txt with some text:

```
$ echo "This is a text file served from netcat" > hello.txt
```

Now, execute this command to make netcat listen for connections on port 8000 and serve the hello.txt file:

```
$ while true; do nc -l 8000 < hello.txt; done
```

This loops indefinitely, listening for connections on port 8000, and then reads in the file, sending its contents to anything that connects. In another terminal, make a request with curl:

```
$ curl localhost:8000
This is a text file served from netcat
```

Return to the original terminal and press Ctrl+c to stop the loop.

You can use this approach to serve a web page. Create a web page named index.html with some text:

```
$ echo "<h1>Hi from netcat</h1>" > index.html
```

To make a browser render the HTML instead of just displaying the source, you'll have to craft a response the browser understands. Instead of just reading in a file, create an HTTP response. Send the text HTTP/1.1 200 OK, followed by two blank lines, followed by the contents of the file:

```
$ while true; \
> do echo -e "HTTP/1.1 200 OK\n\n $(cat index.html)" | \
> nc -l 8000; done
```

With this running, fire up a browser and go to http://localhost:8000 to see your page. This is just one more example of how diverse netcat is. But you're not quite done.

Realtime Chat with Netcat

You can use `nc` as an improvised chat system. This isn't entirely useful, but it's a fun exercise to explore, as it shows how netcat can send data in real time. On your Ubuntu machine, type the following:

```
(ubuntu)$ nc -l 1337
```

This starts a chat server listening on port 1337. You can connect to this server using another machine with `nc`, specifying the IP address of the chat server:

```
(local)$ nc 192.168.99.100 1337
```

At this point, you can type messages on either machine, and the other machine will display them. Pressing `Ctrl+c` breaks the connection for both machines.

You can use netcat for lots more, too. You can use it to send files or create secure internet connections. You've just scratched the surface of this tool. Its primary use is for ad-hoc network diagnostics, but it really is a networking multitool.

Security conscious folks should know that netcat does everything in an unsecured manner. Use this only on trusted networks.

Your Turn

These additional exercises will help you get more comfortable with the tools you used in this chapter.

1. Who is the administrative contact for the wordpress.com domain?

2. Which domain will need to be renewed first; heroku.com or google.com?

3. How many IP addresses are associated with heroku.com?

4. Who has more IP addresses associated with their domain: Facebook, Google, Twitter, Wikipedia, or Amazon?

5. Which of the following IP addresses belongs to a Comcast cable subscriber? Which one of these belongs to Google?

   - 4.2.2.1
   - 137.28.1.17
   - 24.23.51.253
   - 45.23.51.32
   - 8.8.8.8

6. Use traceroute on a few of your favorite websites. What similarities do you see between each? What differences do you see?

7. Use cURL to inspect the headers sent by the following sites.

    * http://twitter.com
    * http://pragprog.com
    * http://news.ycombinator.com
    * http://reddit.com
    * http://automattic.com

    If any sites redirect to a new site, use cURL to make an additional request using the location header.

8. Use netcat to connect to a few of your favorite websites or the sites in the previous question.

9. Use cURL with the Open Weather API[6] to find the weather forecast for your area. You'll need to register for an API key before you can access the API. What command did you end up using?

10. Explain the difference between these two commands:

    * scp -r data username@host:/data
    * scp -r data/* username@host:/data

    When would you use one over the other?

11. Identify all of the established connections on your local machine.

What You Learned

The tools you used in this chapter will become an essential part of your arsenal. You'll revisit a few of them later when you work with networks. You may need these tools to diagnose networking issues of your own, work with APIs, or transfer data between computers on your network.

Next, you will take the commands and concepts you have learned so far and use them to create scripts of commands that you can run over and over to automate tasks.

---

6. https://openweathermap.org/api

## CHAPTER 9

Automation

Throughout this book, you've used various command-line tools to accomplish tasks faster than you could with a GUI. But when you combine those commands with additional logic, you can create reusable workflows. This is the key to unlocking the command line's full potential and a great way to increase your productivity.

To create these workflows, you create scripts, which are lists of instructions or commands you want to run, in the order you want to run them. Every command you've used so far is something you can use in your own scripts. Whether you need to install multiple software packages, create complex file structures, merge a bunch of JavaScript files together, or compile and release software, you can write a script to make that happen.

You're going to work with two common approaches to creating workflows in this chapter. You'll start off working with make, a task-oriented workflow tool often used to compile software. make is a perfect tool for producing output from some input. Then, you'll turn your attention to writing shell scripts, which gives you more flexibility than make.

Automating Tasks with make

make is an automation tool aimed at creating builds for software. It's commonly used to compile and install software. Many times, package managers don't have the very latest version of a particular piece of software available, so the only way to install the most recent version is to download the source code and compile it yourself. The process usually involves downloading the source code archive, extracting it, switching to the directory containing the code, running a script called configure to set some variables based on your environment, and running make to compile the software. It usually looks something like this:

```
$ ./configure
$ make
$ sudo make install
```

make works by reading a file named Makefile and looking for tasks to run. You create these tasks by defining *rules* that tell make what commands to run to produce a desired result. Most of the time, you define rules by specifying files you want to create. These are called *targets*.

Here's an example of a rule. Can you tell what this does by looking at it?

automation/java/Makefile
```
%.class : %.java
        javac $<
```

This rule compiles a Java class from a source file. To run this, you'd type make Hello.class. make would then look for a file named Hello.java and compile it. The $< variable represents the input file.

Here's another example. See if you can figure out what it does before reading on:

automation/book/Makefile
```
book.md:
        cat chapter1.md chapter2.md chapter3.md chapter4.md > $@
```

This rule describes how to make a file named book.md by concatenating four Markdown files. The $@ variable references the name of the output file. To run it, you'd type make book.md.

You can use Makefiles to automate all sorts of tasks. To explore how Makefiles work, you'll create a very basic static site generator. You'll have files containing a generic header and a footer that you'll use on all of your pages. Then you'll have some files that contain just the content you want to use. Your Makefile will let you take the content and apply the template, creating a full HTML page. And for completeness, you'll add a rule that builds all of the pages for the site. The directory structure for the project will look like this:

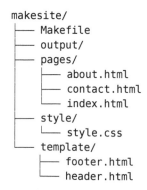

```
makesite/
├── Makefile
├── output/
├── pages/
│       ├── about.html
│       ├── contact.html
│       └── index.html
├── style/
│       └── style.css
└── template/
        ├── footer.html
        └── header.html
```

The pages folder will hold the content for each web page. The template folder will have a header and footer that prepends and appends to each page. You'll place the resulting pieces in the output folder. You'll also add today's date to the footer of all the pages.

First, create the directory structure:

```
$ mkdir -p makesite/{pages,template,style,output}
```

Change to the new makesite directory:

```
$ cd makesite
```

Now, create the template files and the pages, starting with the header template. Create the file template/header.html with the following contents:

```
$ nano template/header.html
```

Add a basic HTML header to the file:

automation/makesite/template/header.html
```
<!DOCTYPE html>
<html lang="en-US">
  <head>
    <meta charset="utf-8">
    <title>My website</title>
    <link rel="stylesheet" href="style/style.css">
  </head>
  <body>
```

Then create the file template/footer.html to define the footer. Use nano to create the file and open it for editing:

```
$ nano template/footer.html
```

Add the footer HTML to the file:

automation/makesite/template/footer.html
```
    <footer><p>@DATE@</p></footer>
  </body>
</html>
```

Save the file and quit nano.

With the templates in place, use nano to create and edit the file pages/index.html, which will hold the content for your site's main page:

```
$ nano pages/index.html
```

Add this content to the file:

automation/makesite/pages/index.html
```
<h1>Welcome</h1>

<p>
  Lorem ipsum dolor sit amet, consectetur adipisicing elit, sed do eiusmod
  tempor incididunt ut labore et dolore magna aliqua. Ut enim ad minim veniam,
  quis nostrud exercitation ullamco laboris nisi ut aliquip ex ea commodo
  consequat. Duis aute irure dolor in reprehenderit in voluptate velit esse
  cillum dolore eu fugiat nulla pariatur. Excepteur sint occaecat cupidatat non
  proident, sunt in culpa qui officia deserunt mollit anim id est laborum.
</p>
```

Save the file and exit nano.

Now make the "About" and "Contact" pages. To save time, use sed to create these files from the index page:

```
$ sed -e 's/Welcome/About Us/' pages/index.html > pages/about.html
$ sed -e 's/Welcome/Contact Us/' pages/index.html > pages/contact.html
```

All of the pieces are in place. Let's review the logic you're about to implement.

For each file in the pages directory, you'll:

- Grab the header and prepend it to the file.
- Grab the footer and append it to the file.
- Replace the date in the footer with today's date.

You'll start by making this work for a single file. After all, if you have many files, it might be nice to be able to generate a single file instead of having to rebuild the entire site every time you change content.

Create the Makefile in the root of the makesite folder:

```
$ nano makefile
```

Define variables at the top of the Makefile to hold the source folder and destination folder:

automation/makesite/Makefile
```
PAGES = pages
OUTPUT = output
```

When you use make to create a file, you specify the file you want to create, rather than the file you already have. So to create the file output/index.html, you'd execute the command make output/index.html. In the Makefile, create a target that gets its files from the pages folder, wraps the file with the header and footer, and places the result in the output folder:

```
automation/makesite/Makefile
$(OUTPUT)/%.html : $(PAGES)/%.html
        @echo "Creating $@ from $<"
        @mkdir -p $(dir $@)
        @cat template/header.html $< template/footer.html > $@.tmp
```

This rule creates the output folder if it doesn't already exist, using the dir function to extract the directory name from the specified path. It then uses the cat command to pull the files together. It saves the new file with a .tmp extension, since you're going to inject today's date next. The commands within this rule must be indented with tabs, not spaces, or it won't work.

Prefixing each command inside of the rule with the @ symbol prevents make from printing the command to the screen. You could leave that character off while you're creating your Makefiles so you can see the commands.

To inject today's date into the file, use sed to replace the @DATE@ markup in the template with today's date. Send the result to the destination filename and then delete the temporary file. Add these lines to the rule:

```
automation/makesite/Makefile
$(OUTPUT)/%.html : $(PAGES)/%.html
        @echo "Creating $@ from $<"
        @mkdir -p $(dir $@)
        @cat template/header.html $< template/footer.html > $@.tmp
➤       @sed s/@DATE@/"$(shell date "+%B %d, %Y")"/ $@.tmp > $@
➤       @rm $@.tmp
```

That's enough to generate the HTML page. Save the Makefile, exit nano, and give it a try:

```
$ make output/index.html
Creating output/index.html from pages/index.html
```

Try running the command again, though:

```
$ make output/index.html
make: `output/index.html' is up to date.
```

make doesn't modify files it doesn't think need to change. Since you didn't modify the source file, make doesn't bother updating it.

Now let's create a clean rule that removes all of the HTML files from the output folder. This is helpful for debugging purposes, and it's also something you'll find in a lot of Makefiles. Open up the Makefile in nano again:

```
$ nano makefile
```

Add this new clean rule which removes the generated files:

```
clean:
        @rm -rf $(OUTPUT)
```

Save the file and run make clean:

```
$ make clean
```

Now generate the index and about files. Chain multiple rules together by separating them with spaces, so you can generate both files at once like this:

```
$ make output/index.html output/about.html
Creating output/index.html from pages/index.html
Creating output/about.html from pages/about.html
```

If you want to regenerate these two files, prepend the clean rule:

```
$ make clean output/index.html output/about.html
Creating output/index.html from pages/index.html
Creating output/about.html from pages/about.html
```

You have three files right now, but if you added more pages, it might make sense to create a rule that only takes everything in the pages folder and runs the rule on each one, building the entire site.

Do this by using a wildcard pattern. Open Makefile in your editor.

After the definition for the OUTPUT variable, define a variable named SOURCE_FILES that looks for all of the files in pages. Use the built-in wildcard function to expand the wildcard into a list of individual filenames. Then define a variable named DEST_FILES that defines a target for each input file by using the built-in patsubst function to take the entries in the SOURCE_FILES list and prepend the output directory to each filename. You can then use that list of targets in a new rule called build:

```
PAGES = pages
OUTPUT = output

➤ SOURCE_FILES = $(wildcard $(PAGES)/*.html)
➤ DEST_FILES = $(patsubst $(PAGES)/%.html, $(OUTPUT)/%.html, $(SOURCE_FILES))
➤
➤ build: $(DEST_FILES)
```

Save the file and exit nano. Then run make build and watch as all of the HTML files are assembled:

```
$ make build
Creating output/contact.html from pages/contact.html
```

The build rule only generated one of the files since the others didn't change. But if you remove the output files and run it again, you will see it builds all three:

```
$ make clean build
Creating output/about.html from pages/about.html
Creating output/contact.html from pages/contact.html
Creating output/index.html from pages/index.html
```

You can use make to automate any build process that relies on command-line tools. You can copy files, create new files, remove files, and even add a rule that uploads files to a remote server using scp or rsync. However, some rules need more customization, and that's where you may want to write your own scripts from scratch.

Writing Bash Scripts

Throughout this book, you've worked with the Bash shell. You've used various commands and programs to work with files, directories, text, and even with data over a network.

A Bash script is a file that contains a list of commands you want the computer to execute. When you run the script, the commands will execute one at a time until all of the commands are run. You can use any command you'd normally type in your terminal, which means you can use everything you've learned about the command-line interface in a script. But Bash scripts support more than just commands. You can use variables, conditional statements, loops, and arrays. You can get input from files, pass command-line arguments in, or even prompt the user for input for a more interactive experience.

To explore these concepts further, you're going to create a script that generates the files and directories for a new website project. When you're done, you'll be able to issue a single command to bootstrap a new project.

But before you dive into the website creation program, you'll get comfortable with creating and running Bash scripts by writing the obligatory "Hello World" program.

Switch to your home directory and create a new file called hello_world.sh. The .sh extension isn't required, but it's handy when developing because text editors use it to enable syntax highlighting for shell scripting.

```
$ cd
$ nano hello_world.sh
```

Add the following statement to the file, which uses the echo command to print "Hello World!":

automation/bash/hello/hello.sh
```
echo "Hello World!"
```

When you run this script, it will execute the script's contents and print the result to the screen.

Rather than saving the file and quitting nano to run the script, press Ctrl+o to save the file. Then suspend nano to the background with Ctrl+z. This will let you jump right back into the file once you've tested it.

At the prompt, use the bash command to run the script:

```
$ bash hello.sh
Hello World!
```

Now modify the program's message so that when you run the program, it produces the following output:

```
Hello World!
This is my first Bash script!
```

To get that output, you'll use an additional echo statement. Bring nano back to the foreground:

```
$ fg
```

Then add the new statement to the file:

automation/bash/hello/hello.sh
```
  echo "Hello World!"
➤ echo "This is my first Bash script!"
```

Save the file, suspend nano, and run the script again:

```
$ bash hello.sh
Hello World!
This is my first Bash script!
```

Now let's make this an executable script so you don't have to run it with the bash command. You saw this a few times back in Chapter 6, The Shell and Environment, on page 125 when you made some quick scripts. Modify the script by adding this line at the top:

automation/bash/hello/hello.sh
```
➤ #!/usr/bin/env bash
  echo "Hello World!"
```

This line is called a "shebang." It's a comment that tells the operating system where to find the interpreter for this script. Save the changes to your script, suspend nano, and then use chmod to make the script executable:

```
$ chmod +x hello.sh
```

Now run the script. Remember, to run a script in the current directory, you have to prefix it with the characters ./, which makes it clear that you want to run the script that exists in the current directory.

```
$ ./hello.sh
Hello World!
This is my first Bash script!
```

That's a basic script. Let's dive deeper and build out that website generator. Use fg to bring nano to the foreground again and then exit the editor.

Automating File and Directory Creation

One of the best things about automation is that you can put in a little extra work up front and get a lot of reward out of that work down the road.

A typical website has a home page, at least one style sheet, a folder for images, and most likely, some JavaScript files. So let's use Bash to automate that. You'll have the script create a root directory for the web site, an index.html file, a scripts directory, an images directory, and a stylesheets directory. And you'll drop a style.css file in the stylesheets directory for good measure:

```
mysite
├── images
├── index.html
├── scripts
└── styles
    └── style.css
```

Using what you learned in Chapter 4, Working with Files and Directories, on page 55, you can probably write this script already. Your first approach might look like this:

```
mkdir -p mysite/{images,scripts,styles}
touch mysite/styles/style.css
cat << 'EOF' > mysite/index.html
<!DOCTYPE html>
<html lang="en-US">
  <head>
    <meta charset="utf-8">
    <title>My Website</title>
    <link rel="stylesheet" href="styles/style.css">
  </head>
  <body>
  </body>
</html>
EOF
```

That would work quite well, but you can make it even more flexible by using variables so you are not repeating website throughout the script. This will also make it easier to change the name of the directory later, which you will do shortly.

Create the file new_site.sh and make it executable:

```
$ touch new_site.sh
$ chmod +x new_site.sh
```

Now open the script with nano:

```
$ nano new_site.sh
```

Add the following content to the file:

automation/bash/website/new_site.sh
```
#!/usr/bin/env bash

set -e

directory="mysite"

mkdir -p ${directory}/{images,scripts,styles}
touch ${directory}/styles/style.css
cat << 'EOF' > ${directory}/index.html
<!DOCTYPE html>
<html lang="en-US">
  <head>
    <meta charset="utf-8">
    <title>My Website</title>
    <link rel="stylesheet" href="styles/style.css">
  </head>
  <body>
  </body>
</html>
EOF
```

The script starts with the shebang line, followed by set -e, which tells Bash that it should exit as soon as some statement fails. Without this option, Bash will attempt to run every command, even if previous ones errored out.

It then initializes a variable called directory with the name of the directory it's going to create to hold the files for the site. In this case, it's using a hardcoded value: mysite. It then uses the directory variable in the paths when it creates the directories and files. Remember that you have to prefix the variable name with the dollar sign. If you don't, Bash will use the literal word directory instead of the value the variable contains. And since we're mixing it with other characters in a string, it's best to use ${directory} here instead of $directory.

Save the file with Ctrl+o. Now test out the script. Suspend nano with Ctrl+z.

Once you're back at a prompt, run the script:

```
$ ./new_site.sh
```

You won't see any output from the script unless you've made a typo when creating the script. But you can verify that it worked by using the tree command to view the mysite directory:

```
$ tree mysite
mysite/
├── images
├── index.html
├── scripts
└── styles
    └── style.css

3 directories, 2 files
```

Bring nano back to the foreground so you can keep editing your script:

```
$ fg
```

The script works, but it's not very flexible. Let's customize the script further by having it prompt for the directory name.

Making an Interactive Script

Currently, the script uses the hardcoded value of mysite for the name of the new website. All of your websites won't have the same name, so you can make the script more flexible by having it prompt you for the directory you want to create.

Modify the variable declaration in your script so it uses the read command to prompt for the directory and assign the value for the directory variable. Then, wrap each use of ${directory} with double quotes so you can support situations where a user might enter a directory name with spaces.

automation/bash/website/new_site_interactive.sh
```
#!/usr/bin/env bash

set -e
➤ read -p "Enter the name of the directory to create: " directory
➤ mkdir -p "${directory}"/{images,scripts,styles}
➤ touch "${directory}"/styles/style.css
➤ cat << 'EOF' > "${directory}"/index.html
```

The read command displays the prompt and pauses the script's execution. The user can then type the directory they want to create. When they press the Enter key, the value gets stored in the directory variable and the script continues.

You might be wondering why we don't just wrap the whole line with double quotes like you've done in previous examples. The reason here is that the brace expansion on the mkdir line wouldn't work. You could use double quotes around the other lines without issue, but it's best to be consistent. We're using the double quotes so we support situations where the variable has spaces in its value, and we control the rest of the path.

Save the file again, and suspend nano with Ctrl+z. Then execute the script again. When prompted for a value, enter mysite2:

```
$ ./new_site.sh
Enter the name of the directory to create: mysite2
```

Verify the new structure was created:

```
$ tree mysite2
mysite2/
├── images
├── index.html
├── scripts
└── styles
    └── style.css

3 directories, 2 files
```

This works reasonably well, but you might run into problems if someone presses Enter without entering a name. If they did, the script would try to create files in the root of the filesystem, because $directory would be an empty string. That's probably not the behavior you want.

Let's add logic to the script that checks if they left the directory name blank. If they did, you'll stop processing the script.

In Creating Shortcuts with Aliases and Functions, on page 146, you wrote a function that used conditional logic to change how a function behaves. You can apply the same approach here by checking to see if the $directory variable is empty.

The expression [-z "$directory"] tests to see if the directory variable is empty. Bring nano back to the foreground with fg and add this code to evaluate the expression and exit the script if the user didn't enter anything:

```
automation/bash/website/new_site_interactive_check.sh
#!/usr/bin/env bash

set -e

read -p "Enter the name of the directory to create: " directory
➤  if [ -z "$directory" ]; then
➤    echo "You didn't enter anything. Exiting."
➤    exit 1
➤  fi
mkdir -p "${directory}"/{images,scripts,styles}
```

In addition to stopping the script, we return an exit code, which ensures that this script can play nice with other programs and commands. Those commands can check if this script executed with errors and respond appropriately.

Save the script, suspend nano, and run the script again. Press Enter when prompted for the directory:

```
$ ./new_site.sh
Enter the name of the directory to create:
You didn't enter anything. Exiting.
```

The current version of the script is friendly, but a lot of the power from the CLI comes from the fact that many commands aren't interactive, which means they can be automated easily. So let's modify this script so you can pass the directory name as an argument to the script. You'll modify the script to check if the script was called with any arguments. If it was, then you can assign the first argument to the directory variable instead of asking the user for it.

Bring nano to the foreground again and modify your script like this:

```
automation/bash/website/new_site_args.sh
#!/usr/bin/env bash

set -e

➤  if [ $# -eq 0 ]; then
    read -p "Enter the name of the directory to create: " directory

    if [ -z "$directory" ]; then
      echo "You didn't enter anything. Exiting."
      exit 1
    fi
➤  else
➤    directory=$1
➤  fi
mkdir -p "${directory}"/{images,scripts,styles}
```

The expression [$# -eq 0] checks that the number of arguments passed to the script is zero. If that's the case, the script executes the original behavior and asks for the name. And if they don't provide it, the script still bails out with an exit code. But if arguments were passed, the script takes the first argument ($1) and assigns it to the value of directory. The rest of the script stays the same.

Save the script. Suspend nano and run the script again with a directory name as the argument:

```
$ ./new_site.sh mysite3
```

The mysite3 directory is created without any interaction. Test that you can still create sites interactively and that your script still exits when someone doesn't enter a directory name. Once you're satisifed that things work as you expect, bring nano to the foreground and exit the editor.

This script becomes even more usable if you move it to /usr/local/bin so it's a system-wide tool:

```
$ sudo mv new_site.sh /usr/local/bin/new_site
```

Now you or any other user can run the new_site command anywhere on the filesystem.

With Bash scripts, you can take the commands you've used throughout this book and create complex workflows. Before you move on to the final chapter of the book, you'll write one more script that ties a few concepts together.

Automating Your Workstation Setup

Throughout this book, you've created a customized environment. You've installed some tools on your machine, created some directories, and wrote some configuration files. Once you get something just the way you like it, you might want to keep it that way. You can create a script that will set things up for you. That way, when you get a new machine, you can run your script and hit the ground running.

Let's create a script that does just that. You'll install the handful of utilities you've installed throughout the book and create a ~/.bashrc file with some basic options. To keep this exercise short, the script won't contain everything you've done, but it will contain enough that you'll be able to add everything else on your own. You'll start by creating a script to set up an Ubuntu environment, which you can test with the Ubuntu virtual machine you created. If you're on a Mac, follow along anyway because once you're done, you'll alter the script so that it works on macOS.

To build this script, you'll leverage many of the techniques you learned in this book, along with a few new ones. You'll use some conditional statements to check exit codes from commands, you'll install programs with the package manager, and you'll create files with cat. You'll also use variable expansion throughout the script, a small bit of command substitution, and use a for loop to iterate over a collection of packages.

Create a new file named ubuntu_setup.sh and make it executable:

```
$ touch ubuntu_setup.sh
$ chmod +x ubuntu_setup.sh
```

Now open the file with nano:

```
$ nano ubuntu_setup.sh
```

Start out your script with the shebang line and declare a variable that holds a datestamp you'll use as a suffix when creating backups of files. Then add a call to sudo which will cause the script to prompt for the sudo password right away:

automation/bash/setup/ubuntu_setup.sh
```
#!/usr/bin/env bash
datestamp=$(date +"%Y%m%d%H%M")

sudo -v
```

You're not using set -e this time because you're going to trap errors yourself.

The commands in this script will generate a lot of text output. Let's colorize information messages, error messages, and success messages so they'll stand out from the other text. Add this code to create variables to hold the color values:

automation/bash/setup/ubuntu_setup.sh
```
ERRORCOLOR=$(tput setaf 1)     # Red
SUCCESSCOLOR=$(tput setaf 2)   # Green
INFOCOLOR=$(tput setaf 3)      # Yellow
RESET=$(tput sgr0)
```

This is similar to how you defined the colors for your shell prompt in your .bashrc file, except this time you don't need to include square braces in the output, since these won't be used as part of the prompt. And just like with the prompt, include a variable named RESET so you can put the shell colors back to normal.

To use these colors, you'll print them out using variable expansion inside of echo statements. That'll get messy quickly, so define functions you can call instead to print info, success, and error messages:

automation/bash/setup/ubuntu_setup.sh
```
function info()    { echo "${INFOCOLOR}${@}${RESET}"; }
function success() { echo "${SUCCESSCOLOR}${@}${RESET}"; }
function error()   { echo "${ERRORCOLOR}${@}${RESET}" >&2; }
```

Each function prints the color code to the terminal, then prints all the arguments passed to the function (${@}), and then resets the terminal's text settings. The error function is slightly different though. It redirects the output to STDERR instead of to STDOUT, which is echo's default output.

Next, display a message that informs the user you're starting the script. Use the info function you just defined, and use command substitution with the date command to get the date to display:

automation/bash/setup/ubuntu_setup.sh
```
info "Starting install at $(date)"
```

Now add this code to the script which installs some of the software packages you used in this book.

automation/bash/setup/ubuntu_setup.sh
```
declare -a apps=(tree curl unzip make)

info "Updating Package list"
sudo apt-get update

info "Installing apps:"
for app in ${apps[@]}; do
  info "Installing ${app}"
  sudo apt-get -y install $app
  result=$?
  if [ $result -ne 0 ]; then
    error "Error: failed to install ${app}"
    exit 1
  else
    success "Installed ${app}"
  fi
done
```

First, you define a variable named apps which contains a list of apps you want to install. You then iterate over each entry in the list using a for loop, displaying the app's name and passing the app to the apt-get command to install it. The -y option tells apt-get to install the program without confirmation, which is perfect for a script.

Throughout the book, you've used apt install instead of apt-get install. The apt command is a newer, high-level user interface for installing packages interactively. It sets some default options for package installation and looks a little nicer. The apt-get command is the legacy command and is a good fit for scripts because it has a more stable user interface. In fact, if you use apt in a script, you'll see this warning:

```
WARNING: apt does not have a stable CLI interface. Use with caution in scripts.
```

You could install these packages without using the list of packages and the for loop, as the apt-get command supports supplying a list of packages to install all at once. But with this structure you have a little more control.

In Working with Web APIs, on page 211, you installed Node.js. Let's add that to this setup script as well. You'll use cURL to grab the installation script and execute it directly this time. This "pipe a script from the Internet to Bash" approach does pose a security risk, but you're going to roll with it here because you're trying to automate the process anyway, so downloading it and inspecting it like you did previously doesn't make sense here. You'll just have to trust that the servers holding the script haven't been compromised.

Add this code to the script:

```
automation/bash/setup/ubuntu_setup.sh
echo "Installing Node.js from Nodesource"
curl -sL https://deb.nodesource.com/setup_11.x | sudo -E bash -
sudo apt-get -y install nodejs
result=$?
if [ $result -ne 0 ]; then
  error "Error: Couldn't install Node.js."
  exit 1
else
  success "Installed Node.js"
fi
```

Once again, you check the exit status from the apt-get command and display an error message if it failed.

Now that the software is installed, let's create a ~/.bashrc file containing some of the settings you configured in Chapter 6, The Shell and Environment, on page 125. The code that follows won't have everything you did previously, but as you work through this, feel free to add more. Let's back up any existing ~/.bashrc file first. Add this code to check if one exists, if it does, back it up:

```
automation/bash/setup/ubuntu_setup.sh
info "Setting up ~/.bashrc"

if [ -f ~/.bashrc ]; then
  oldbashrc=~/.bashrc.${datestamp}
  info "Found existing ~/.bashrc file. Backing up to ${oldbashrc}."
  mv ~/.bashrc ${oldbashrc}
fi
```

To create the backup filename, use the datestamp variable that you defined at the top of the script as a suffix for the file. Notice that we are not using any quotes around the value we are creating. The tilde isn't expanded to the full path in a double-quoted string. It's stored as a literal character. If you used double quotes here, the command to move the script would fail because the destination path would be invalid. As an alternative, you could replace all occurrences of the tilde with ${HOME}. That value would be expanded in the double-quoted string.

Now use cat to create the new ~/.bashrc file and then check the status of the command:

```
automation/bash/setup/ubuntu_setup.sh
cat << 'EOF' > ~/.bashrc
[ -z "$PS1" ] && return

shopt -s histappend
HISTCONTROL=ignoreboth
HISTSIZE=1000
HISTFILESIZE=2000
HISTIGNORE="exit:clear"

export EDITOR=nano
export VISUAL=nano

export PATH=~/bin:$PATH
EOF

result=$?
if [ $result -ne 0 ]; then
  error "Error: failed to create ~/.bashrc"
  exit 1
else
  success "Created ~/.bashrc"
fi
```

By using single quotes around the EOF in the cat line, you ensure that the variables in the body of the heredoc aren't interpreted.

Finally, add a message at the end of the script that confirms things are finished and tells the user what to do next:

```
automation/bash/setup/ubuntu_setup.sh
success "Done! Run   source ~/.bashrc   to apply changes."
```

Save your file. To test it out, suspend nano (Ctrl+z). Then, at the prompt, run the script with ./ubuntu_setup.sh. It'll produce a lot of output, truncated here to save space:

```
$ ./ubuntu_setup.sh
Starting install at Sun Mar  3 03:01:55 IST 2019
Updating Package list
Hit:1 http://in.archive.ubuntu.com/ubuntu bionic InRelease
Get:2 http://security.ubuntu.com/ubuntu bionic-security InRelease [83.2 kB]
Hit:3 https://deb.nodesource.com/node_11.x bionic InRelease
...

Installed Node.js
Setting up bashrc
Found existing bashrc file. Backing up
to /home/brian/.bashrc.201903030301.
Created ~/.bashrc
Done! Run  source ~/.bashrc   to apply changes.
```

Your logging statements throughout the script display with color, and you can see the responses from the other commands as well.

If you want to run your script silently, redirect all output to a log file:

```
$ ./ubuntu_setup.sh > log.txt 2>&1
```

This won't capture the commands, but you can add set -x to the script and Bash will print all of the commands executed. Alternatively, use bash to execute the script and pass the -x option, like this:

```
$ bash -x ubuntu_setup.sh > log.txt 2>&1
```

The log now contain all executed commands.

Bash scripting offers so much more that you haven't covered yet. Bash has while loops you can use either in scripts or on the command line, which you saw an example of in Serving Files with Netcat, on page 227:

```
$ while true; do nc -l 8000 < hello.txt; done
```

And remember that you can take advantage of tools like sed, cut, or awk to manipulate input and output in your scripts. And instead of using cat to write your files, you could host your files online and use curl to pull them down directly. You can even host your script online, making it even easier to use on a new machine.

Unfortunately, this installation script only works on an Ubuntu system. But read on to find out how to make things work on macOS. It's not much different.

Making a Mac Version

If you're using a Mac, you may want a similar script. To make it, replace apt-get update with brew update, and apt-get install with brew install. Node.js is available through Homebrew, so add nodejs to the list of packages to install and remove the manual installation steps. And since macOS uses ./bash_profile instead of .bashrc, you'll want to make that change as well. Let's walk through it.

Copy the existing script and open it in your editor:

```
$ cp ubuntu_setup.sh mac_setup.sh
$ nano mac_setup.sh
```

Since Homebrew isn't installed by default on a Mac, let's add it as a step to the script:

automation/bash/setup/mac_setup.sh
```
info "Starting install at $(date)"

➤ info "Checking for Homebrew"
➤ if which -s brew; then
➤   info "Homebrew installed"
➤ else
➤   info "Installing Homebrew"
➤   /usr/bin/ruby -e \
➤   "$(curl -fsSL
➤        https://raw.githubusercontent.com/Homebrew/install/master/install)"
➤ fi
```

You first check for the existence of the brew command. which -s will silently look for the command, so you won't see output. Then you check the exit status and install Homebrew if it's not available. We'll use the method that Homebrew recommends,[1] which involves downloading a script from their site and sending it to the Ruby interpreter installed on macOS. Like the Node.js install for Ubuntu, we're trading security for the ability to automate the installation.

Next, modify the section where the script installs apps. Add nodejs to the list of packages and change the apt-get references to brew references.

automation/bash/setup/mac_setup.sh
```
➤ declare -a apps=(tree curl unzip make nodejs)

info "Updating Package list"
➤ brew update

info "Installing apps:"
for app in ${apps[@]}; do
  info "Installing ${app}"
➤  if brew list $app > /dev/null; then
➤    info "${app} is already installed"
➤  else
➤    brew install $app
```

---

1.   https://brew.sh

```
➤    fi
     result=$?
     if [ $result -ne 0 ]; then
       error "Error: failed to install ${app}"
       exit 1
     else
       success "Installed ${app}"
     fi
done
```

The apt-get command returned an exit status of 0 if the package was already installed, so a nonzero exit status would only happen if something else went wrong. Unfortunately, brew returns an exit status of 1 if the package is already installed, so you first check to see if the package is already available on the system using the brew list command. You can suppress its output since all you care about is its exit status. If the package is installed, you move on. If it's not, you install it.

You can completely remove the Node.js section from the script now that you've added the nodejs package to the list of packages in the previous step. Find this section and comment it out or remove it:

automation/bash/setup/mac_setup.sh
```
➤ # echo "Installing Node.js from Nodesource"
➤ # curl -sL https://deb.nodesource.com/setup_11.x | sudo -E bash -
➤ # sudo apt-get -y install nodejs
➤ # result=$?
➤ # if [ $result -ne 0 ]; then
➤ #   error "Error: Couldn't install Node.js."
➤ #   exit 1
➤ # else
➤ #   success "Installed Node.js"
➤ # fi
```

The rest of the script stays the same, except that macOS uses ~/.bash_profile by default, so you'll modify that file instead. Change the references for the backups and change the output of the cat command:

automation/bash/setup/mac_setup.sh
```
➤ info "Setting up ~/bash_profile"
➤
➤ if [ -f ~/.bash_profile ]; then
➤   oldprofile=~/.bash_profile.${datestamp}
➤   info "Found existing ~/.bash_profile file. Backing up to ${oldprofile}."
➤   mv ~/.bash_profile ${oldprofile}
➤ fi
➤
➤ cat << 'EOF' > ~/.bash_profile
```

Then change the check at the end of the file as well as the confirmation message:

automation/bash/setup/mac_setup.sh
```
result=$?
if [ $result -ne 0 ]; then
➤   error "Error: failed to create ~/.bash_profile"
    exit 1
else
➤   success "Created ~/.bash_profile"
fi

➤ success "Done! Run   source ~/.bash_profile   to apply changes."
```

You now have a script that lets you set up a Mac. Save the file, exit the editor, and run the script:

```
$ ./mac_setup.sh
Starting install at Sun Mar  3 20:13:31 CST 2019
Homebrew installed
Updating Package list
...
Done! Run   source ~/.bash_profile   to apply changes.
```

You can go further than this with macOS. You can manipulate a ton of macOS settings through the terminal. For example, if you always want to show hidden files in Finder, you can add this line:

```
defaults write com.apple.finder AppleShowAllFiles -bool YES
```

Since it's a change to Finder's settings, you'll have to restart Finder, which you can do with this line:

```
killall Finder
```

You can set a lot more options like this through a script, but you'll have to find them on your own as Apple doesn't maintain a master list. However, you can execute defaults read | less and read through its output for some clues.

Your Turn

These exercises will help you build on what you learned in this chapter. They'll help you improve your scripts, too.

1. Add a rule to your Makefile that uses scp or rsync to transfer the files to your web server.

2. Modify your website creation script to create a default CSS file with some basic styles.

3. Modify your website creation script to accept a value for the site's name and inject it into the <title> tag of the template.

4. Use the date command to embed a copyright date in the footer of the site's template.

5. Combine the Makefile with the website creation script so that each new site has a templates and pages directory, as well as the Makefile.

6. In your setup script, add code that looks for .bash_profile, backs it up, and replaces it with code that loads the .bashrc file. Use the same technique you learned in this chapter, and refer to Handling .bash_profile, on page 145, for an example of what the .bash_profile file should contain. If you're on a Mac, you can use this technique, too, instead of having the script write the ~/.bash_profile file.

7. In your setup script, include an .inputrc file as well.

8. Modify your setup script to install your configuration files into its own directory and create symlinks to the files instead of creating actual files.

9. Create an isMac function to determine if you're on macOS and use it along with your two existing scripts to create a single script for both Ubuntu and macOS. You can use the check ["$(uname)" == "Darwin"], which will return 0 if you're on a Mac and 1 if you aren't.

What You Learned

You worked with two approaches to automate tasks: Makefiles and Bash scripts. Makefiles are great for situations where you're creating output files. Scripts, on the other hand, offer more flexibility. In both cases, you're able to use all the command-line tools and techniques you've learned so far.

To make creating your scripts easier, use the contents of your Bash history as a starting point. You can dump your history to a file with history > script.sh and then use your editor to turn it into a script. Or you can use the script command to record a shell session and then convert the log to a script.

You're not limited to these choices. If you find Bash scripting too obtuse for your liking, you can use other languages to get the same results. Perl and Python are available on most systems out of the box and make great choices for creating scripts, as it's very easy to call out to external programs.

In the next chapter, you'll install and explore some additional tools that make it easier to manage files, manage environment variables, and much more. Then you can incorporate those into your scripts too.

## CHAPTER 10

Additional Programs

You've used a lot of general-purpose tools so far; you can manage files, manipulate streams of text, and communicate over the Internet all through the CLI. You've learned how much you can speed up your workflow using these kinds of tools, but that's just the beginning. In this chapter, you'll install some additional programs that will let you get even more done, leveraging the concepts you've already learned. You'll do some document conversion and file management, add a tool to make managing environment variables easier, and then work with web-based APIs from the command line.

Some of the tools in this chapter require that you have the Python interpreter installed, along with pip, Python's package manager. macOS has Python 2 installed by default, while Ubuntu 18.04 has Python 3 installed by default. You'll be using Python 3 in this chapter.

On Ubuntu, since Python 3 is already installed, install pip using the python3-pip package:

```
$ sudo apt install python3-pip
```

Programs you install with pip are stored in ~/.local/bin on Ubuntu, so modify your PATH to include that directory. Open your ~/.bashrc file in nano:

```
$ nano ~/.bashrc
```

Change the PATH variable so it includes ~/.local/bin before the other entries:

additional_programs/bashrc
```
export PATH=~/.local/bin:~/bin:$PATH
```

Save the file, exit the editor, and source the file to apply the new settings:

```
$ source ~/.bashrc
```

On macOS, install Python 3 using Homebrew, which also installs pip and ensures that programs installed with pip are added to your path:

```
$ brew install python3
```

With everything installed, it's time to play with some new CLI tools, starting with ones that make it easier to manage files and content.

Working with Text and Files

By now you're pretty comfortable creating and manipulating files and folders from the CLI. But with some additional tools, you can solve more complex problems while building on the skills you've already learned.

Managing Files with ranger

ranger is a terminal-based graphical file manager. While this book is all about working on the command line, ranger makes it easier to work with files in batches, and it also makes previewing files a breeze. To use it, you first need to install it. On Ubuntu, use apt:

```
$ sudo apt install ranger
```

On macOS, use brew:

```
$ brew install ranger
```

Then execute the following command to generate ranger's default configuration, which will be stored in ~/.config/ranger:

```
$ ranger --copy-config=all
```

After that, start ranger:

```
$ ranger
```

You will be greeted with a three-pane interface that looks like the first image on page 257.

The middle pane shows the current directory's files and directories. The left pane shows the contents of the parent directory, with the current directory highlighted. The right pane shows the contents of the item selected in the middle pane. If the item in the middle pane is a directory, the right pane shows the directory's contents. If it's a file, the right pane shows the file's contents.

Use the j key to move down one item in the middle pane. Use the k key to move up one folder. As you navigate through each directory or file, its contents automatically appear in the right pane. This makes ranger great for reviewing a directory full of code or documentation.

```
brian@puzzles /home/brian/Desktop
 brian          bin                     1   website
                Desktop                 2   greetings.txt
                dir1                    3
                dir2                    3
                Documents               0
                Downloads               0
                files                   6
                greeting_script         0
                Music                   0
                Pictures                0
                Public                  0
                secret_files            0
                sharptools              2
                Templates               0
                testdir                 0
                testsite                3
                testsite2               3
                Videos                  0
                website                 5
                brian_history.txt    8.74 K
                commands.txt         6.24 K
                commented_urls.txt     80 B
                contacts.txt           49 B
drwxr-xr-x 3 brian brian 2 2019-03-03 09:45              1.33M sum, 21.8G free  2/49  Top
```

To navigate into a directory, press l or your right arrow key. To navigate to
the parent directory, use h or your left arrow key. Each time you navigate,
the panes update to reflect where you are and what you see.

You already know how to navigate around your filesystem, but ranger makes
things a little easier if you have more complex operations you need to perform.
For example, pressing the g key displays a list of predefined destinations:

```
brian@puzzles /home/brian/Desktop                                              g
 brian          bin                     1   website
                Desktop                 2   greetings.txt
key             command
 L              cd -r %f
 l              cd -r .
 r              cd /
 /              cd /
 d              cd /dev
 e              cd /etc
 m              cd /media
 M              cd /mnt
 o              cd /opt
 s              cd /srv
 u              cd /usr
 ?              cd /usr/share/doc/ranger
 v              cd /var
 h              cd ~
 R              eval fm.cd(ranger.RANGERDIR)
 g              move to=0
 c              tab_close
 T              tab_move -1
 t              tab_move 1
 n              tab_new ~
drwxr-xr-x 3 brian brian 2 2019-03-03 09:45              1.33M sum, 21.8G free  2/49  Top
```

If you type `gv`, ranger switches to the /var directory. If you type `gh`, you'll end up back in your home directory.

You can use ranger to create new directories and files. Try it out. Use `gh` to go to your home directory. Then, type : to enter ranger's command mode. Type `mkdir testing`, press `Enter` and ranger displays the new directory.

Use the `j` key to navigate to the testing directory. Then, press `Enter` to switch to the directory. Create a new file by typing : to enter Command mode, and enter the command `touch test.txt`. Press `Enter` to create the file.

The new file appears in ranger. Press `Enter` on the file. If you have the VISUAL environment variable set to `nano`, the file opens in the `nano` text editor so you can modify it. If you don't have that variable set, ranger will ask you what text editor you'd like to use.

With the file open in `nano`, enter these lines into the file:

```
# This is a simple document.

There's nothing too special about it.
```

Save the file by pressing `Ctrl+x`, followed by `y` to confirm you want to save the file. `nano` displays the current filename, so press `Enter` to save the file and exit `nano`.

When you return to ranger, it displays the contents of the file you just saved in the right-hand pane:

Now let's take a look at how you can use ranger to copy and move files. In the testing directory, create a new directory named backup. Again, type : followed by mkdir backup.

Now, use ranger to copy the test.txt file into the backup folder. First, ensure the test.txt file is highlighted. Then, type yy which copies the text.txt file. Navigate into the backup folder and type pp. The text.txt file appears in the backup.txt folder.

Duplicate this file a few times by pressing pp. ranger will create copies of the file.

You should now have these four files:

```
test.txt
test.txt_
test.txt_0
test.txt_1
```

ranger lets you perform actions on multiple files if you mark them. Select the first file and press the Spacebar. Do the same for the other three files.

Rename these files. Press :, followed by the command bulkrename.

This launches nano again with the filenames in the editor window:

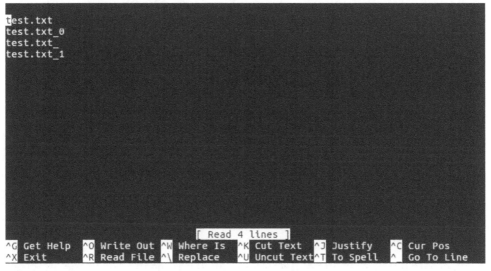

Modify the file so it looks like this:

```
one.txt
two.txt
three.txt
four.txt
```

Press Ctrl+x, followed by y to save the file. Accept the default filename by pressing Enter.

ranger determines the commands needed to rename the files and displays a script in nano for you to review:

```
# This file will be executed when you close the editor.
# Please double-check everything, clear the file to abort.
mv -vi -- test.txt one.txt
mv -vi -- test.txt_0 two.txt
mv -vi -- test.txt_ three.txt
mv -vi -- test.txt_1 four.txt
```

Press Ctrl+x to close nano. ranger renames the files and displays the new filenames.

```
brian@puzzles:/home/brian/testing/backup/two.txt
 backup      four.txt          69 B  # This is a simple document.
 test.txt    one.txt           69 B
             three.txt         69 B  There's nothing too special about it.
             two.txt           69 B
```

Move these files back to the testing directory. Mark each of these files again by selecting each file and pressing the Spacebar key. Now, press dd. Then, navigate back to the testing directory and press pp. The files move to the new location.

You can delete these files by marking them and using the :delete command.

ranger is a great way to work with files and directories in a more graphical way while still integrating with the command-line interface.

Managing Documents with pandoc

If you work with text-based documents, you'll find pandoc to be a lifesaver. pandoc can convert documents from one format to another. Let's use it to convert a Markdown document to HTML and back.

Install pandoc with your package manager:

```
$ sudo apt install pandoc
```

Now, create a new Markdown document called hello.md in your home directory with this content:

additional_programs/hello.md
```
# Welcome

This is a simple Markdown document.

It has a [link to Google](http://google.com) in it.
```

Use pandoc to convert this file to HTML:

```
$ pandoc -f markdown -t html -o hello.html hello.md
```

The -f and -t arguments specify the source and destination formats. You can think of this as "from Markdown to HTML." The -o argument specifies the output file.

pandoc converts the file. View it with the cat command:

```
$ cat hello.html
<h1 id="welcome">Welcome</h1>
<p>This is a simple Markdown document.</p>
<p>It has a <a href="http://google.com">link to Google</a> in it.</p>
```

You can go the other direction too. Create an HTML file called hello2.html with this content:

```
additional_programs/hello2.html
<h1>Testing</h1>
<p>This is an HTML document.</p>
<ul>
  <li>It has a list.</li>
  <li>With <a href="http://google.com">a link</a>.</li>
  <li>And some <em>emphasized</em> text!</li>
</ul>
<h2>And a subheading.</h2>
<p>And there's even some extra <span class="keyword">markup.</span></p>
```

Now, use pandoc to convert it. Use the -t markdown_mmd option this time to tell pandoc to use MultiMarkdown in the output:

```
$ pandoc -f html -t markdown_mmd -o hello2.md hello2.html
```

Look at the new hello2.md file:

```
$ cat hello2.md
Testing
=======

This is an HTML document.

-   It has a list.
-   With [a link](http://google.com).
-   And some *emphasized* text!

And a subheading.
-----------------

And there's even some extra <span class="keyword">markup.</span>
```

pandoc converted most of the HTML elements, but it left the inline markup alone. pandoc tries to make intelligent choices on how to handle the document. It is not always perfect, but it does keep showing improvement with each new version.

If you leave off the output filename, pandoc sends its output to STDOUT, which means you can pipe it to another program to transform it further. It also will take input from STDIN, meaning you can use it in the middle of a pipeline:

```
$ echo "# hello" | pandoc -t html | sed s/hello/Goodbye/g
<h1 id="Goodbye">Goodbye</h1>
```

Try it out. Using ls, awk, and pandoc, transform a directory listing into an HTML list:

```
$ ls -1 | awk '{print "* " $0};' | pandoc -t html
```

In this example, you use ls -1 to get a listing of files, one per line. You then use awk to print out the line with an asterisk in front of the filename, which creates a bulleted list in Markdown.

Then, you send the output to pandoc, transforming it into an HTML list.

pandoc can also convert documents to PDFs if you install the necessary components. That's something for you to look into on your own, though.

Running Tasks When Files Change

The entr command[1] can watch files for changes and execute any command you need. There are plenty of other utilities available, but entr is one of the most flexible options, and it requires no configuration to use.

Install entr using the package manager. On Ubuntu, run this:

```
$ sudo apt install entr
```

On macOS, run this:

```
$ brew install entr
```

entr takes a list of files from STDIN and executes the given command when the files change. Let's use entr to watch a Markdown document for changes and use pandoc to convert it to an HTML file.

---

1. http://entrproject.org/

First, create a Markdown document to watch called watchme.md:

additional_programs/watchme.md
```
# Hello world

This is a paragraph

## This is a a heading

This is [a link](http://google.com).

### This is a third heading
```

entr accepts a list of files as input. The easiest way to provide that input is to pipe the results of an ls command to entr. After that, you can tell entr what to do with those files. Execute the following command to tell entr to create the file watchme.html from the watchme.md file any time watchme.md changes:

```
$ ls watchme.md | entr pandoc -t html -f markdown -o watchme.html /_
```

The /_ at the end is a special entr argument that refers to the first file that changed. This way, you don't have to specify the watchme.md filename to pass it to pandoc.

The command runs the pandoc command immediately, creating the watchme.html output file. It then watches watchme.md for any changes.

This command takes over your terminal session until you stop it with Ctrl + c, which means you can't do anything else right now. Go ahead and stop it now so you can verify it did create the output file.

Back at the prompt, use the ls command to see if the watchme.html file exists:

```
$ ls -l watchme.html
-rw-r--r-- 1 brian brian 236 Mar  3 22:02 watchme.html
```

It's there, so view it with cat:

```
$ cat watchme.html
<h1 id="hello-world">Hello world</h1>
<p>This is a paragraph</p>
<h2 id="this-is-a-a-heading">This is a a heading</h2>
<p>This is <a href="http://google.com">a link</a>.</p>
<h3 id="this-is-a-third-heading">This is a third heading</h3>
```

Now, start up entr again so it's watching the file for changes. To keep it from taking over your terminal, run it as a background task in a subshell:

```
$ (ls watchme.md | entr pandoc -t html -f markdown -o watchme.html /_ &)
```

With entr running in the background, add a blank line and a new paragraph to the watchme.md with echo. Use the -e flag so echo interprets newline characters:

```
$ echo -e "\nThis is a new paragraph." >> watchme.md
```

This change triggers entr to regenerate the watchme.html file. Use cat to view the watchme.html file. It now has a new paragraph at the end:

```
$ cat watchme.html
<h1 id="hello-world">Hello world</h1>
<p>This is a paragraph</p>
<h2 id="this-is-a-a-heading">This is a a heading</h2>
<p>This is <a href="http://google.com">a link</a>.</p>
<h3 id="this-is-a-third-heading">This is a third heading</h3>
<p>This is a new paragraph.</p>
```

entr will continue to watch this file for changes until you stop it. Locate the entr process and send it a SIGINT signal, which is equivalent to pressing Ctrl+c. You can use ps -ef | grep entr to find the process, and kill -SIGINT followed by the process ID, or you can use pkill if your system supports it:

```
$ pkill -SIGINT entr
```

If managing entr as a background process like this seems more complicated, you can always use multiple terminal sessions, or leverage screen like you did in Keeping Commands Running with GNU Screen, on page 193.

You can use entr to transform documents, reload your web browser when files change, watch entire directories, or even relaunch a process. Use the man page for entr to learn more.

Next, you'll explore tools you can use to manage environment variables, manage processes, and move around your environment faster.

Managing Your Environment

You've used environment variables to store data, managed processes, and created your own shortcuts to make your environment more personal, but there are a few additional tools you can use to go to the next level.

Using direnv to Manage Environment Variables

If your experiences with software development are anything like mine, you're probably juggling a few different API keys for things. Perhaps your application uses a token to keep cookies secure or an API token for managing cloud servers. Many apps push developers to place these tokens in environment variables, but this can clog up your .bashrc files.

The direnv program lets you keep environment variables with your project. When you enter the directory, direnv sets the environment variables you need. When you leave the directory, those variables are removed.

Install direnv with the package manager. On Ubuntu, use this command:

```
$ sudo apt install direnv
```

On macOS, use the following:

```
$ brew install direnv
```

This installs direnv, but you also need to activate it by adding some code to your .bashrc file:

```
$ echo 'eval "$(direnv hook bash)"' >> .bashrc
```

If you want to handle situations where direnv isn't installed, you could instead add this section to your file, which tests if direnv is installed and activates it:

additional_programs/bashrc
```
if hash direnv 2>/dev/null; then
  eval "$(direnv hook bash)"
fi
```

Apply the changes to your environment:

```
$ source ~/.bashrc
```

direnv works by looking for a file named .envrc in your current working directory. If it finds it, it loads the file. For safety and security reasons, it won't do it the first time without asking you.

Try it out. Create a new directory named project and create the file .envrc in that directory. Add an export statement to that file to set a SHIELD_PASSWORD environment variable:

```
$ mkdir project
$ cd project/
$ echo 'export SHIELD_PASSWORD=12345' > .envrc
direnv: error .envrc is blocked. Run `direnv allow` to approve its content.
```

When you create the file, direnv notices and says it's blocked. It needs your permission to load it. Run direnv allow and it'll load the file:

```
$ direnv allow
direnv: loading .envrc
direnv: export +SHIELD_PASSWORD
```

Print out the value with echo:

```
$ echo $SHIELD_PASSWORD
12345
```

Now, leave the directory and print the value again. It'll be gone:

```
$ cd ..
direnv: unloading
$ echo $SHIELD_PASSWORD
```

Switch back to the directory again and your value is reloaded:

```
$ cd -
/home/brian/project
direnv: loading .envrc
direnv: export +SHIELD_PASSWORD
```

```
$ echo $SHIELD_PASSWORD
12345
```

If you change the file, direnv alerts you again. Add a new value to the file:

```
$ echo 'export LUGGAGE_COMBO=12345' > .envrc
direnv: error .envrc is blocked. Run `direnv allow` to approve its content.
```

Run direnv allow again to load the changes:

```
$ direnv allow
direnv: loading .envrc
direnv: export +LUGGAGE_COMBO
```

Whenever direnv notices something's different in your file, it lets you know. If you see this warning and you didn't make a change, you should open up .envrc and find out what changed.

One final note: if you're going to use direnv to store sensitive information, be sure to tell your version control software to ignore the .envrc file so you don't accidentally check it in to version control. If you're using Git, add .envrc to your project's .gitignore file.

Monitor and Manage Resources with htop

The top command gives you a basic overview of your system, but it's limited to just displaying data. The htop program lets you see more detailed information, but also lets you filter the process list and even stop processes that may have gotten out of control.

Install htop on Ubuntu with apt:

```
$ sudo apt install htop
```

And on macOS, install it with brew:

```
$ brew install htop
```

Then, launch htop:

```
$ htop
```

The htop interface appears, which looks like this:

The interface shows graphs for memory and CPU usage and shows a list of processes.

Press u to see a list of users. Select your user to see only the processes owned by your user.

You can also search for a process by pressing `F3`. You can then type the name of the process to highlight it. Pressing `Enter` selects the process. From here, you can send signals to the process by pressing `k`, or press `F9` to kill the selected process.

htop gives you a lightweight control panel for working with the processes on your machine, and it can come in handy if your graphical process manager isn't responding.

Autocompleting Files, Directories, Processes, and More with fzf

Navigating a more complex filesystem, like a codebase, can be challenging, even with tab completion. fzf is a tool that lets you navigate your filesystem, history, and even processes by searching for partial words. It's a *fuzzy finder* for your shell.

On macOS, you can install it with Homebrew.

```
$ brew install fzf
```

Once installed, run the following command to install scripts that enable default keybindings:

```
$ /usr/local/opt/fzf/install
```

Unfortunately, fzf isn't available through Ubuntu's package manager. To install fzf on Ubuntu, you'll grab its source code from Github[2] and run an installer script. The easiest way to do this is to install Git on your Ubuntu machine and use it to clone the source code repository. Git isn't covered in this book; you're just going to use it to fetch the fzf program.

First, use apt to install the git package:

```
$ sudo apt install git
```

Next, use git to download fzf to the ~/.fzf directory:

```
$ git clone --depth 1 https://github.com/junegunn/fzf.git ~/.fzf
Cloning into '/home/brian/.fzf'...
remote: Enumerating objects: 95, done.
remote: Counting objects: 100% (95/95), done.
remote: Compressing objects: 100% (88/88), done.
remote: Total 95 (delta 4), reused 22 (delta 2), pack-reused 0
Unpacking objects: 100% (95/95), done.
```

When you use git clone, you download the current version of the files along with all previous versions. The --depth 1 option tells Git to only grab the current version.

---

2. https://github.com/junegunn/fzf

Now run the installer:

```
$ ~/.fzf/install
```

When asked if you want to enable fuzzy autocompletion, press `y` and press `Enter`. Do the same when asked if you want to enable keybindings, and again when asked to update your shell configuration files.

Time to start using this tool. First, reload your shell configuration files to activate the keybindings and shortcuts fzf installed for you:

```
$ source ~/.bashrc
```

In Creating Directories, on page 65, you created this directory structure:

```
files
├── code
│   ├── elm
│   ├── go
│   └── js
├── docs
│   ├── diagrams
│   └── markdown
├── movies
├── music
└── photos
```

If you've deleted it, create it again with this command:

```
$ mkdir -p files/{movies,music,photos,docs/{diagrams,markdown},code/{go,js,elm}}
```

Now, use fzf to navigate to the files/code/elm directory. Press `Alt+c`. This brings up a menu for changing directories:

```
$ `__fzf_cd__`
>
  42/42
> Templates
  Downloads
  Desktop
  Public
  Videos
...
```

Type elm at the prompt, and the result shrinks:

```
$ `__fzf_cd__`
> elm
  1/42
> files/code/elm
```

The path files/code/elm fills in. Press Enter and the current working directory changes.

Switch back to your home directory:

```
$ cd
```

Let's use fzf to copy files/code/elm to ~/elm.

Type cp -r, followed by a space, followed by Ctrl+t. The fzf menu appears. Type elm into the box:

```
> elm
  11/104
> files/code/elm
...
```

Press Enter on the path and the path fills in. You can then type the rest of the copy command:

```
$ cp -r files/code/elm ~/elm
```

You can use fzf in conjunction with commands like cat, cd, and more. The sequence **, followed by the Tab key will use fzf instead of the normal tab-completion behavior you're used to. Try it out by using cat to display the ~/.inputrc file:

```
$ cat **<Tab>
```

The fzf menu appears, displaying several files:

```
>
  724/724
> .
  .inputrc
  Templates
  test.html
  Downloads
  ...
```

Select .inputrc from the list by using the arrow keys and press Enter to add the file to the line. If you don't see it, type a few characters of the filename, and ensure you're in your home directory. fzf can only look in the current directory and subdirectories; it's not able to look at parent directories.

Not every command works with this out of the box. For example, if you try this with nano instead of cat, you'll get the default tab completion. fzf has a built-in list of commands it supports, but you can add others.

Open your ~/.bashrc file and add this command after the existing fzf line:

```
additional_programs/bashrc
[ -f ~/.fzf.bash ] && source ~/.fzf.bash
➤ # Add additional completion commands
➤ complete -F _fzf_path_completion -o default -o bashdefault nano
```

Save the file, source it with source ~/.bashrc to apply the changes, and try using nano to open a file using fzf:

```
$ nano **<Tab>
>
  724/724
> .
  .inputrc
  bhcldev-code.zip
  Templates
  test.html
  Downloads
  ...
```

The keybindings you installed with fzf remapped Ctrl+r, so you can use this same interface to search through your command history. Give it a try and you'll see something like this:

```
$ `__fzf_history__`
  410  sudo apt update
  411  git
  412  sudo apt install git
  413  git clone --depth 1 https://github.com/junegunn/fzf.git ~/.fzf
  414  ~/.fzf/install
  415  mkdir -p files/{movies,music,photos,docs/{diagrams,markdown}....
  416  source ~/.bashrc
> 417  cd files/code/elm
```

Type source at the prompt, and watch as the results filter down. You can use the Up and Down arrows to select entries in the list as well, or press Esc to cancel.

Finally, you can use fzf to locate processes and kill them. Launch the responder program located in the book's code download:

```
$ ~/sharptools/code/responder/linux/responder start &
[1] 3155
```

Type kill -9, followed by a space, then press Tab. fzf displays a list of processes:

```
>
  231/231
> root        1     0  0 00:49 ?        00:00:00 /sbin/init splash
  root        2     0  0 00:49 ?        00:00:00 [kthreadd]
  root        3     2  0 00:49 ?        00:00:00 [kworker/0:0]
  ...
```

Use this to locate responder. When you find it, press Enter and the process ID is entered on the line.

```
$ kill -9 3155
```

Verify it's been killed with jobs:

```
$ jobs
[1]+  Killed                  ~/code/running_commands/responder/linux/responder start
```

fzf gives you an incredible amount of power in a lightweight tool.

Serving a Directory with Python

If you have a directory full of files and you want to serve them over the network, you don't have to install and configure a web server if you already have Python installed. Python has a built-in web server module you can invoke directly from the command line. This is great for testing a single-page application locally or sharing some files with others quickly.

Try it out. Create a new directory named pythonsite and switch to it:

```
$ mkdir pythonsite
$ cd pythonsite
```

Then, create an HTML page named index.html:

```
$ cat << 'EOF' > index.html
> <h1>My Website</h1>
> <p>This is served from Python!</p>
> EOF
```

With the file in place, you can start the web server:

```
$ python3 -m http.server
```

This starts a web server running on port 8000. Open your browser and visit http://localbost:8000, and you'll see your file.

The terminal displays the web request:

```
Serving HTTP on 0.0.0.0 port 8000 (http://0.0.0.0:8000/) ...
127.0.0.1 - - [03/Mar/2019 22:10:07] "GET / HTTP/1.1" 200 -
127.0.0.1 - - [03/Mar/2019 22:10:07] code 404, message File not found
127.0.0.1 - - [03/Mar/2019 22:10:07] "GET /favicon.ico HTTP/1.1" 404 -
```

This server is listening on all interfaces by default, which means you can provide your IP address to others and they can access your server, provided you've allowed traffic through any firewalls.

Stop the server with Ctrl+c. Return to your home directory before moving on.

Viewing Colored Source Code with Pygments

Commands like cat and less are great for viewing the contents of a file, but when you're looking at code, syntax coloring makes things easier to see. This comes in handy especially when previewing a diff file before applying it.

The Pygments library for Python can scan code and produce colored output. When you install it globally, you'll get a pygmentize command that can print a file to your screen with color.

Install Pygments using the pip3 command:

```
$ pip3 install Pygments
```

Once installed, use it to read a file. Create the following Ruby file named person.rb in your current directory:

additional_programs/person.rb
```ruby
class Person

  attr_accessor :first_name, :last_name

  def initialize(first_name, last_name)
    @first_name = first_name
    @last_name = last_name
  end

  def full_name
    "#{self.first_name} #{self.last_name}"
  end

end
```

Then, use pygmentize to view the file in color.

```
$ pygmentize -g person.rb
```

The output displays on the screen. If the default is too difficult to see, you can use a different color scheme. Use pygmentize -L styles to list the color schemes. Test each one with the -O switch to find the one you like. The native scheme is a nice choice:

```
$ pygmentize -O style=native -g person.rb
```

If your terminal can support 256 colors, you can make things look even nicer:

```
$ pygmentize -O style=native -g -f terminal256 person.rb
```

Since that command is a lot to type, make a shell alias for it. Add this to your .bashrc file:

additional_programs/bashrc
```
alias colorize="pygmentize -O style=native -g -f terminal256"
```

Remember to reload your shell settings with source ~/.bashrc.

If you have a larger file you want to view, you can pipe the output to less, but you have to use the -R option so that the less command interprets the colors:

```
$ pygmentize -O style=native -g -f terminal256 person.rb | less -R
```

Or, with your alias, use this:

```
$ colorize person.rb | less -R
```

This lets you use all of less's features to navigate through the code, including its search feature.

Keeping a Log with jrnl

Keeping a log of what you worked on throughout the day will help you identify where you're spending your time and help you see your accomplishments. If you make this a habit, you can use it as a reference when your boss inevitably asks you what you worked on all quarter. In addition, taking some time to reflect on the work you've done at the end of your day can help you collect your thoughts and prepare for the future. jrnl[3] lets you keep a journal of your thoughts right from your terminal and lets you query your entries for search terms and tags.

jrnl is written in Python. On Ubuntu, install it with pip:

```
$ pip3 install jrnl
```

If you want to be able to create encrypted journals, install jrnl like this:

```
$ pip3 install --upgrade keyrings.alt
$ pip3 install jrnl[encrypted]
```

The first command ensures that the keyrings.alt library is up to date. The second installs jrnl with support for encryption.

On macOS, you should install jrnl with Homebrew instead. This method installs encrypted journal support too:

```
$ brew install jrnl
```

Now that jrnl is installed, you can create your first journal entry. Create an entry like this:

```
$ jrnl Set up my first journal
```

---

3.   http://jrnl.sh/

Since this is the first journal entry, jrnl asks you where you'd like to save your journal and if you want to encrypt its contents:

```
Path to your journal file (leave blank for ~/journal.txt):
```

```
Enter password for journal (leave blank for no encryption):
[Journal created at /home/brian/journal.txt]
[Entry added to default journal]
```

Make another journal entry with some more context:

```
$ jrnl This is a short title. This is a note that goes with the journal entry.
```

This creates a note with a short title, followed by some additional notes. jrnl uses sentence-ending punctuation to separate the journal entry from its notes.

Now, view the journal contents for today:

```
$ jrnl -on today
2019-03-03 22:04 Set up my first journal

2019-03-03 22:04 This is a short title.
| This is a note that goes with the journal entry.
```

To make modifications to these entries, pass the --edit flag, which opens the journal entries in your text editor. Once you save the changes and exit, the entries update.

If you forgot about a meeting earlier in the week, you can still add an entry for it:

```
$ jrnl last monday at 9am: Meeting with the team.
```

To view it, tell jrnl to show you the entries for last Monday:

```
$ jrnl -on "last monday"
2019-02-18 09:00 Meeting with the team.
```

Or view the entries from the beginning of your journal to today using -until:

```
$ jrnl -until today
2019-02-18 09:00 Meeting with the team.

2019-03-03 22:04 Set up my first journal

2019-03-03 22:04 This is a short title.
| This is a note that goes with the journal entry.
```

In addition, you can use tags to organize your entries so you can find them faster. Just add the @ symbol to a word in your journal entry:

```
$ jrnl last Tuesday at 4pm: Deployed the @awesomeco app to production.
```

Then, look for any entries with that tag:

```
$ jrnl -until today @awesomeco
2019-02-19 16:00 Deployed the @awesomeco app to production.
```

Or count the tags:

```
$ jrnl --tags @awesomeco
@awesomeco          : 1
```

Finally, you can customize jrnl by editing the file ~/.jrnl_config and modifying the settings. You can even configure it to have multiple journals, like a default journal for work and another one for a diary of your personal thoughts:

```
{
  "default_hour": 9,
  "linewrap": 79,
  "encrypt": false,
  "default_minute": 0,
  "tagsymbols": "@",
  "editor": "nano",
  "timeformat": "%Y-%m-%d %H:%M",
  "highlight": true,
  "journals": {
    "default": "~/Dropbox/journal/work.txt",
    "diary": "~/Dropbox/journal/diary.txt"
  }
}
```

That's just the beginning. You can perform more complex searches, export your journal, and even star items you want to find more quickly.

jrnl reduces the friction in creating a journal of your thoughts that's portable and searchable. Make using it a habit, and three months from now you'll be glad you did.

Next, you'll look at a few tools that make working with external APIs easier.

Working with Data and External APIs

If you develop web-based APIs, or just consume them, there are several tools that can make your life a little easier. The jq command is a command-line utility for parsing JSON responses. The HTTPie program makes reading results easier, and the Siege program lets you test how responsive your APIs are.

In Working with Web APIs, on page 211, you used json-server[4] as a fake web API. You'll use that in this section, too, along with the data.json file you created in that section. If you don't have the file handy, create it again:

```
$ cat << 'EOF' > ~/data.json
> {
>   "notes": [
>     { "id": 1, "title": "Hello" }
>   ]
> }
> EOF
```

Then start up json-server with npx and tell it to watch the data.json file:

```
$ npx json-server -w ~/data.json
```

After the server starts, open a new terminal window and use curl to add some new notes:

```
$ curl -X POST http://localhost:3000/notes \
> -H 'Content-type: application/json' \
> -d '{"title": "This is another note."}'

$ curl -X POST http://localhost:3000/notes \
> -H 'Content-type: application/json' \
> -d '{"title": "This is a third note."}'
```

Now, access http://localhost:3000/notes and verify that you see all three notes:

```
$ curl http://localhost:3000/notes
[
  {
    "id": 1,
    "title": "Hello"
  },
  {
    "title": "This is another note.",
    "id": 2
  },
  {
    "title": "This is a third note.",
    "id": 3
  }
]
```

With the server running and displaying data, let's look at some tools for accessing it.

---

4. https://github.com/typicode/json-server

Manipulating JSON with jq

The jq command-line program lets you format and manipulate JSON data. It's perfect when exploring APIs from the command line. You provide jq some JSON to process and a filter to apply. It transforms the JSON and displays the results.

Install jq from the package manager. On Ubuntu, use apt:

```
$ sudo apt install jq
```

On macOS, use brew:

```
$ brew install jq
```

One of the most common uses is to "pretty-print" JSON results from curl. When you execute curl http://localhost:3000/notes, the results are already nicely formatted. But not every API returns formatted results.

Open Notify[5] has several free APIs you can query to find information about the International Space Station. If you use curl to request data from this endpoint, which displays the current location of the ISS, the output might not be very readable:

```
$ curl http://api.open-notify.org/iss-now.json
{"timestamp": 1556777805, "iss_position": {"latitude": "29.0539",
"longitude": "-58.5050"}, "message": "success"}
```

But jq can format the output. Take the output from curl and pipe it to the jq command, applying the "dot" filter, which doesn't do any processing:

```
$ curl http://api.open-notify.org/iss-now.json | jq '.'
...
{
  "timestamp": 1556777874,
  "iss_position": {
    "latitude": "32.1566",
    "longitude": "-55.0392"
  },
  "message": "success"
}
```

That by itself is incredibly helpful, but it's not very nice to repeatedly hit an external API when you're testing something. You should make a local cache of this data if you want to play with it more. When you make that local cache, you can format the text too. If you combine the previous command with output redirection, you can save this nicely formatted output to a local file:

---

5.   http://open-notify.org/

```
$ curl http://api.open-notify.org/iss-now.json | jq '.' > space.json
```

Now you can use space.json locally instead of pounding on someone else's API:

```
$ cat space.json
{
  "timestamp": 1556777915,
  "iss_position": {
    "latitude": "33.9239",
    "longitude": "-52.8864"
  },
  "message": "success"
}
```

Let's go back to your JSON API of notes to explore a few other features. First, you might have noticed that when you fetch data from the JSON API, the first record has the id field first, followed by the title field, but the other records have the title field first, like this:

```
$ curl http://localhost:3000/notes
[
  {
    "id": 1,
    "title": "Hello"
  },
  {
    "title": "This is another note.",
    "id": 2
  },
  ...
```

If you use the -S argument, jq will sort the fields in the output, which puts each record's fields in the same order:

```
$ curl localhost:3000/notes | jq -S '.'
[
  {
    "id": 1,
    "title": "Hello"
  },
  {
    "id": 2,
    "title": "This is another note."
  },
  {
    "id": 3,
    "title": "This is a third note."
  }
]
```

This is a handy way of cleaning up output.

You can use jq to extract little bits of data from the API. To display just the first note, use the filter .[0], like this:

```
$ curl localhost:3000/notes | jq '.[0]'
{
  "id": 1,
  "title": "Hello"
}
```

Constantly using curl to re-fetch this data is getting a little repetitive—and like with the Open Notify API, it's not a great practice to keep hitting an API unless you are looking for changes. Save the notes data to a local file:

```
$ curl localhost:3000/notes > notes.json
```

To use jq with a local file, pass the file as the last argument, after you specify the filter. Test it out by retrieving the first note from the data.json file:

```
$ jq '.[0]' notes.json
{
  "id": 1,
  "title": "Hello"
}
```

Many times you're not interested in all of the data in a record. You can use jq to filter out fields as well as records.

Execute this command to tell jq to return all of the results, but only show the title:

```
$ jq '.[] | {title: .title}' notes.json
{
  "title": "Hello"
}
{
  "title": "This is another note."
}
{
  "title": "This is a third note."
}
```

Here, you're telling jq to grab all of the records, then you're piping the results to another filter which runs on each record.

With this filter, you're not just specifying what you want, you're specifying that you want it to have the label title. But you can change that. Use this filter to get all of the note titles, but change the label for each title from title to Name:

```
$ jq '.[] | {Name: .title}' notes.json
{
  "Name": "Hello"
}
{
  "Name": "This is another note."
}
{
  "Name": "This is a third note."
}
```

This is handy if you need to take data from one source and merge it into another with different keys.

And if you just want the values of the fields, you can extract those:

```
$ jq '.[] | .title' notes.json
"Hello"
"This is another note."
"This is a third note."
```

The output has quotes around each entry, as jq has preserved it as JSON strings. But if you use the -r switch, jq prints out raw output instead:

```
$ jq -r '.[] | .title' notes.json
Hello
This is another note.
This is a third note.
```

The filter .[] | .title is taking every row and extracting the title. If you provide a specific index, you can extract a single row. Grab the second note's title from the file:

```
$ jq -r '.[1] | .title' notes.json
This is another note.
```

Remember, the indexes are zero-based.

This is a small example of what you can do with jq. You have a data.json file and a space.json file. Try to use jq to transform and manipulate the data in these files. Then, try it out with other JSON data sources.

Inspecting Requests with HTTPie

curl is a fine multipurpose tool for interacting with web APIs. But it's a little cumbersome if you're going to do it a lot. HTTPie is an alternative that makes working with web requests a little easier.

Install it through the package manager. On Ubuntu, use apt:

```
$ sudo apt install httpie
```

And on macOS, use brew:

```
$ brew install httpie
```

HTTPie supports downloading files, submitting forms, and even interacting with web apps that use sessions. But it really shines when making API requests.

Use it to get the list of notes from the API:

```
$ http localhost:3000/notes
HTTP/1.1 200 OK
Access-Control-Allow-Credentials: true
Cache-Control: no-cache
Connection: keep-alive
Content-Length: 163
Content-Type: application/json; charset=utf-8
Date: Mon, 04 Mar 2019 04:21:25 GMT
ETag: W/"a3-/ia+coieeQEhK+/GBIyl5YP/4Ns"
Expires: -1
Pragma: no-cache
Vary: Origin, Accept-Encoding
X-Content-Type-Options: nosniff
X-Powered-By: Express

[
    {
        "id": 1,
        "title": "Hello"
    },
    {
        "id": 2,
        "title": "This is another note."
    },
    {
        "id": 3,
        "title": "This is a third note."
    }
]
```

By default, HTTPie shows the headers and the response all at once. The command itself looks almost like what you'd type in a web browser.

If you only want to see the body, use the -b switch:

```
$ http -b localhost:3000/notes
```

Let's add a fourth note. Here's what the command would look like if you used curl to do that. Don't run this yet though:

```
$ curl -X POST http://localhost:3000/notes \
> -H "Content-type: application/json" \
> -d '{"title": "This is a fourth note."}'
```

Instead, run this command to use HTTPie to create the new note:

```
$ http POST localhost:3000/notes title="This is a fourth note."
HTTP/1.1 201 Created
...
{
    "id": 4,
    "title": "This is a fourth note."
}
```

You don't need to specify headers or content type. Most web APIs use JSON now, so HTTPie just assumes that's what you want to do by default.

Updating the note in the API is a nearly identical command. Use PUT for the HTTP method and use /notes/4 as the endpoint:

```
$ http PUT localhost:3000/notes/4 title="This is the fourth note."
HTTP/1.1 200 OK
...
{
    "id": 4,
    "title": "This is the fourth note."
}
```

You can remove the note with the DELETE method.

Finally, it's often helpful to see the request that HTTPie is sending. If you use the -v switch, you'll see the request headers too. Create a fifth note using the -v switch:

```
$ http -v POST localhost:3000/notes title="This is a fifth note."
POST /notes HTTP/1.1
Accept: application/json
Accept-Encoding: gzip, deflate
Connection: keep-alive
Content-Length: 34
Content-Type: application/json
Host: localhost:3000
User-Agent: HTTPie/0.9.2

{
    "title": "This is a fifth note."
}
...
```

Testing Performance with Siege

If you're building a web app, you've probably wondered how well it performs under load. There are several tools that can help you figure this out, but Seige is one of the most flexible. It has an interface similar to curl, and you can automate it.

Don't run Siege against servers you don't manage. Use it to stress-test your own stuff. You'll use the Notes API for this.

Install Siege on Ubuntu with apt:

```
$ sudo apt install siege
```

Or install it on macOS with brew:

```
$ brew install siege
```

To use Siege with its default values, give it a URL:

```
$ siege http://localhost:3000/notes
New configuration template added to /home/brian/.siege
Run siege -C to view the current settings in that file
** SIEGE 4.0.4
** Preparing 25 concurrent users for battle.
The server is now under siege...
```

Siege makes concurrent connections to your API over and over until you tell it to stop by pressing Ctrl+c.

When you do, Siege generates a report on the screen:

```
Lifting the server siege...
Transactions:                  9762 hits
Availability:                100.00 %
Elapsed time:                 13.95 secs
Data transferred:              2.64 MB
Response time:                 0.04 secs
Transaction rate:            699.78 trans/sec
Throughput:                    0.19 MB/sec
Concurrency:                  24.93
Successful transactions:       9762
Failed transactions:              0
Longest transaction:           0.10
Shortest transaction:          0.01
```

It shows how many transactions it was able to make before it stopped, and it shows the success rate. In this example, Siege received successful responses 100 percent of the time. If this number was lower, you could look at the Successful transactions and Failed transactions output.

Sometimes people will report that their connections took a long time. Siege shows you the times of the longest and shortest transactions. This can help you verify that some resources might have trouble under stress.

Siege uses a configuration file to control its options. It created one for you at ~/.siege/siege.conf on your first run.

Siege can keep a log of your runs, but the default logfile location is in the /var directory, and you'd need to modify permissions there or run siege as a superuser to write results there.

So, enable logging and change the log location to your home directory. Set the value of the logfile entry in the configuration file to $HOME/siege.log and set the value of logging to true. You can do this with nano, or you can do it quickly with sed, which you learned how to use in Chapter 5, Streams of Text, on page 91. To avoid escaping slashes in pathnames, use a pipe as the delimiter for your expression:

```
$ sed -i -e 's|^# logfile =|logfile = $HOME/siege.log|' ~/.siege/siege.conf
$ sed -i -e 's|^logging = false|logging = true|' ~/.siege/siege.conf
```

Use siege -C to verify the changes:

```
$ siege -C
...
URLs file:                    /etc/siege/urls.txt
thread limit:                 255
➤ logging:                     true
➤ log file:                    /home/brian/siege.log
resource file:                /home/brian/.siege/siege.conf
...
```

Now you can look in ~/siege.log for your results.

Like curl and HTTPie, you can use Siege to make JSON requests, which means you can test the more intense parts of your web application.

Try this out: Tell Siege to make 50 concurrent connections update the fifth note's title:

```
$ siege --concurrent=50 \
> --time=10s \
> --content-type="application/json" \
> 'http://localhost:3000/notes/5 PUT {"title":"A fifth note."}'
```

Finally, you can use Siege to simulate real Internet users. Siege can load a list of URLs from a file and hit them randomly.

Create a file named urls.txt and add some URLs to the file that hit various endpoints in the notes API:

```
$ cat << 'EOF' > urls.txt
> http://localhost:3000/notes
> http://localhost:3000/notes/1
> http://localhost:3000/notes/2
> http://localhost:3000/notes/3
> http://localhost:3000/notes/4
> EOF
```

Execute this command to have 50 concurrent users hit these URLs randomly:

```
$ siege --concurrent=50 --delay=5 --internet --file=urls.txt --time=1m
```

The --internet switch tells Siege to have each connection grab a random entry from the urls.txt file. The --delay switch tells Siege to make each connection wait for a random duration from zero to the specified number. With these options, you can simulate more realistic traffic.

Siege is a powerful tool for ensuring your applications hold up under pressure.

Wrapping Up

In this chapter, you explored a handful of additional tools you can incorporate into your workflow, but there are so many more tools out there, each solving a specific purpose. From here, explore using tmux to manage your terminal sessions in *tmux 2: Productive Mouse-Free Development [Hog16]*, or look into editing text with Vim and NeoVim in *Modern Vim [Nei18]*. Explore the command-line tools for your cloud infrastructure provider, or take advantage of front-end development tools.

And who knows, you might even consider building your own command-line tools. The Go programming language makes it easy to create command-line tools that work on all platforms, and Python or JavaScript are popular options as well. And of course, you could just create a simple Bash script that leverages what you've learned in this book to build even more complex workflows.

Be on the lookout for new small, sharp tools to add to your collection, or opportunities to create your own. You'll find so much more to explore.

Command Quick Reference

This is a quick reference of all commands used in this book. Some of these commands need to be installed via the package manager to use them. You can use this list to refresh your memory, or use it to quiz a friend and test their knowledge of various CLI tools.

- apt: Package manager for Ubuntu

- awk: Pattern scanning and text processing language

- bash: The Bash shell

- bc: An arbitrary precision calculator language

- bg: Background a job

- bind: Define a keybinding in Bash

- brew: Open-source macOS package manager

- cat: Concatenate files and print on the standard output

- cd: Change directory

- chmod: Change file mode bits

- chown: Change file owner

- column: Columnate lists

- cp: Copy files and directories

- curl: Transfer a URL

- cut: Remove sections from each line of files

- date: Print or set the system date and time

- df: Report file system disk space usage

- dig: DNS lookup utility

- direnv: Environment variable manager for your shell

- dirs: Display the directory stack

- du: Estimate file space usage

- echo: Display a line of text

- entr: Run arbitrary commands when files change

- env: Run a program in a modified environment or display environment variables

- exit: Cause normal process termination

- export: Create an environment variable

- fc: Fix a previous command by opening it in your visual editor

- fg: Foreground a task

- file: Determine file type

- find: Search for files in a directory hierarchy

- fzf: Command-line fuzzy finder

- git: Distributed version control system

- grep: Print lines matching a pattern

- head: Output the first part of files

- history: Show the command history

- host: DNS lookup utility

- htop: Interactive process viewer similar to top

- http: HTTPie, a command-line tool similar to curl

- ifconfig: View or configure a network interface

- ip: Show/manipulate routing, network devices, interfaces, and tunnels

- jobs: List current background jobs

- jq: Command-line JSON processor

- jrnl: Command-line journal written in Python

- kill: Send a signal to a process

- less: View file or text one page at a time

- ln: Make links between files

- ls: List directory contents

- make: GNU make utility to maintain groups of programs

- man: An interface to the online reference manuals

- mkdir: Make directories

- more: View file or text one page at a time

- mv: Move or rename files

- nano: A terminal-based text editor

- nc: Netcat: Create arbitrary TCP and UDP connections

- nohup: Run a command immune to hangups, with output to a non-tty

- npx: Node.js utility used to download and run a Node.js-based executable program

- pandoc: Library for converting from one markup format to another

- pgrep: Look up or signal processes bascd on name and other attributes

- ping: Send ICMP ECHO_REQUEST to network hosts

- pkill: Look up or signal processes based on name and other attributes

- popd: Remove a directory from the directory stack

- printenv: Print all or part of the environment

- ps: Report a snapshot of the current processes

- pushd: Add a directory to the directory stack

- pwd: Print name of current/working directory

- pip3: A tool for installing and managing Python packages

- pygmentize: Colorize source code

- python3: Interpreter for version 3 of the Python programming language

- ranger: Visual file manager

- rm: Remove files or directories

- screen: Screen manager with VT100/ANSI terminal emulation

- script: Save a log of the terminal session
- sed: Stream editor for filtering and transforming text
- seq: Print a sequence of numbers
- set: Set a shell variable
- siege: An HTTP/FTP load tester and benchmarking utility
- sleep: Delay for a specified amount of time
- sort: Sort lines of text files
- source: Load a shell configuration file
- stat: Display file or file system status
- sudo: Execute a command as another user
- tail: Output the last part of files
- time: Run programs and summarize system resource usage
- top: Display Linux processes
- touch: Change file timestamps
- traceroute: Print the route packets trace to network host
- tree: List contents of directories in a tree-like format.
- unalias: Remove an alias
- unset: Unset a variable
- unzip: List, test, and extract compressed files in a ZIP archive
- which: Locate a command on the PATH
- while: Looping construct in Bash
- whois: Look up domain name information
- xargs: Build and execute commands from standard input

Installing GNU Utilities on macOS

macOS systems are based on BSD, rather than on GNU/Linux like RedHat, Debian, and Ubuntu. As a result, a lot of the command-line tools that ship with macOS aren't 100 percent compatible with the ones you've learned about in this book. If you are interested in leveraging what you learned in this book and you don't want to keep track of the differences, follow the steps in this appendix to install the GNU versions on your Mac.

Installing coreutils

The coreutils[1] package contains GNU versions of many tools, including sort, stat, cat, date, and many more.

Install coreutils with the following command:

```
$ brew install coreutils
```

Commands in this package are all prefixed with a g. For example, to use the stat command, you'd use gstat.

To make these commands override their BSD counterparts, modify your .bash_profile file to include the path, and then apply the changes to your current environment:

```
$ echo 'export PATH="$(brew --prefix coreutils)/libexec/gnubin:$PATH"' \
> >> ~/.bash_profile
$ source ~/.bash_profile
```

Verify that the changes are applied by using the which comand to verify that the stat command comes from the coreutils package:

```
$ which stat
```

1.　http://en.wikipedia.org/wiki/GNU_Core_Utilities

You'll see this output:

```
/usr/local/opt/coreutils/libexec/gnubin/stat
```

Since these files are now at the front of your PATH, they'll be used first.

Installing diffutils and findutils

The diffutils[2] package includes programs like diff, cmp, and diff3 that let you see differences between files.

Install them with this command:

```
$ brew install diffutils
```

These commands will be placed in /usr/local/bin, which will override the built-in tools due to how Homebrew modifies your PATH.

The findutils[3] package includes find, locate, updatedb, and xargs.

```
$ brew install findutils
```

To use these tools instead of the built-in tools, you'll have to either prefix each with a g, or add another entry to your PATH:

```
$ echo 'export PATH="$(brew --prefix findutils)/libexec/gnubin:$PATH"' \
> >> ~/.bash_profile
$ source ~/.bash_profile
```

When you use which find, the GNU version will show up instead of the built-in one.

Installing GNU Versions of awk, sed, and grep

The awk, grep, and sed programs included on macOS work very differently than their GNU counterparts.

Install the GNU version of awk with the following command:

```
$ brew install awk
```

This installs to /usr/local/bin, overriding the built-in BSD version, as it will be first in your PATH.

Install the GNU version of sed with this command:

```
$ brew install gnu-sed
```

---

2. https://www.gnu.org/s/diffutils/
3. https://www.gnu.org/software/findutils/

This installs the command gsed. To use it in place of your existing sed command, add it to your PATH by modifying your .bash_profile file again and applying the changes to your local environment:

```
$ echo 'export PATH="$(brew --prefix grep)/libexec/gnubin:$PATH"' \
> >> ~/.bash_profile
$ source ~/.bash_profile
```

Install grep with this command:

```
$ brew install grep
```

Like sed, grep installs as ggrep, so if you want it to override your existing grep command, add it to your PATH in both your .bash_profile and your current session:

```
$ echo 'export PATH="$(brew --prefix grep)/libexec/gnubin:$PATH"' \
> >> ~/.bash_profile
$ source ~/.bash_profile
```

You now have the most essential GNU versions of popular utilities.

In addition, your Mac comes with versions of nano, git, and less that aren't as up to date as you might like. Use Homebrew to install those too:

```
$ brew install nano git less
```

These will install to /usr/local/bin which will override the versions that ship with macOS.

Index

Thank you!

How did you enjoy this book? Please let us know. Take a moment and email us at support@pragprog.com with your feedback. Tell us your story and you could win free ebooks. Please use the subject line "Book Feedback."

Ready for your next great Pragmatic Bookshelf book? Come on over to https://pragprog.com and use the coupon code BUYANOTHER2019 to save 30% on your next ebook.

Void where prohibited, restricted, or otherwise unwelcome. Do not use ebooks near water. If rash persists, see a doctor. Doesn't apply to *The Pragmatic Programmer* ebook because it's older than the Pragmatic Bookshelf itself. Side effects may include increased knowledge and skill, increased marketability, and deep satisfaction. Increase dosage regularly.

And thank you for your continued support,

Andy Hunt, Publisher

SAVE 30%!
Use coupon code
BUYANOTHER2019

tmux 2

Your mouse is slowing you down. The time you spend
context switching between your editor and your con-
soles eats away at your productivity. Take control of
your environment with tmux, a terminal multiplexer
that you can tailor to your workflow. With this updated
second edition for tmux 2.3, you'll customize, script,
and leverage tmux's unique abilities to craft a productive terminal environment that lets you keep your fin-
gers on your keyboard's home row.

Brian P. Hogan
(102 pages) ISBN: 9781680502213. $21.95
https://pragprog.com/book/bhtmux2

Exercises for Programmers

When you write software, you need to be at the top of
your game. Great programmers practice to keep their
skills sharp. Get sharp and stay sharp with more than
fifty practice exercises rooted in real-world scenarios.
If you're a new programmer, these challenges will help
you learn what you need to break into the field, and if
you're a seasoned pro, you can use these exercises to
learn that hot new language for your next gig.

Brian P. Hogan
(118 pages) ISBN: 9781680501223. $24
https://pragprog.com/book/bhwb

Modern Vim

Turn Vim into a full-blown development environment
using Vim 8's new features and this sequel to the
beloved bestseller *Practical Vim*. Integrate your editor
with tools for building, testing, linting, indexing, and
searching your codebase. Discover the future of Vim
with Neovim: a fork of Vim that includes a built-in
terminal emulator that will transform your workflow.
Whether you choose to switch to Neovim or stick with
Vim 8, you'll be a better developer.

Drew Neil
(166 pages) ISBN: 9781680502626. $39.95
https://pragprog.com/book/modvim

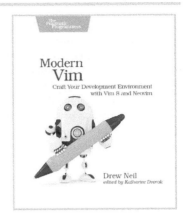

Practical Vim, Second Edition

Vim is a fast and efficient text editor that will make
you a faster and more efficient developer. It's available
on almost every OS, and if you master the techniques
in this book, you'll never need another text editor. In
more than 120 Vim tips, you'll quickly learn the editor's
core functionality and tackle your trickiest editing and
writing tasks. This beloved bestseller has been revised
and updated to Vim 8 and includes three brand-new
tips and five fully revised tips.

Drew Neil
(354 pages) ISBN: 9781680501278. $29
https://pragprog.com/book/dnvim2

Practical Security

Most security professionals don't have the words "security" or "hacker" in their job title. Instead, as a developer or admin you often have to fit in security alongside your official responsibilities — building and maintaining computer systems. Implement the basics of good security now, and you'll have a solid foundation if you bring in a dedicated security staff later. Identify the weaknesses in your system, and defend against the attacks most likely to compromise your organization, without needing to become a trained security professional.

Roman Zabicki
(132 pages) ISBN: 9781680506341. $26.95
https://pragprog.com/book/rzsecur

Forge Your Future with Open Source

Free and open source is the foundation of software development, and it's built by people just like you. Discover the fundamental tenets that drive the movement. Take control of your career by selecting the right project to meet your professional goals. Master the language and avoid the pitfalls that typically ensnare new contributors. Join a community of like-minded people and change the world. Programmers, writers, designers, and everyone interested in software will make their mark through free and open source software contributions.

VM (Vicky) Brasseur
(222 pages) ISBN: 9781680503012. $33.95
https://pragprog.com/book/vbopens

A Common-Sense Guide to Data Structures and Algorithms

If you last saw algorithms in a university course or at a job interview, you're missing out on what they can do for your code. Learn different sorting and searching techniques, and when to use each. Find out how to use recursion effectively. Discover structures for specialized applications, such as trees and graphs. Use Big O notation to decide which algorithms are best for your production environment. Beginners will learn how to use these techniques from the start, and experienced developers will rediscover approaches they may have forgotten.

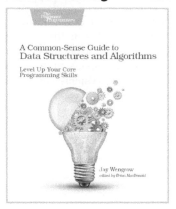

Jay Wengrow

(220 pages) ISBN: 9781680502442. $45.95

https://pragprog.com/book/jwdsal

Design It!

Don't engineer by coincidence—design it like you mean it! Grounded by fundamentals and filled with practical design methods, this is the perfect introduction to software architecture for programmers who are ready to grow their design skills. Ask the right stakeholders the right questions, explore design options, share your design decisions, and facilitate collaborative workshops that are fast, effective, and fun. Become a better programmer, leader, and designer. Use your new skills to lead your team in implementing software with the right capabilities—and develop awesome software!

Michael Keeling

(358 pages) ISBN: 9781680502091. $41.95

https://pragprog.com/book/mkdsa

Your Code as a Crime Scene

Jack the Ripper and legacy codebases have more in common than you'd think. Inspired by forensic psychology methods, this book teaches you strategies to predict the future of your codebase, assess refactoring direction, and understand how your team influences the design. With its unique blend of forensic psychology and code analysis, this book arms you with the strategies you need, no matter what programming language you use.

Adam Tornhill
(218 pages) ISBN: 9781680500387. $36
https://pragprog.com/book/atcrime

The Nature of Software Development

You need to get value from your software project. You need it "free, now, and perfect." We can't get you there, but we can help you get to "cheaper, sooner, and better." This book leads you from the desire for value down to the specific activities that help good Agile projects deliver better software sooner, and at a lower cost. Using simple sketches and a few words, the author invites you to follow his path of learning and understanding from a half century of software development and from his engagement with Agile methods from their very beginning.

Ron Jeffries
(176 pages) ISBN: 9781941222379. $24
https://pragprog.com/book/rjnsd

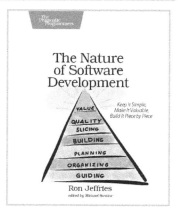

The Pragmatic Bookshelf

The Pragmatic Bookshelf features books written by developers for developers. The titles continue the well-known Pragmatic Programmer style and continue to garner awards and rave reviews. As development gets more and more difficult, the Pragmatic Programmers will be there with more titles and products to help you stay on top of your game.

Visit Us Online

This Book's Home Page
https://pragprog.com/book/bhcldev
Source code from this book, errata, and other resources. Come give us feedback, too!

Keep Up to Date
https://pragprog.com
Join our announcement mailing list (low volume) or follow us on twitter @pragprog for new titles, sales, coupons, hot tips, and more.

New and Noteworthy
https://pragprog.com/news
Check out the latest pragmatic developments, new titles and other offerings.

Save on the eBook

Save on the eBook versions of this title. Owning the paper version of this book entitles you to purchase the electronic versions at a terrific discount.

PDFs are great for carrying around on your laptop—they are hyperlinked, have color, and are fully searchable. Most titles are also available for the iPhone and iPod touch, Amazon Kindle, and other popular e-book readers.

Buy now at *https://pragprog.com/coupon*

Contact Us

Online Orders:	*https://pragprog.com/catalog*
Customer Service:	*support@pragprog.com*
International Rights:	*translations@pragprog.com*
Academic Use:	*academic@pragprog.com*
Write for Us:	*http://write-for-us.pragprog.com*
Or Call:	+1 800-699-7764

Milton Keynes UK
Ingram Content Group UK Ltd.
UKHW012036270824
447508UK00009B/204

9 781680 502961